Live to Make a Difference

The Legacy of a Servant Leader Rev. Lloyd E. Dees in Bermuda and Beyond

Shangri-La Durham-Thompson, Ed.D.

PB ISBN: 978-1-939237-04-0

HB ISBN: 978-1-964143-13-2

EBOOK ISBN: 978-1-964143-12-5

Suncoast Digital Press, Inc.

Sarasota, Florida

www.suncoastdigitalpress.com

Printed in the United States of America

The photographs and image reproductions in this book were generously provided by Rev. Dees and his family, drawn from their collection of historical documents and memorabilia. While some images lack modern photographic quality, each one holds significant historical value and contributes to preserving the story and purpose of this book.

Royal Gazette photo on cover courtesy of Dexter Smith, Editor of the *Royal Gazette*.

Dedication

This book is dedicated to the memory of the late Rev. Lloyd E. Dees, my mentor, former pastor, and dear friend and to his devoted wife, Mrs. Dolores Dees.

Rev. Lloyd Dees profoundly impacted my life, and this work is a testament to the countless others he influenced. My hope is that readers will be as inspired by his story as I have been, and, in turn, strive to make a meaningful difference in the lives of others.

"If I love you, I must make you conscious of the things you don't see."

– James Baldwin

Contents

Preface ix

Foreword xi

The Reverend Howard H.L. Dill xi

Part 1 xiii

Chapter One: Black Dolls and Self-Identity 1

The Bermuda of the 1960s [Rolfe Commissiong] 7

A Mammoth Task 10

Chapter Two: The Impact of Rev. Dees 13

His Impact on Me 13

His Impact on Bermuda 18

Protection for the Consumer 29

New Rent Commissioner 31

Bermuda's Budget 33

Big Debate on the Budget 36

Record Budget Ups Tax on Liquor, Cigarettes 45

Assemblymen Debate Role of Church [Rev. Trevor Woolridge]... 50

Bermudians for Reconciliation Reply to Members' Reply 54

Meetings with the Reverends [Mr. Phil Perinchief] 57

Another Perspective [Mr. Phil Perinchief] 63

Chapter Three: Overview of ***The Protest*** Magazine 71
- The Protest Magazine, 1969 75
- The Protest Magazine, January - March 1970 77
- The Protest Magazine, October - December 1970 82
- The Protest Magazine, March 1971 85
- The Protest Magazine, September 1971 89

Chapter Four: Beyond Bermuda. 93
- Rev. Dees in North Carolina (North Carolina Agricultural & Technical State University) . 93
- Rev. Dees in West Virginia (Human Rights Director) 98
- Rev. Dees in White Plains, N.Y. (Standing Up for Firefighters) 102
- Rev. Dees in Georgia (A Lifetime of Advocacy) 106
- A Lasting Voice 108
- Black Man's Struggle Not Over 116

Chapter Five: A Forever Bond with Bermuda. 119
- In Honor of Our Fathers 120
- Retirement Celebration 123
- Stand Tall for Justice by Shangri-La Durham-Thompson. 124
- Return Visits to Bermuda 127
- Visit to House of Assembly 133
- The Bermuda Industrial Union (BIU). 134
- The Chimes of Hope Concert. 134
- Prospect Primary School 137

Chapter 6: The Speeches 143
- Drugs (date unknown). 144
- The Fantastic Mind (date unknown) 145
- A Better Goodbye for the Babies (April 24, 1990) 146
- On the Passing of Time (date unknown) 146
- "Lo These Many Years" (date unknown). 147
- My Prayer (date unknown) 148
- I Have Known Wars (date unknown) 148

Chapter Seven: Overview of the Letters 151

Chapter Eight: A Life Well Spent 161

Memorial 162

Memorial Service Celebrating the Life of The Reverend Lloyd E. Dees 166

Remembering Rev. Dees. 168

Hope Springs Eternal 174

Part II—Anthology of Reference Material 177

Chapter 9: The Protest Magazines. 179

November 1969 179

January – March 1970. 189

October – December 1970 203

March 1971 217

September 1971 233

Chapter Ten: Letters 249

Chapter 11: Pictures/News Articles 291

Acknowledgments. 305

About the Author 307

Other works by the Author:. 308

Children's Books. 309

Poetry From the Heart 309

Plays. 309

References 311

Index. 313

Dawn of a New Day: A Poem. 319

Preface

On his deathbed, I promised Rev. Dees I would tell his story, because of how profoundly he had impacted my life and the lives of countless others. I had already been writing and previewing the information he sent me, never imagining that he would not live to see the completion of this project.

When Rev. Dees first sent me his materials, he expressed no particular expectations for their use. Yet the wealth of information was overwhelming. As I explain in Chapter One, he entrusted the documents to my sister Shelby, asking her to pass them on to me. This book, *Live to Make a Difference: The Legacy of Servant Leader, Rev. Lloyd E. Dees, in Bermuda and Beyond* has taken nearly a decade to complete. Throughout this journey, I have spent countless hours in prayer and communion with God, whose guidance made this work possible. I have come to appreciate the truth in the saying, "It is not the destination, but the journey." Writing this book has been a test of faith and a spiritual awakening. At every step, God has been present, revealing the purpose and scope of this work.

My intent has been to capture how Rev. Dees shaped my life, his community in Bermuda, and everywhere he lived. In fact, his legacy is that his bold and profound stand for justice reached across and around the globe. In the following chapters, I have sought to portray his character, ethics, and unwavering faith. Above all, I hope to highlight a vital truth: only what we do for God endures. Rev. Dees followed his calling with conviction, and through his example, I have gained a deeper understanding of my own purpose. Like him, I, too, must strive to make a difference. A sign in my church reads, "Count not the blessings you have received, but the blessings you have shared." This book is one way I share the blessing of God.

Rev. Dees faced many challenges, yet his love for people and his dedication to justice remained steadfast. His hunger strike protesting the rising cost of living in Bermuda, his efforts to inspire, unite, and mobilize individuals including my mother, Mrs. Julia Durham, Mr. Randolph Hayward, and the Reconciliation Group, and his role in establishing the Consumer Affairs Bureau all speak to his unwavering commitment. He listened, empathized, and stood by those in need. People depended on him because of his humanity.

The arts, poetry, and music were central to his life, and he used these gifts to provoke thought and inspire change. Through *The Protest* magazines, co-written with Rev. John Brandon, he challenged institutions—whether the A.M.E. Church, the United Methodist Church, bishops, or politicians. He volunteered his time, uplifted the downtrodden, encouraged senators and fellow clergy, and cherished his family and the family of God.

I hope his story moves you as it has moved me. We are all placed on this earth to make a difference. The question for each of us when we awake to the gift of a new day of life is, "What will I do today to make a difference?"

My deepest hope is that this book will inspire readers to serve others, to recognize that we all have a purpose, and to use our unique gifts not for ourselves alone, but to uplift those around us and draw them closer to Christ. I am profoundly grateful to have been entrusted with this work and to have known Rev. Lloyd E. Dees. This book title *Live to Make a Difference* serves as an intentional reminder to all of us.

Foreword

by

The Reverend Howard H.L. Dill

Rev. Lloyd E. Dees was more than a pastor—he was a force for justice and unity in every community he served. With a ministry spanning decades and continents, including Bermuda, West Virginia, New Jersey, and New York, Rev. Dees brought together spiritual leadership and a deep commitment to social change.

His appointment as a human rights commissioner reflected a lifelong dedication to standing up for the marginalized and challenging systems of injustice. Whether he was preaching from the pulpit or advocating in public forums, Rev. Dees used his voice to speak truth to power.

Live to Make a Difference is a superbly written tribute, helping to ensure that his legacy endures in the lives he touched and the communities he helped uplift. Rev. Dees was not only a spiritual guide—he was an activist whose faith inspired action.

I have known the author, Dr. Durham-Thompson, since my youth. We have worked together on community and church projects, too many to count. As the Bermuda Annual Conference Church School Superintendent, Shan (as we call her) brought energy and enthusiasm to an otherwise dull ministry. She has made a difference that inspires the listener as she speaks and teaches with excitement.

One of her previous publications, "Battle for Freedom," was eventually turned into a stage play held at the Bermuda Botanical Gardens—I recited an antebellum poem as part of that performance. This production drew over 6,000 people. That play made a phenomenal mark on the lives of many people, who to this day still reflect on the production.

Presently, she has a radio show that focuses on interviewing persons in leadership. The information shared by a cross-section of people is a valuable source for her listeners. Her keen interest in our Bermuda history, in people who have profoundly impacted Bermudians and others, and her own deep-rooted Christian faith make her uniquely qualified to write *Live to Make a Difference: The Legacy of Servant Leader, Rev. Lloyd E. Dees, in Bermuda and Beyond.*

Dr. Durham-Thompson has made more than a difference with in-depth research of Rev. Dees' journey. The documentation revealed is fascinating to those curious about that historical time of civil rights and social justice, as well as Bermuda's most renowned leaders.

While this book is the trajectory of one individual and his consortium of people, you, dear reader, will be spiritually challenged to engage in making a difference in your own life and the lives of others. You will realize that there are no limits on your opportunities to be influential and to live your own legacy of making a difference.

Be encouraged, changed, and inspired: Read on!

Rev. Howard H.L. Dill, JP

Presiding Elder EW District, Bermuda

Pastor of Allen Temple A.M.E. Church, Bermuda

Part I

Chapter One

Black Dolls and Self-Identity

"Wow! She looks like us," my friend blurted out. "And she walks!" As a young child growing up on Radnor Road in Shelly Bay, Bermuda, my sisters and I were excited to receive three Black dolls brought to Bermuda from America by my Aunt Curlene (Furbert) Warmbrun. My mother had sent her the funds to purchase the dolls for us as Christmas presents, and I vividly recall that those dolls made quite an impression in our neighbourhood. My sisters and I, along with the numerous neighbourhood children, were mesmerized by these exceptional dolls, which were as tall as me. Also, they were walking dolls. Imagine! But, walking or not, the dolls were beautiful and, for many in my neighbourhood, quite extraordinary—white dolls were the norm.

It was no surprise that my mother wanted those dolls for us since she had always been concerned about our self-identity. As a young teen, my mother had hair that reached her bottom—a local paper had written an article about her hair. I have never seen my mother with hair longer than her shoulders. She told us a story about when she had once worn an Afro wig on the local bus, and someone made a nasty remark that the hair wasn't even hers. She told us how she took the wig off to reveal her natural hair. Hair length, texture, and skin colour were all very important in the Bermuda of the 1950s and this, in some cases, remains the fact today.

The issue of self-identity was the first predicament Rev. Dees tackled upon arriving in Bermuda. In December of 1970, he felt it necessary to speak out about the importance of self-identity and he proposed that the shopping public's preferred purchase of white dolls was in fact a result of the lack of advertising. While he agreed that Black children who were given white dolls were appreciative of them, they should have the opportunity to also have dolls of their own skin colour.

In the December 1970 edition of *The Mid-Ocean News*, a Bermudian newspaper, headlined, "There ARE dolls with Afros in local toy shops." The somewhat lengthy article was in response to the inquiries made by Rev. Lloyd E. Dees about the importance of having Black dolls also available to children. Rev. Lloyd E. Dees was an American minister who had arrived in Bermuda in 1968, to become the new pastor for Bethel African Methodist Episcopal (A.M.E.) Church in Shelly Bay. The article demonstrated that the Bermudian merchants did not appreciate the importance of identity as it pertained to Black children, nor were they held accountable for this obvious oversight.

There ARE dolls with Afros in local toy shops

The toy shops of Hamilton have news for the Rev. Lloyd Dees, the A.M.E. pastor who earlier this week urged the public to stop buying dolls for their children until manufacturers went over to the production of "black dolls with Afros".

For their shelves are stacked high with black dolls — some with Afro hair styles, some without. "I have 250 in stock. I would be pleased to give Mr. Dees one if he came in," said one store owner.

The pastor launched his attack on "blonde-haired, white dolls" at a meeting of the Bermudians for Reconciliation group recently formed to fight price rises.

Bermuda's stores seemed only to sell white dolls, he declared, saying: "Our girls have been playing with little white dolls too long. Why can't a black kid play with a black doll — what is racist about that?"

But according to the store owners Mr. Dees is a little out of touch with the latest doll-buying trends. For, generally speaking, the great doll-owning public doesn't appear to think too deeply about the meaningful complexities of colour.

Little white girls fall violently in love with black dolls; little back girls become equally attached to flaxen-haired, blue-eyed dolls. Colour seems a secondary consideration — the frilly pants and inter-changeable outfits are really much more important.

The Annex on Reid Street carries a comprehensive selection of dolls of both colours. Sales are fairly even, reported the manager.

A large consignment of coloured dolls with Afro hair styles and "psychedelic clothing" arrived at the store last May from Germany.

Sales have not been at all brisk. But this is attributed more to lack of intensive advertising than racial dollmanship.

"Children want what they see advertised" added the spokesman. "Colour doesn't come into it at all when it comes to buying dolls."

LARGER DOLLS

Another consignment of larger dolls with more extreme Afro hair styles was on its way from the States, he said.

It was the same story at Masters toy department where black and white dolls perch on shelves in roughly equal numbers.

"A doll is a doll," said a spokesman. "The Rev. Dees can't have been in here recently."

And there are no signs that the Pastor's message is having much impact at this stage — "the dolls are going very fast, we will be sold out long before Christmas," she added.

The Mid-Ocean News, December 1970

Rev. Lloyd Dees, a soft-spoken gentleman, was fearless in colonial Bermuda where the white minority had continued to rule even after the Emancipation Proclamation of 1834 and after the Progressive Labour Party (P.L.P.) was formed on February 10, 1963. The article pointed out that Bermuda had good news for Rev. Lloyd Dees, who had urged the public to stop buying dolls for their children until manufacturers produced "Black dolls with Afros." At the time, this was quite a provocative statement that the merchants could not ignore. In response, one merchant proclaimed that his shelves were stocked with at least 250 Black dolls, some with Afro hairstyles and some without. He said he would be pleased to give one to Rev. Dees.

It is important to consider that prior to this response from the merchants, there was a meeting of the Bermudians for Reconciliation, a group that had recently formed to fight price increases. It was stated that Rev. Dees had launched a racist attack concerning the selling of "blond-haired, white dolls." Because Rev. Dees believed in equality for all people and felt that Black children had a right to self-identity, he met the issue of identity head-on.

In the Bermuda Population Trend report, we learned that there were 55,019 people living in Bermuda during the 1970s, where Blacks represented 52.3%, whites represented 30.5%, mixed race represented 9.1%, Asians represented 4.1%, and Other represented 4%. Rev. Dees stood for justice and equality and believed in the worth of all men. He felt it was of great importance that Black children had the opportunity to play with Black dolls. Merchants made it clear they didn't place the same importance on this idea as Rev. Dees.

The fact that Rev. Dees was called a racist provoked him to respond that, "Our girls have been playing with only little white dolls for too long. Why can't a Black kid play with a Black doll—what is racist about that?"

While Rev. Dees had arrived in Bermuda only a short time before, he felt it was important to speak up. Store owners stated that he was a little out of touch with the latest doll-buying trends and said that the doll-buying public didn't appear to be very concerned with the complexities of colour. "Little white girls fall violently in love with Black dolls; little Black girls become equally attached to flaxen-haired, blue-eyed dolls. Colour seems a secondary consideration—the frilly pants and inter-changeable outfits are much more important."

The Annex Store on Reid Street noted that they carried a comprehensive selection of dolls of both colours and stated that the sales were fairly even. They had received a consignment of coloured dolls with Afro hairstyles and "psychedelic clothing" that had arrived at their store in

May from Germany. They noted that sales had not been brisk and that "children want what they see advertised." "Colour," they said, "doesn't come into it at all when it comes to buying dolls." Yet, the merchant noted, "Another consignment of larger dolls with more extreme Afro hairstyles was on its way from the States."

At yet another store, Master's Toy Department, Black dolls and white dolls could be found on the shelves in equal numbers, a spokesperson for the store told Rev. Dees. They also noted that, "a doll is a doll," and that if Rev. Dees had been in the store recently, he would have been aware of that. Although Rev. Dees had raised the issue, the merchants felt that there were "no signs that the pastor's message was having much impact at this stage…the dolls are going very fast. We will be sold out long before Christmas."

In the 1970's Bermuda, the call for Black dolls was not simply a call on behalf of children by Rev. Dees, but a demand for recognition that Blacks were worthy and Black consciousness was being raised throughout the community. What struck me about this was the statement that read, "…the great doll-buying public doesn't appear to think too deeply about the meaningful complexities of colour as relevant."

It was interesting to acquire some insight as to why Rev. Dees was so focused on improving the self-identity of Bermudian children by pushing to get Black dolls into toy stores. According to Rev. Dees' daughter, Janet, her father had learned about the "The Doll Study" designed by Black psychologists Drs. Maimie and Kenneth Clark, who first conducted the study in 1943. Interestingly, Dr. Mamie Clark was the first Black student to enter the doctoral program at Columbia University. The study was designed to measure the psychological effects of segregation on African American children and was believed to have had a profound impact on the Civil Rights Movement.

Their experiments focused on assessing children's racial perceptions, and they discovered that Black children often preferred white dolls and attributed positive characteristics to them, while assigning negative traits to the Black dolls. Their research also played a crucial role in the landmark Supreme Court case Brown v. Board of Education, which led to the desegregation of American schools. The Clarks' work highlighted the damaging effects of racial segregation on children's self-esteem and was instrumental in the fight for equality. The Clarks' "Doll Study" became the first psychological research to be cited by the Supreme Court and was significant in the Court's decision to end school segregation.

There is an interesting article, "How a Psychologist's Work on Race Identity Helped Overturn School Segregation in 1950s America," in the *Smithsonian* magazine written on October 26, 2017, by Leila McNeill, explaining the significance of this Black doll study. It also reveals how Mamie Phipps Clark originally thought of the idea for the oft-cited "doll study" and provided expert testimony in the Brown v. Board of Education case.

The shop merchant's statement that "sales have not been all that brisk" was unacceptable to Rev. Dees, as not only were Black dolls unavailable, but during that period many Blacks would have preferred to give their Black children white dolls because the public perception of beauty was still blond hair and blue eyes. Rev. Dees believed that the shop merchants should begin to understand the importance of self-identity of Black children and that they were actively participating in a practice that devalued others. This point may have been a bit embarrassing or irritating to the merchants as their only concern was to sell and promote products that they deemed necessary and knew would sell. That Rev. Dees thought Black girls playing with Black dolls affirmed identity and that a sense of pride was more important was perhaps not as important to the merchants. It is interesting that Rev. Dees also noted that "without Black stores with funding to advertise and sell products to Black consumers, Blacks were at the mercy of others who saw no real value in purchasing what they did not deem important."

Rev. Lloyd Dees was an iconoclast. He was a man who stood up to power, faced issues, and raised concerns that others accepted or did not raise. He was not content to sit back and accept the status quo, but he provoked thought and acted to make the necessary changes. He was a man who was compelled to "let justice roll." He was my mentor and a man who helped chart the course of my life.

Rev. Lloyd Dees was a man of character, and he proved to be unafraid to tackle any issue that dealt with injustice and inequality. Certainly, he was not afraid to tackle the issues of the day, even if he had to stand alone. Therefore, it is important that I introduce to some and reintroduce to others, as we say when introducing people in the A.M.E. Church, Rev. Lloyd E. Dees, "A Fearless Warrior" for justice and equality. He was first and foremost my mentor and friend. Although he was the pastor of Bethel A.M.E. Church and, consequently, my pastor, he became so much more and had a great impact on my life and the lives of others.

In 2015, I became the host of a one-hour radio show in Bermuda titled *The Need to Lead* on Magic 102.7, which still airs each Saturday at 10:00 a.m. I take this opportunity to thank Mr. Glenn Blakeney, the owner of Inter-Island Communications for affording me the opportunity. The show is a Christian-based program designed to expose listeners to leadership principles and people with an intention to enhance servant leadership skills, initially using John C. Maxwell's book, *The 21 Irrefutable Laws of Leadership* as my guide. During the first few minutes of the program, I introduce the topic, which is determined from the bio/resume provided by the interviewee. In recent years I started reading one of my poems that pertains to the topic, and then I pose questions that highlight the guest's servant leadership skills. This allows me to reveal who my guest is and all that he/she has done as a servant leader. I will use this format to introduce Rev. Lloyd E. Dees. His resume was one of the documents sent to me in July of 2015. By that time, I had known Rev. Dees for over 40 years, and yet reading his bio impacted me, as it revealed why he was who he was.

Rev. Lloyd E. Dees was ordained an elder in the A.M.E. Church in 1968, which means he came to Bermuda as a neophyte. He was married to Dolores Dees, and they had two children, Jason and Janet. Rev. Dees obtained a Bachelor of Arts degree from Shelton College in Ringwood, New Jersey, where he majored in philosophy. He received a Master of Divinity degree from the Interdenominational Theological Center in Atlanta, Georgia where he studied the Old Testament. He also studied at Princeton Theological Seminary and received a Master of Sacred Theology with an emphasis on Christian Social Ethics. Additionally, Rev. Dees studied at the Congress of Evangelism at the United Methodist Church in Chicago in 1990, the United Methodist Church in Atlanta in 1991, and at the United Methodist Church in Houston in 1993. He went to workshops on preaching at Auburn Theological Seminary in New York City in the spring of 1986, 1987, 1989, and 1993. He studied at the Institute on Religion and Social Studies, Jewish Theological Seminary, in New York City, and was part of the United Methodist Bishops' Convocation on "Critical Issues" in 1986 and 1994.

Rev. Dees was stationed in Berlin, Germany for ten months and from May 1951-1953 he served in the U.S. Army. He had served as a Social Investigator for the New York Department of Social Justice from 1963-1965 and was responsible for determining the eligibility of persons to receive public assistance and maintained an active caseload of clients. In the summer of 1966, he was a youth counsellor for a city-wide coordinating committee in New York. His first pastoral responsibility was at Fisk Chapel African Methodist Episcopal Church in Fair Haven, New Jersey, from June of 1968 to June of 1969. Soon after he was sent to pastor Bethel A.M.E. Church in Shelly Bay, Bermuda, and this is where we first met.

The Bermuda of the 1960s

I believe it is important to understand the Bermuda of the 1960s and 1970s, for it was that Bermuda Rev. Dees encountered when he arrived. Past minister of the government Mr. Rolfe Commissiong, JP is a contributor to the daily newspaper and a past consultant for two of Bermuda's premiers, and is known for his dedication to justice. As a program director for the Government's "Big Conversation" from 2007-2010, he held wide discussions on racism and its impact on Bermuda and he explains the Bermuda of that period as follows:

> The 1960s were a tumultuous time in Bermuda and no less globally. In fact, Bermuda was not immune to the same issues that were impacting societies at that time. These included civil rights, the right to vote, and questions around self-determination. Throughout the region from Bermuda down to Trinidad and Tobago and Guyana, the fight for independence in many of the British colonies, and the ongoing destructive impact of white supremacy and its chief weapon, racism, were ever present.
>
> Bermuda, it must be said, suffered from many of these afflictions. It was a society that much like the American South and South Africa had its own brand of apartheid—albeit a milder version for the most part but no less destructive to the souls and psyches of Black Bermudians. It was a system designed to keep Black Bermudians, who comprised the majority of the population, both economically and politically at the margins of this society. In Bermuda, Blacks were subordinate to the mostly white, Anglo minority of British descent.
>
> However, like in many of its sister islands to the south by the 1960s, Black Bermudians would also resist the racial oppression of colonial authorities and in Bermuda's case its rather large and powerful white minority. In the post emancipation era of the 1960s

and 1970s, the Black Bermudian population created and developed a number of tools in the form of organizations. These included churches, schools, friendly societies, a labour organization named The Bermuda Industrial Union, and the first political party formed in Bermuda named The Progressive Labour Party in order to address their overall marginalization within this society.

One such organization was the African Methodist Episcopal (A.M.E.) Church. The A.M.E. Church in Bermuda had a tradition of having African American pastors along with Bermudian preachers since its inception in Bermuda. It was known to be a church committed to social and racial justice and activism in Bermuda and throughout its conferences worldwide. This was amply demonstrated by Rev. Theopolis Monk. He is legendary for his work in Bermuda fighting on behalf of Jamaican workers who were ruthlessly exploited while the workers were employed by the British Navy at the Dockyard base.

Shortly before the arrival of Rev. Dees, an activist group was formed and named The Progressive Group. This group was made up of relatively young African Bermudians who formed the group to dismantle the Bermuda-style, colonial Apartheid system in the British colony of Bermuda. Their courageous efforts to boycott the racially segregated cinemas led to the effective end, in 1959, of racial discrimination of public places in Bermuda.

But that along with the fight for labour rights would only be the first steps in creating a more equitable society. Little known at the time, some of the members of The Progressive Group became interested in activism by attending an A.M.E. youth group organized in the 1950s at St. Paul A.M.E. Church in Hamilton. The youth group was under the guidance of Rev. Thomas Forster who served from 1957 to 1959 at St. Paul A.M.E.

Rev. Dees' work that resulted in the creation of the consumer affairs bureau was noteworthy. Many of his parishioners, in addition to many Bermudians, were suffering under the weight of the high cost of living and the abuse of merchants who had no reluctance in raising prices beyond what was reasonable. Many of whom were also known to indulge in dubious practices in the absence of what we would now call consumer protection.

During this time around the world, and especially in America, the world watched while recently enslaved Blacks sought to make a life for themselves and their families. In Bermuda, Blacks had very recently attained the right to vote. They struggled to get enough funds to purchase land to build their own homes. While Black men were attempting to sustain their families, they endured hardship and strife. As a British Dependent Territory, Bermudians, who appeared to be acceptable to the oligarchy, had greater chances of advancement. Many Blacks were not accepted or respected and those with British ties received the lion's share of the wealth.

As someone who has been involved in social activism since the early 1990s, I routinely took inspiration and guidance from those who walked this path before me. Persons such as my parents Rudolph and Vera Commissiong who were civil rights icons and founding members of The Progressive Group, Dr. Eva Hodgson and so many others. Bermudians today are facing challenges no less existential than those faced by prior generations. Dr. Hodgson, for example, believed that until racial inequality is eliminated none of us will be free. I too share that view and have committed my life to that proposition. Clearly, the lesson is that we must continue to fight to ensure a just society not only for those here today but also for future generations. That was the ethos of those who came before us and it must be our own.

A Mammoth Task

As I began this book, I realized the mammoth task before me. Because I believe that this work must be recorded with authenticity, the second part of this book includes actual news and magazine articles, sermons, and letters that substantiate this information. I am humbled that Rev. Dees chose to share his life's work of achievements, trials, and frustrations with me to make known to others. This story is retold from his and my perspectives. Although this is his story, I cannot tell it without interjecting the impact he had on my life. My mother, after reading my opening commentary, asked if this story was about me or Rev. Dees. This question made me realize that this story is being written for many reasons. It is my hope that this book will make a difference in the lives of all those who read it. In this way, God's Great Commission will be fulfilled.

Because of how zealously and fearlessly Rev. Dees lived his life, I hope to be able to show his work for God and inspire others to do what they can for Christ. As John Maxwell states in the "Law of the Picture" from *The 21 Irrefutable Laws of Leadership:* "People do as people see." Rev. Dees did what he could to help eliminate injustice. There is still injustice in the world, and we can do our part as there is still so much to do. We must appreciate who we are in Christ and know that because He is, we are. We are worthy and everyone, made in His image, is worthy. Rev. Dees worked throughout his life to help people believe in their own self-worth, and that of others. The under-appreciation of self-worth is something Rev. Dees knew had a huge impact on people.

I hope that by reading his story there will be an understanding of what it takes to make a difference. As my mother always said, "nothing worth doing is without difficulty." We are on this earth to fulfill our destiny, and God has a plan for our lives. The Bible says in Jeremiah 29:11, "'I know the plans I have for you,' declares the Lord. 'Plans to prosper you and not harm you, plans to give you hope and a future.'"

God had a plan for Rev. Dees' life. His arrival in Bermuda was no accident and he accepted God's command "to go into all the world and preach His gospel." Rev. Dees, a messenger of God, spent his life fulfilling his purpose without wavering, without murmuring, without questioning. He worked tirelessly for his heavenly Father, and I am convinced that when he was finally called home, he heard, "Well done my good and faithful servant." Rev. Dees wanted me to fulfill my purpose. He understood my gifts and he knew that if I allowed God to direct my life, I, too, could make a difference. It is my greatest desire that all who read this book will be inspired to use their gifts and talents for the benefit of humanity and in this way positively impact the lives of others. In the final analysis, we must be focused on our Father's business.

Hopefully this book will be read with an open mind and an open heart. Rev. Dees worked so tirelessly for justice and equality and hopefully his loving nature and conviction will shine through. Rev. Dees realized that what is written in Matthew 25:40 is true—for "truly I tell you, whatever you did for the least of these brothers and sisters of mine, you did for me."

As both Rev. Dees and I are Christians, this book is filled with references to God and the church. This book is written to record what Rev. Dees attempted to do for the people of Bermuda and for those he encountered wherever he lived. This book is his legacy and the documentation of his efforts to make the world a better place for his family and the people he served. Therefore, in the second half of this book I have recorded, as best I can, his speeches, his *Protest* magazines, newspaper and magazine articles, letters, and recognitions he received, in their entirety.

This work began on July 10, 2015, when my sister Shelby received a bundle of papers sent to her home in Philadelphia. Inside was a note which read:

Dear Shelby,
I hope all is well with you! The enclosed items are for your dear sister, Dr. Shangri-la Durham-Thompson.
Thank you for passing them on,
Rev. Dees

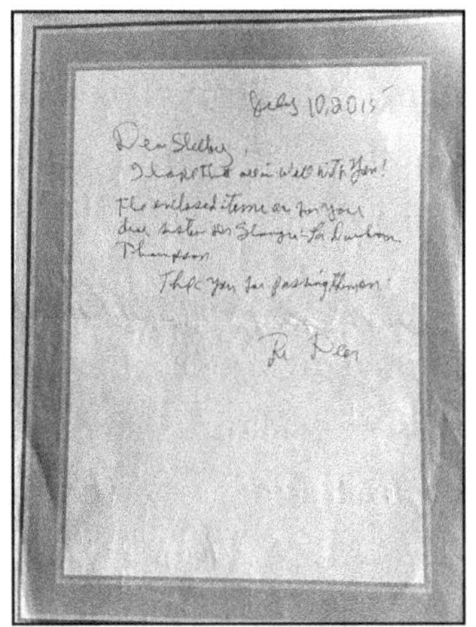

July 10, 2015

Dear Shelby,
I hope that all is well with you!
The enclosed items are for your dear sister Dr. Shangri-la Durham-Thompson.
Thank you for passing them on!

Rev. Dees

Note to Shelby, July 11, 2015

When I visited my sister in 2015, she helped me arrange the many pages that he had sent in chronological order. She knew, like I did, that I had to write his story. I also knew that his story would be inexplicably intertwined with mine. I telephoned Rev. Dees shortly after receiving the documents to let him know that they had arrived and that I would write his story. I asked if there was a deadline and he laughed and said, "No." He continued, "Whatever you want to do with the material is fine with me."

At the time I received his documents, my sister and I were working on a book for the A.M.E. Church School. In fact, I spent my whole summer on that book, as did the Bermuda Church School superintendents. I had begun the book the year before and *The Bermuda A.M.E. Church Schools' Memoirs* was published shortly thereafter. In the book there was a picture of Rev. Dees and his wife Dolores visiting my aunt Hilda Smith, who was, at the time, Bermuda's oldest resident (and was actually my great cousin). I had hoped to surprise him with a copy of the *Book of Memoirs* as a Christmas present because he was identified in that book as the previous Pastor of Bethel A.M.E. Church. I always spoke to him at length when he called, and he loved hearing news about Bermuda. I decided not to communicate with him until he saw the book, as I wanted it to be my Christmas surprise. After 2015, *The Bermuda A.M.E. Church Schools' Memoirs* was completed and I began to work on the information he had sent to my sister Shelby.

Unfortunately, my first attempt to put this story on paper resulted in one paragraph and when I spoke with him in October, I profusely apologized, embarrassed about my lack of progress. He graciously assured me that there was no rush…no rush. In the intervening weeks, I only spoke with him a few times, feeling guilty that I had not completed more.

I believe it was in January 2016 that I received a devastating phone call that made me think the idea to surprise him had not been a good one. Rev. Dees usually called me before I could call him. Even though I vowed to be the one to call first the next time, it seldom happened. It seemed life always intervened and every other month or so he would call and ask, "Shangri-La, what's going on in Bermuda?"

One can only imagine how I felt when I received the call from his wife, his son Jason, and his daughter Janet. They haltingly explained that their father—my mentor, friend, confidant, my pastor—had only a few weeks to live. I was not only shocked but felt horrible that I had let him down. The man who had helped shape my life and the lives of countless others was dying. This was very sad news to many, many people, and tragic to me personally. His family apologized for not informing me sooner.

His wife, Dolores, explained, "Shangri-La, I told Lloyd he had to tell you. I reminded him that he had already told Randolph [Hayward] and that if he didn't tell you himself, Randolph would." It seemed that for some reason, Rev. Dees did not want me to know that he had taken ill. "Shangri-La," she continued, "I am putting the telephone to his ear. He can hear you. Go ahead and talk."

With tears streaming down my face and a huge lump in my throat, I thanked him for all he had done for me. I promised I would write his story. I emphasized that his life had made a tremendous difference, especially in mine. I understood, at that moment, that the phrase *pay it forward* is not cliché. If our world is to be a better place, if we are to be all that God wants us to be, if we are to fulfill God's purpose in our lives, we too must strive to make a difference, as did my mentor, The Rev. Lloyd E. Dees.

Chapter Two

The Impact of Rev. Dees

His Impact on Me

I vaguely recall meeting Rev. Dees and his wife Dolores for the first time as they stepped out of a car into the Bethel A.M.E. Church parking lot. I had been told that he was going to be the new pastor of Bethel A.M.E. Church. I observed that both he and his wife were of slim build. He had a deep voice and she was very soft spoken, and somewhat shy. Without hesitation, my precocious and gregarious self asked if they had children. When they said no, undaunted, I exclaimed, "Well, you're going to have a baby while you are here and I'm going to be the babysitter!" Rev. Dees smiled while his wife looked at the ground. I was right though, and Jason was born in Bermuda and I was eventually his babysitter. I believed Rev. Dees liked that I had an outgoing personality and so when he had to leave the island to attend church meetings abroad, I kept his wife company. I don't recall babysitting Jason until I attended college in North Carolina, where they went to live after leaving Bermuda.

I'll share a little more about myself, who I am, and who I was when Rev. and Mrs. Dees first met me. I have described myself as precocious. I am told that I first recited the entire Lord's Prayer in church at the age of three, and I always spoke at recitals, church services, and other special events from that time on. In day school I always came first in reading. I remember learning to recite "Paul Revere's Ride" in standard two with Mrs. Veronica Phillips. I read "The Song of Hiawatha" by

Henry Wadsworth Longfellow for my reading exam with the principal, Mrs. Rosalyn Robinson—"By the shores of…" When I entered standard five, my teacher Mrs. Lillian Woolridge often gave me recitations to read in church for special occasions like Easter and Christmas. She was also my Sunday school teacher and my YPD leader, which meant I often saw her almost every day of my life.

As I mentioned, as a child I demonstrated the ability to speak in public at an early age, and this gift was refined through participating in all church activities. Although my father, Coolidge George Durham, a bartender, periodically attended church, my mother, Julia Durham, was an active member, as she, too, had grown up in Bethel A.M.E. She had helped her grandmother, Julia Furbert, to clean the church, and my great-great-grandfather had been the church school superintendent. It was interesting to be told by my cousin, Norris Burgess, that I followed in the footsteps of my forefathers when I later became a Bethel Church School Superintendent.

My mother was the first female trustee in Bethel A.M.E. Church (and perhaps in the Bermuda A.M.E. Conference) and participated actively by reading the scripture at Sunday services or praying for the congregation. Because my mother wanted me to hone my skills as a speaker, she would often have me speak in her place on special occasions. In this way, I and my siblings were always active. Soon, though, it was me who they called upon to participate in Sunday school, to explain the lesson, or debate an issue, as speaking in public came naturally to me. When others did not wish to participate, were too shy, would forget their lines, or not show up for rehearsals, I was asked to fill in. I read the scriptures, prayed, and led the worship services on "Children's Days." At Easter and Christmas, we would all be given poems and other materials to recite or read. I loved reciting everything they suggested and the encouragement from members of the congregation, especially Mr. Leroy T. Pyke, Bethel's elocutionist, always motivated me.

My mother would have my sisters and me memorize our parts and practice at home. We took part in church plays and I was once directed by one of Bermuda's most outstanding drama directors, Ms. Carol Hill. I performed around the island in a play called *As Easter Dawns*. I was ten at the time and played the wife of a pastor of a dying church. Coincidentally, Charles Smith, the young man who played the part of the pastor, is today Rev. Charles Smith, the pastor of Bright Temple A.M.E. Church where I am currently an associate member.

After I left for college, my mother tried to have my sisters Shelby and Donna fill my public speaking role and had them recite some materials for a programme, but they forgot their lines.

Years later they laughed uproariously when they recalled the faces of the congregation. My mother was not impressed. After that, my sisters focused on singing. All four of us were members of the junior choir until we were "kicked out" because we failed to attend a practice one evening when my mother was working. We went to church that Sunday without our uniforms, as we had been called and told specifically not to wear them because we would not be singing. The person who called had on her uniform, as did everyone, except us! My mother was livid, and at the next church conference she gave those Christian members "a piece of her mind," as she would not stand by and have others discourage her children!

So, when Rev. Dees arrived, he found a mother, a protector of her children, an outspoken woman with whom he could enjoy fellowship, and me, who had a talent that he could and did use. Then, to the chagrin of the congregation, he introduced me to a wide variety of literature... Black literature. Perhaps he saw me as a conduit to impact the hearts and minds of the people. To say our church was conservative would be an understatement. I believe that many, if not most of the members—except my mother, who was P.L.P.—voted for The United Bermuda Party. Rev. Dees, with his penchant for self-respect and self-identity, wanted his congregation to be a thinking people, people who could influence their own destiny, and people who could appreciate their value as Black people. I don't think the congregation appreciated the direction my speaking took. In fact, years later, one of my peers told me that she thought I was radical with my large Afro and a bandanna tied around my head.

The first work I recall Rev. Dees giving me to recite was "That Word Black," by Langston Hughes. I still have a ragged copy of that work today. It was and still is a provocative piece. I am not sure that I fully appreciated my Blackness when the work was first introduced to me. I remember Rev. Dees giving me a sheet of paper and telling me to become familiar with it, as he wanted me to read it on a Friday night. We had a small stage in the church hall, and I remember reading it to a small audience. The play's essence is summed up by a character named Simple, as follows:

"Now as I were saying, the word *black*, white folks have done used that word to mean something bad so often until now when the N.A.A.C.P. asks for civil rights for the black man,...I reckon it all started with a black cat meaning bad luck. Don't let one cross your path! Next, somebody got up a blacklist on which you get if you don't vote right."

This work explained all the words that were identified with being Black which were really negative. For example, being blackballed, blackmailed, black-market, black sheep, black magic, having a black heart. "According to white folks, black is bad. Wait till my day comes! In my language, bad will be white." The person named Simple in Langston Hughes' piece goes on to point out that the earth is black, and all kinds of good things come from the earth, including coal, the night with the "moon, and a million stars, and is beautiful. Sleep is black, which gives you rest, so you wake up feeling good. I am black. 'What is wrong with black?'"

Unfortunately, some people may have thought that being taught to appreciate Blackness was to teach hatred for whites. Nothing could have been farther from the truth. Rev. Dees taught us to appreciate and love who we were, but he was no racist. He valued people, all people. Certainly, the word Black, during my teen years, held certain connotations and evoked feelings of being less than. Rev. Dees attempted to get his congregation to appreciate their Blackness. He showed me through Hughes' piece that being Black had so many positive aspects.

I don't think that until that point I had considered the word "black" in all its aspects, and I was new to the works of Langston Hughes. This work taught me more about the meanings of the word Black. Obviously, I knew little about the history in some of Langston Hughes selections, like the corner of 125th and Lenox. This corner was described as "Harlem's heartbeat" by Langston Hughes in his poem, "Juke Box Love Song." I knew nothing about the Black Hand Society in Chicago, but I did know about black cats crossing my path and I tried not to let that happen. After this exposure, I tried to believe that a black cat crossing my path was good luck, but it took a great deal of self-convincing.

When I was around ten, I had an incident occur concerning my Blackness. I was walking home from Francis Patton Elementary School. A bus passed me carrying white children to the Roger B. Chaffee School on the U.S. military base. As they passed, they spat on me and called me derogatory names. I also remember a time when I called an aunt a "black monkey" and I received an angry reprimand. So, like the character Simple in Langston Hughes' "That Word Black," I had some negative experiences with the word *black*, but had never heard it presented so poignantly through the character Simple. This work opened my eyes to other works by Langston Hughes.

Soon I was researching works by other Black poets and came across the poem "Black Mother Praying" by Owen Dodson. I was so enthralled that I memorized it in one afternoon while in The Berkeley Institute's school library, which was also my high school. At a later date, I recited it at church and around the island as people asked me to recite it at various events. I was then asked to recite it at St. Paul A.M.E. Church and, as their services were broadcast on the radio, my Black studies teacher, Mrs. Sharon Parris, heard about it and asked me to recite other works such as "I Dream a World," "Mother to Son," "The Ballad of the Landlord," and "Dream Deferred" (by Langston Hughes), and also "I Know Why the Caged Bird Sings," (by Maya Angelou) during our high school assemblies.

I recall Rev. Dees giving me "Letter from a Birmingham Jail" to read for a concert held in the church lecture hall. This letter, written by Dr. Martin Luther King, Jr. in the spring of 1963, is considered protest literature and a classic document of civil disobedience. The letter was smuggled out of the Birmingham prison, in sections, over time, first on pieces of newspaper given to Dr. King by a Black trustee and then on pieces of paper given to him by his attorneys. Reading it myself so many years later, I understood the impact it had on Rev. Dees, given how he felt about injustice. I do not recall reading the entire excerpt, but the letter demonstrated how Rev. Dees attempted to bring awareness to the actions of Dr. King and his efforts for nonviolence. This letter explained the city of Birmingham's white power structure and how it left the Negro community with no alternative but to protest.

In the letter, Dr. King explained the four basic steps for a nonviolent campaign: collection of the facts to determine whether injustices exist, negotiation, self-purification, and direct action. Dr. King noted that Birmingham was probably the most thoroughly segregated city in the United States where "Negroes had experienced grossly unjust treatment in the courts. There have been more unresolved bombings of Negro homes and churches in Birmingham than in any other city in the nation. On the basis of those conditions, Negro leaders sought to negotiate with the city fathers. But the latter consistently refused to engage in good faith negotiation."

Rev. Dees had a similar view about the injustices he encountered while in Bermuda and he took action. He had arrived in a colonized Bermuda where Blacks were marginalized, as explained earlier by Mr. Rolfe Commissiong.

Around the time of Rev. Dee's arrival in Bermuda, the students at my high school, The Berkeley Institute, held similar views about the lack of teaching of Black history in our textbook, *Tudors and Stuarts*. Without a knowledge of our past, we felt that we had no fundamental self-identity. The student body held a sit-in, refusing to return to class until a Black Studies teacher was hired. I remember students like Ottiwell Simmons, Jr., Julian Hall, and Dale Butler being leaders in this effort. Julian Hall became one of Bermuda's finest lawyers but unfortunately died too young. Dale Butler later published my first book of poetry and plays, titled *Battle for Freedom*, and the works of many other Bermudians. My mother said she watched on television as students at The Berkeley Institute ignored the schools' principal, Mr. Shirley Furbert, as he tried unsuccessfully to get us to return to class. As a past student of The Berkeley Institute, my mother remembered a school where students respectfully did as they were told, although she expressed with pride that the students of my generation were standing up for their rights—a right to know who they were. The sit-in was successful and our first ever Black Studies teacher, Mrs. Sharon Parris, was hired.

So you can see that when Rev. Dees arrived in Bermuda, his thoughts and actions were in line with our efforts to bring about positive change, as well as the importance of identity.

His Impact on Bermuda

I can only imagine how Rev. Dees felt after his arrival in Bermuda and his first visit to the grocery store. Usually, ministers do not make large salaries, with the exception of those who have mega churches. I am certain that Rev. Dees did not make enough money as a pastor of Bethel A.M.E. Church to afford the fresh fruits and vegetables that he had perhaps been accustomed to in the U.S. As a man who listened more than he talked, he must have heard the rumblings of his congregation concerning the high cost of living in Bermuda. He had made a friend in Rev. John Brandon, another young A.M.E. pastor new to Bermuda, and who would have encountered the same alarming plight. They got together to discuss how they could combat what they considered "taking advantage of the people."

In any effort to make change, people need assistance and Rev. Dees found an ally in Rev. John Brandon. I was interested to learn how Rev. Dees and Rev. Brandon met, so I contacted Rev. Brandon's son Marcus and on June 14, 2023, he sent me the following information: "Rev. Dees and my father met in 1969 in Atlantic City, N.J. at an A.M.E. Church conference where they both received assignments to pastorates in Bermuda. At the completion of that conference, my father indicated that Rev. Dees and his wife, Dolores, took a flight to Bermuda. My father and my mother took a flight to Bermuda at the completion of that conference also." (Marcus mentioned that their airline ticket cost $99 at that time!)

Marcus recounted that his father and Rev. Dees were both social activists. They were each other's confidant and friend. Marcus noted also that while they served as pastors, their social interests led them to work together, to organize and serve as advisers for The Bermudians for Reconciliation Group who worked with them to combat the high cost of living. The establishment of The Consumer Affairs Bureau was a direct result of their efforts. Today, The Consumer Affairs Bureau portfolio is part of the government budget regardless of which party is in office. Rev. Brandon suggested that if anyone needed to know the history of The Consumer Affairs Bureau, they could find it in The Consumer Affairs Bureau archives. Marcus provided the following names and parishes of the Bureau members (other than Mr. Randolph and my mother Julia). They included Rosalie Douglas (Somerset), Richard Powell (Southampton), Lois Brown-Evan's sister Leonie Richards (Devonshire), and Walter Seymour (Southampton).

Marcus noted that his father left Bermuda in 1975 with his wife and sons, Micah and Marcus, to pursue other endeavours in the Ministry. Rev. Dees had left Bermuda a few years before, in 1972.

In an effort to increase the awareness of the high price of food and housing, Rev. Dees and Rev. Brandon joined forces and proved they were two pastors with a purpose.

On March 24, 1970, "a joint statement, for immediate release" was issued by Rev. Dees and Rev. Brandon. They stated that "As ministers of the gospel of Jesus, the Christ, who are concerned about every aspect of the lives of the people who we serve, we have resolved to take the following action: We will begin a fast on Wednesday, March 25, 1970, at midnight and continuing through Easter Sunday. During this period, we will eat only bread and drink only water." The announcement from these pastors stated that this action was being taken for two reasons: 1) "We hope that the general public will become more aware of the increasing high prices being paid for such basic commodities as food and housing and 2) We hope that the government will be moved to take some action in regulating prices and instituting a degree of price control."

The next day, *The Royal Gazette,* Bermuda's daily newspaper, boldly captioned "Prices too High—pastors to stage a fast over Easter." The article noted that the "two A.M.E. pastors would undergo a four day fast as a protest against increasingly high prices for food and housing. The fast is to begin at midnight on Thursday and continue through to midnight on Sunday. They were to eat sparingly of bread and drink a little water. Rev. Dees said that he and his colleague would be confined to their parsonages as much as possible."

It is amazing what events we remember and how we remember them. I recall this event, but in my mind, the fast was much longer than the time specified. I observed Rev. Dees, who was already a thin man, grow visibly thinner—but how much thinner could he have gotten in four days? Many have stated that ministers of the gospel should refrain from political activism even while they

FOR IMMEDIATE RELEASE
March 24, 1970

JOINT STATEMENT

AS MINISTERS OF THE GOSPEL OF JESUS, THE CHRIST, WHO ARE CONCERNED ABOUT EVERY ASPECT OF THE LIVES OF THE PEOPLE WHOM WE SERVE, WE HAVE RESOLVED TO TAKE THE FOLLOWING ACTION: WE WILL BEGIN A FAST ON WEDNESDAY, MARCH 25, 1970 AT MIDNIGHT AND CONTINUING THROUGH EASTER SUNDAY. DURING THIS PERIOD, WE WILL EAT ONLY BREAD AND DRINK WATER.

WE ARE TAKING THIS ACTION MAINLY FOR TWO REASONS: (1) WE HOPE THAT THE GENERAL PUBLIC WILL BECOME MORE AWARE OF THE INCREASING HIGH PRICES BEING PAID FOR SUCH BASIC COMMODITIES AS FOOD AND HOUSING, (2) WE HOPE THAT THE GOVERNMENT WILL BE MOVED TO TAKE SOME ACTION IN REGULATING PRICES, AND INSTITUTING A DEGREE OF PRICE CONTROL.

The Reverend Lloyd E. Dees, Pastor
Bethel A.M.E. Church, Shelly Bay

The Reverend John E. Brandon, Pastor
Allen Temple A.M.E. Church, Somerset

The Joint Statement from Rev. Dees and Rev. Brandon, March 24, 1970

applauded Rev. Dr. Martin Luther King, Jr. for the stance he took with non-violence. This article reported that Rev. Dees and Rev. Brandon felt that the action they were taking was "very much a part of their job." "We," the article continued, "are not trying to start a petition of protest. We will let people be led by their own consciences. There is no question of a mass demonstration."

On Monday, March 30, 1970, *The Royal Gazette* reported on page three, "Pastors' appeal for costs cut." It noted that, "The two ministers who last night ended a four day fast in protest of the rising prices appealed to Bermuda merchants to voluntarily reduce costs." The two ministers had declined an open invitation to have talks with the Member for Finance, The Hon. Jack Sharpe. The pastors stated that, "We do not intend to confuse our position as ministers of the Gospel, for we are not politicians. We, as pastors, speaking on behalf of those who suffer under the present price crisis would first of all call on the merchants of the community to take some voluntary steps to reduce the crisis. Secondly, we urgently implore the Government to begin immediately to set up guidelines for some regulatory procedures to halt spiraling prices in Bermuda. The important question is not whether some kind of price control will work, but rather how people are being affected under the present situation."

The pastors asked, "What happens to the average citizen when he has to suffer outrageous discrepancies in prices from week to week and place to place when his wages remain unchanged?" The article noted that: "Although the fast ended at midnight, Mr. Brandon said he would only be eating soup and crackers for the next few days before going back to regular eating." Perhaps Rev. Dees did likewise, which may explain why I recalled him as being visibly thinner. Rev. Brandon stated that he had "not suffered any adverse effects, just a feeling of being tired." But, he added, "It has made me more determined than anything else to see this thing through."

In April of 1970, *The Royal Gazette* headline, "On Parliament Hill" told the story of the pastors' appeal to supporters, as they proposed to stage a "silent vigil" outside of the House of Assembly. Their action was in protest of the "rising food and housing prices." Rev. Brandon told *The Royal Gazette* that the Hamilton Corporation had given permission for the vigil to take place inside a wall surrounding the grounds of the House. "We are asking people to observe the vigil with us, but we are asking them to keep silent and not to obstruct the passageway of the Members of the House." The pastors intended to maintain their vigil during the whole period that the House was in session, and they wanted supporters to stay that long as well, or at least to stay as long as they could.

—ON PARLIAMENT HILL—

"Vigil" pastors make appeal to supporters

"No noise and no obstruction" — that is the plea sent out to their supporters by the two A.M.E. pastors, the Rev. John Brandon (Allen Temple) and the Rev. Lloyd Dees (Bethel) who are staging a "silent vigil" outside the House of Assembly this morning.

Their action is in protest against "rising food and housing prices."

Mr. Brandon told The Royal Gazette yesterday that Hamilton Corporation had given permission for the vigil to take place inside a wall surrounding the grounds of the House.

"We are asking people to observe the vigil with us," he said "but we are asking them to keep silent and not to obstruct the passageway of Members of the House."

The two pastors intend to maintain their vigil during the whole period the House is in session.

They would like their supporters to stay that long, too, but any who can't are asked "to stay as long as possible."

The Royal Gazette, April 1970

Ministers protest at House of Assembly

LED BY REV. JOHN BRANDON (Allen Temple A.M.E.) and Rev. Lloyd Dees (Bethel A.M.E.) a group of young men, many wearing the regalia of the Black Berets, stage their silent protest against high prices in front of the House of Assembly yesterday. The demonstration was extremely orderly. The A.M.E. ministers had hoped others would join the "silent vigil" but few turned up.

The Mid-Ocean News, circa April, 1970

These two young ministers indeed were making an impact and doing what they could to create a more just and liveable Bermuda. They knew firsthand the impact on the ordinary man as they, too, had to use their meager funds to support their families. I am certain that they had spoken with their respective congregations, and they were working to make their lives easier. *The Mid-Ocean News* displayed a wonderful picture of their demonstration. Not surprisingly, there were only about ten people in the photograph, as perhaps only a few people had turned out in support. One member of Bethel's A.M.E. congregation told me on April 5, 2022, that he did not think that the vigil made the impact the young ministers would have liked. The fact that Bermuda is still a British colony today may shed some light on understanding their dilemma. However, the vigil received recognition and years later I am awed by the resolve of two young pastors who tried, against all odds, to right wrongs and make a difference. Bermuda's talk shows today state that Bermudians talk and complain, but seldom act. My mother says that we, as a people, have been discussing the same issues since she was a young adult and she hopes that before she leaves this earth, we will be credited with more than great discussions. Action is required for things to change.

The Mid-Ocean News article stated that "A group of young men, many wearing the regalia of the Black Berets, staged their silent protest against the high prices in front of the House of Assembly the day before and although the demonstration was extremely orderly, the A.M.E. ministers had hoped others would join the 'silent vigil'."

On Saturday, April 11, 1970, *The Royal Gazette* headline read, "Demonstrations and Petition" and talked about how younger voters were protesting for Black Studies, and showed a picture of Black students making their way to protest at City Hall. The students also wanted a lowered voting age.

A second picture on the front page, in that same news article read, "Desire...Lower food and housing prices." In the picture was my esteemed mentor, the valiant Rev. Lloyd Dees with a sign around his neck, standing tall for us! The caption read as follows: "Commissioner of police Mr. George Duckett talks to one of the Black Beret Cadre members while Deputy Commissioner Frank Williams clears a way for Mr. deForest Trimingham, M.C.P. Placard-carrying the Rev. Lloyd Dees stands on the steps in the centre of the picture."

Across from the picture is a story revealing that inside the House of Assembly, M.C.P.s discussed high prices. Despite the low supporter turnout, the two ministers were making an impact. The report stated that the ministers' protests "naturally led to a discussion inside the building on the cost of living." First to speak on the adjournment motion was Mr. Austin Thomas of the Opposition Progressive Labour Party, (P.L.P.). Mr. Thomas hoped the "silent vigil" outside "would prick the consciousness of Government Members" and make them realize that something had to be done about high prices of food and housing. Mr. Thomas stated, "It was all very well for Government to say many price increases were caused because of the rising prices of goods from abroad, but no one knew the percentage markup by merchants here, nor the profits made..." He proposed that more statistics were needed so that the correct facts and figures could be known.

Outside the House of Assembly, the newspaper noted, "Some members of the Black Beret Cadre joined two A.M.E. ministers…Detectives watched the group, also supported by a few members of the public as they formed two lines on the pathway leading to the main entrance. The demonstrators were cautioned twice when they refused to move to allow Mr. Harry Viera, M.C.P. and George Duckett to squeeze through the line-up. Detective Chief Inspector John Sheehy spoke to two young men as Mr. Viera, who arrived with the Government Leader Sir Henry Tucker, waited to get through the ranks. Sir Henry managed to slip through without trouble. A few minutes later, Mr. Duckett accompanied by Deputy Commissioner, F.B. Williams…" While there was no confusion, a silent vigil led by A.M.E. ministers, with the support of a few members of the Black Beret Cadre, needed watching by detectives. Perhaps the next news article explains better why this occurred.

On October 14 or 19, 1970 (the date on the news article was unreadable), a report in *The Royal Gazette* stated, "We are willing to die: Cadre' highlights another issue of concern to some in the community." This article reported: "A meeting held at Vernon Temple A.M.E. Church in Southampton and opened by Rev. John Brandon stated that Mr. Mel Saltus of the Black Beret Cadre told a packed hall the previous night, 'We the Black Beret Cadre are willing to make the supreme sacrifice to bring about changes and make sure our children get what they should.' He told the audience that the Black Beret Cadre took a stand against the Bermuda government earlier in the year because they had remained idle on the issue of arms being sold to South Africa by Britain. 'We feel if the Government thinks it is all right for arms to be sold to South Africa which practices openly discrimination against black people, then they would feel alright to have arms sent there to kill black people.' Mr. Saltus went on to say, 'We must work to destroy the system of injustice which has been placed on us by our British Colonial Masters. We might have to break unjust laws to accomplish this and even if it hurts the tourist industry, we must be willing to pay some price to get the right people in the right places to run this country. Christ fought against unjust laws and even died in the struggle. We must do the same. We are not joking about this. We are very serious.'"

Mr. Philip Perinchief also spoke at this event, but the article did not mention his comments. It did report, however, that Rev. Brandon said, "Many people are saying today it is too late for talk but perhaps one of the problems is that we haven't really begun to talk." He stated that the purpose of the meeting was to try to bridge the gap of communication, "for as long as there is misunderstanding and mistrust, we must talk with and hear people of varying views so we may together better be able to reason."

Rev. Dees nor Rev. Brandon could never be accused of being idle, or of restricting their ministerial activities to Sunday morning worship services and church activities that took place in their respective buildings. They were concerned for the people, all people, but especially those in need, and as servant leaders, they listened and acted on their beliefs.

Bermudians For Reconciliation Organization

CITIZENS OF BERMUDA

Do Something About The High Cost of Living!

SIGN THE PETITION

Calling for Price Controls and Consumer Protection Legislation

at

THE TOWNE HALL, ST. GEORGE

TOMORROW NIGHT — 8.30 - 10.30 p.m.

The Petition will be available for signatures until late October

10/1970

The Royal Gazette, October 1970

In October of 1970, a notice appeared in another news article, I believe it was *The Royal Gazette*, as the name of the news article was not available. The notice headlined, "Bermudians for Reconciliation Organization." It asked that "Citizens of Bermuda…do something about the rising cost of living!" People were asked to sign a petition calling for price controls and Consumer Protection Legislation. A meeting was held at the Town Hall in St. George from 8:30 p.m. - 10:30 p.m. My mother, who became a member of this group, spoke often about the efforts of this organization as she was proud to lend her support.

On Saturday, October 24, *The Royal Gazette* reported "2nd balloting against high prices yesterday." The article read as follows:

> Protest ballots against rising prices were again cast in Bermuda last night when a second "vote in" was staged on the steps of the House of Assembly by the Bermudians for Reconciliation Group headed by two A.M.E. ministers, the Rev. John Brandon and the Rev. Lloyd Dees. The group again set up their ballot box and said that on Wednesday about 300 people voted. "After the count last night," Rev. Brandon said, in a statement, "that the people who had voted had shown that something must be done to change the 'unstable prices situation' in Bermuda." We are referring to the price spiral as being unjust…and indeed it is, but unjust conditions don't go away voluntarily. Particularly, if someone is making a profit. Therefore, we are only in the beginning of a long hard fight. This ballot box and the ballots you have cast are symbolic of the fact that you are asking for a change from exploitation and seeming unconcern on the part

2nd balloting against high prices yesterday

The Royal Gazette, October 24, 1970

of supposedly responsible persons who have been elected by you to look after your welfare in this regard.

You who have come are in a sense indicating that you are willing to go the second mile to rid this island of the kind of thinking that says whatever the traffic will bear let it be—when it comes to unstable vacillating high prices. Rev. Brandon declared: "May those who sit comfortable in places of business where people are being exploited, know that in the very near future—the people have the power. If they will not see that power, then they will have to feel it. When enough people stand up and say prices are too high—prices will come down. The number of those who would stand up is growing." The group announced that they intended to stage two additional voting sessions the following Tuesday and Wednesday at the House of Assembly but this time they will run from midday to 1 p.m.

As we can see, these two ministers refused to give up.

In December of 1970, momentum for the cause was evident. *The Bermuda Recorder* (now defunct), a "Pro Bono Publico" published by the Union Printery on Court Street, in Hamilton, Bermuda every Saturday, headlined, "Living Costs Prohibitive." On page two of the newspaper the following was reported:

> In recent months the walks leading to the House of Assembly have been the scene of frequent demonstrations against the high cost of living. These protests have been spearheaded by the Reverends Lloyd Dees and John Brandon. The protests have been very orderly and something of a novelty for Bermudians. As with most changes to the status quo, the cries could be heard miles away that the Bermudian himself was not interested in nor a part of such behaviour; but that this was the action of "foreign elements" on our soil who were labelled "trouble makers." This was quickly dispelled as more and more Bermudians got caught up in the action. The Bermudians for Reconciliation Organization—a group dedicated to combating the high cost of living—has been setting up meetings designed to educate the consumer concerning the facts and figures.
>
> It appears to us that whether those concerned about the welfare of "the man in the street" are black, green, blue; or whether they be Indian, Jew, British or American, should not prejudice the irrefutable facts.
>
> The merchants whimper that the cost-of-living index has risen because of labour cost which they attributed to Unionism. On the other hand, the workers are equally as vociferous about their claim that the cost of the barest necessities dictate that they band themselves together; so that they can be assured of a share of the profits.
>
> Bermuda, because of its insular nature and a dearth of raw materials and consequently a lack of many industries, must import a very high percentage of its foodstuffs. This adds to the cost to the

> consumer; but it would seem that such an increase would be slight. It appears to us that a visit to the market or the vegetable cart leaves one spending more and more money for less food.
>
> We have noted that quite a few of black members of the House of Assembly have challenged the Government's stand that there is not much that it can do about the matter. It seems that Government is unwilling to approach the issue.
>
> However, since we do not live in a vacuum and in view of the fact that the news media get the facts before the people, it is inconceivable that the Government is not aware that the United States Government has made it quite clear to the merchants that it will not tolerate any further abuse of the consumers by their inflationary actions. The Bermuda Government must be willing to see the problem for what it is and find ways to solve it.
>
> It has been suggested that the consumer refrain from purchasing all but the barest necessities, also that housewives should take a hard look at their dilemma. A speed assessment should move them in the direction to abate the continual increase in the cost-of-living index. Are the housewives willing to put themselves on the line in protest of these conditions? Will we continue to live in a world of make believe? Can we count on the silent majority to come forth and show their colours? Or must we wait for Government to wake up and face the issues squarely?

The people were becoming more aware of the efforts spearheaded by the two "foreign entities" to awaken the consciousness of the merchants and housewives who were on the front line of the purchasing debacle. They were being asked to lend support and change their selling and purchasing behaviour in the face of high prices.

Protection for the Consumer

On Saturday, November 13, 1971, on page four, *The Bermuda Sun* reported in an article captioned, "Protection for the Consumer:"

> A Commissioner of Consumer affairs? Well, why not? It is a post most shoppers will probably be happy to see filled. And that means practically everybody. For about a year now we have been hearing from Government and the Chamber of Commerce about the possibility of lowering profits on basic items which are sold in great quantity. The parallel suggestion has usually been made that this would probably mean higher mark-ups on less basic items, to compensate the traders for lower profits on basics. But the possibility never becomes reality. The hang up, we are told, is over the question of what constitutes basic items. Is toothpaste, for instance, a basic?
>
> It is undoubtedly a tricky list to draw up, but it would also seem to the onlooker that both sides are using that fact in order to let the issue drag on unresolved. Perhaps a commissioner of consumer affairs with horse-sense could come up with a list which would go beyond bread, milk, potatoes, flour, sugar and eggs, but stop short of the shoe polish and the potato chips.
>
> Bermudians for Reconciliation, the organization which suggests a consumer affairs commissioner be appointed, seem at long last to be getting down to some concrete proposals for frequent protests but few constructive ideas. And even now they skirt the question of the basic foods list by suggesting that they "be determined," rather than making a start by suggesting a list themselves.
>
> The group's suggestion that frozen meat and milk should be date-stamped would meet with the approval of every housewife. Their idea that stores should provide scales on the premises for customers to check weights should be seized upon by any supermarket with an eye to its image. Whether it is justified or not, Bermuda's food

> sellers in particular face a big credibility gap and this sort of gesture would do something to reduce it. The group's suggestion that credit payments should be clearly spelt out has long been anticipated by reputable stores which also give the cash price, so that no one can claim to have been misled. Shoppers could keep clear of the others, which, incidentally, would be the surest way of bringing them into line.
>
> A consumer affairs commissioner would be a good gathering point for information from customers who buy mechanical products and then find it impossible to buy spare parts when there is a breakdown. One firm is notorious for its attitude and disrespect. An annual report by the commissioner listing valid complaints of this nature according to store, would quickly put a painful and reforming spotlight on the chief offenders.

The Bermudians for Reconciliation must have felt some satisfaction to finally make progress on their fight to bring awareness concerning the high cost of living in Bermuda. Their proposal for a consumer affairs commissioner was getting some traction. It is important to note that when you believe in something, you should be prepared to fight for it. Rev. Dees and Rev. Brandon first brought awareness to a problem that existed in Bermuda long before they arrived. When they were made aware of it, they sought out people they could motivate to act. This is not to say that the people were unaware but perhaps they just needed someone to inspire them to greater action. Rev. Dees and Rev. Brandon were prepared to go the extra mile. The group seemed to be successful in creating concrete proposals and didn't simply stop at protesting. In any case their protests paid dividends as can be seen in the next section.

New Rent Commissioner

In *The Royal Gazette* newspaper dated Saturday, February 26, 1972, pages of information appeared devoted to the cost of living. The information included numerous charts, but the first article that caught my attention was the following, captioned "New Rent Commissioner takes over—and issues warning to landlords." The article reads as follows:

Mr. Hector Barcilon, Bermuda's former Puisne Judge, took up his post as Rent Commissioner yesterday—and issued a warning to landlords to safeguard themselves in cases of agreed rent increases. Facing Mr. Barcilon in his new job is a backlog of work, and the task of coping with initial inquiries.

"We are trying to tackle the problems as we think of them," he told The Royal Gazette, and cited one situation under which a landlord could leave himself unprotected. He explained: "Under the act, if the landlord and the tenant agree to an increase, all they have to do is to notify us, and we endorse the agreed increase and send the forms back."

If the landlord has failed to take this action, however, even if he has the agreement of his tenant, the latter, at some later stage, could turn nasty and try to recover all he has paid in the way of increases.

It is in everyone's interest and particularly the landlord's, to send in these forms when there is an agreed increase. Some landlords may not bother. They have the tenant's agreement, but one day some row occurs, and the tenant realizes the forms have not been sent in and he can claim against the landlord.

Mr. Barcilon added, "From the rather few such agreement increases that we have been notified about so far, it seems obvious that this has been occurring, and the landlord is without any protection whatsoever." Mr. Barcilon is expected to be a week or two in establishing the running of his office which is in the Burnaby building.

He said, "At the moment we are trying to think out some way of preventing the spiral in rent increases, but if tenants are merrily agreeing left, right and centre to these increases, they are doing this situation no good at all. We have no alternative if there is an increase agreed to by a tenant. We have no discretion at all to

> refuse it—unless it appears to us that the tenant has been pressured into accepting the increase."
>
> What I am saying are just the right thoughts that are going through my mind. I feel sure that there will be other problems, and we will have to get round to them all.
>
> As far as the public is concerned, a lot of people at the moment look upon us as legal advisors on their tenancy problems. But we must not be asked to give legal advice. We must tell people what forms to fill in and so on, but anyone with any legal query on the new Act should go straight to his lawyer. A specific ruling, we might give—but I may well have to refer a matter to the Attorney General. I have to keep reminding myself at the moment that I am no longer a judge.

Once again Rev. Dees and Rev. Brandon worked to have the government institute protection against rising costs and the cost of housing, which was a grave problem. I suppose that they were aware that some people, especially those I know from the Black community, used rents as a way to make money and a rent commission could put limits on how much a landlord could increase their rent. This was a double-edged sword, as those who needed rent most and who had invested in securing their homes fell under rent control. Unfortunately, many others who had property did not fall under the control of the rent commission and could benefit extensively from the properties they rented. The ruling government of the day, the United Bermuda Party (U.B.P.), and those associated with this government, which included the local merchants, would have done all they could to protect their own interests. This is the government which had formed on August 21, 1964, and who ruled the country for over thirty years—winning eight straight elections until the Progressive Labour Party finally won the government in 1998.

For those who did not know, Sir Henry Tucker was the first leader of the U.B.P. party and was considered a shrewd and personable businessman. I met him in person in 1987 when he pleasantly asked me to speak at his caucus meeting. Certainly, for many, Bermuda was a wonderful place to live and the ruling party would have been pleased about the following headline in *The Royal Gazette* on Saturday, February 26, 1972, "Record $48.4 Million to Spend. Beautiful day."

Bermuda's Budget

What follows is what was reported in *The Royal Gazette* at the time. According to the article "A record $48.4 million Budget, which includes tax increases of nearly four-and-a-half million dollars, was presented to the House of Assembly yesterday by the Member for Finance the Hon. Jack Sharpe. It called for:

- Higher import duties on liquor, beer and cigarettes, to raise an extra million dollars.
- Upward adjustment of land tax rates to realise an additional $1.7 million.
- An over-100 percent increase in annual exempted company fees to produce $700,000 more.
- A rise from $2.40 to $4 in the "head tax" to increase revenue by $800,000.
- Raising the cost of licenses to non-Bermudians acquiring property here to realize an extra $200,000.

The Member told the House: "I am satisfied that this year's Budget provides a good basis for another record year in the advance of the Bermuda economy, on which we all depend for the fulfillment of our personal and community goals."

"It has been possible to achieve a financially strong and responsible budgetary position without premature ventures into new taxation before we can be satisfied about all the consequences." He said later the Government believes that the thorough study of the tax system now underway will enable the Government to propose changes in the existing structure in ways which can strengthen Bermuda's economy, ensure fairness and encourage fuller participation by Bermudians in their own economy. The Budget is nearly $3 million higher than last year's and allows for a "small surplus" of just under $2 million.

On the land tax issue, Mr. Sharpe commented, "Because there has been some misunderstanding about the effect of the new valuations, the Member for Planning has agreed to extend the period for lodging objections for a further two weeks, ending Friday, March 10." The original deadline had been today. As has been the case in recent years, education calls for the single largest expenditure, being allowed nearly 20 percent of the total budget, $9.8 million—an increase of $1.2 million.

Teacher salaries take up more than half of that amount, while $1.7 million has been earmarked for the school building program. The other major capital expenditure in this department will be $66,000 for development of recreational facilities at Bernard Park.

Under education there are other allocations for sports organizations and facilities.

Major capital expenditures here are $75,000 for continued renovations at Lefroy House and $36,000 for conversion of the Haven into a community home for boys.

Agriculture and Works is close behind Health, being allocated 15.3 percent of the total, or $7.4 million. On the revenue side, Customs duties are the biggest source of income, being estimated to raise $25.4 million or 50 percent of Government receipts.

"It's a beautiful day today," said the beaming Member for Finance the Hon. Jack Sharpe, as the House of Assembly opened yesterday. "I think it's a beautiful day for a beautiful budget." As a few members groaned he added, "I hope that at the end I will get a better reception then I did at the beginning—though I appreciate that members may be a little apprehensive."

He then read out his formal budget statement, "This budget can properly be regarded as a catching up budget." When he reached the section calling for higher customs duties on cigarettes and liquors, he remarked, "The last time I was in the House of Commons when

> the Chancellor was presenting his budget, announcing changes in customs duties, I recall very vividly and dramatically his making a gesture that I am not going to make." He reached into his hip pocket, pulled out a small flash containing an amber liquid, poured some into a glass in front of him and said, "This is probably the last drink at this price that I will have." Observing that this anecdote "gives a clue" to what would follow, Mr. Sharpe remarked, "I know it will affect some honourable members more personally than others."
>
> After reading his formal statement the Member moved adoption of the estimates of revenue and expenditure for the financial year 1972-73. The speaker, Lt. Col. J.C. Astwood, pointed out, "The motion will not be put until the Committee of Supply have discussed the whole thing and report it back." The Committee of Supply is the name for the committee of the whole House when the budget for appropriations are under discussion.
>
> Mr. Sharpe then sat down the estimates, together with the budget statement, as the first order to be taken up at next Friday's meeting. Member for Agriculture and Works the Hon. John Patton announced that "as an anticlimax" he was submitting for the information of the House a survey of the agricultural industry in Bermuda for 1971, prepared by the Department of Agriculture and Fisheries.

On the surface this looked like a good budget, however a country as profitable as Bermuda should have, in the opinion of many, given greater relief to the working classes. It is interesting to note that in the same newspaper there was a full-page report on the cost of living and the debate on the budget as referenced below.

Big Debate on the Budget

On Saturday February 26, 1972, *The Royal Gazette* also reported: "Big debate on cost of living." The extensive article ran for several pages and listed the retail prices for the cost of items per pound, package, can, bag, or jar. Beside the Bermuda prices were the prices for the cost of the same goods in America. I found this article absolutely fascinating. It noted how the Bermudians for Reconciliation members were considered an unfavourable pressure group. Obviously, the group was making an impact after all, as the article reported:

> The cost-of-living petition signed by 2,900 local people and presented to the Bermudians for Reconciliation Group, was given the unusual distinction of being debated in the House of Assembly yesterday, together with the reply of the Member for Finance, the Hon. Jack Sharpe.
>
> The petition, which was introduced by Mr. Ralph Marshall (U.B.P.) called essentially for price controls and consumer protection. Mr. Sharpe's reply, which rejects the former and supports the latter, was eventually adopted. The debate started with the speaker informing the house in his ruling against the petition being admitted as a subject for debate but reminding them that they could overrule him by simply agreeing to the motion that "the question now be put." Member in charge, Mr. Ralph Marshall (U.B.P.) accordingly made his motion and the House agreed to it unanimously.
>
> Mr. Sharpe, moving that his reply to the petition be adopted, stated that at Thursday's caucus meeting of the U.B.P., it had been agreed that debate should be permitted on the petition, but that it should be restricted to the House as a whole and not taken "into committee." This has the effect of permitting the member in charge and, in this case, Mr. Sharpe, to open and close the debate, and for each member of the House to speak only once on the subject. Once in committee individual members can speak as often as they wish.

In his opening remarks, the Member for Finance began by doubting if the Bermudians for Reconciliation were really interested in reconciliation. He noted where the group had accused Government of attempting to shunt the matter aside, when in fact parliamentary procedure was being followed closely, as any one genuinely interested in being constructive could have ascertained.

MEETING

Mr. Sharpe added that at Mr. Marshall's suggestion he had instigated a meeting with the group and offered his Finance Department offices for the get-together. He was somewhat upset when the person at the other end of the telephone suggested, instead of City Hall, that the Bermuda Library, or the Vernon Temple Church could be the meeting place.

"I was again disconcerted when the time came for the meeting in my office, and I saw who was coming through the door," said the Member. First in was the former parliamentary leader of the P.L.P., Mr. Walter Robinson, followed by a former candidate for the P.L.P., then a person who was not a Bermudian (Rev. Dees), and finally a professional stenographer with a notebook and a tape recorder.

Although he found this inhibiting, Mr. Sharpe said, the discussion took place, for what it was worth. "Then when I had my reply ready and was unable to present it because the House was not sitting that Friday, instead of calling me to ask what was happening, the so-called Bermudians for Reconciliation threatened to expose me by publicizing the transcript of our discussion. And this was two days before their letter on the subject."

Mr. Sharpe said he found such conduct irregular, unethical and, as far as the tape recording was concerned, not very helpful to the public.

CONTRAST

"Their conduct, and I say this with all due respect, contrasts markedly, for the instance, with the Committee for Social Concern of the Ministerial Association," he went on. "They investigated their facts and met with the Chamber of Commerce, the grocers, myself and other interested parties."

Bermudians for Reconciliation have refused to meet with anyone who might be able to supply them with the sort of information they must have, to be able to make the kind of statements they delight in.

At this point Mr. Sharpe turned to the petition itself and his reply, and produced the list of comparative prices which he describes as "a pleasant surprise." He said, "Unless their minds are made-up and they don't want to hear the facts, I do urge members of the opposition to take a look at these figures."

"If they look at them dispassionately, they will see that prices in Bermuda are really most reasonable and that in some cases we do better than other countries." He pointed out that some items abroad were called lost leaders and only had to profit margin of 3.7 to 4.8 percent so that they moved quickly and in large quantities. Locally this was difficult to do, and grocers preferred instead an across-the-board margin. In a free enterprise society, anyone could run a grocery business, and it was his understanding that the officers of the B.I.U., had one near Spanish Point. He himself had helped develop a farm linked very closely to the food industry, and although he no longer took part in its everyday running, he was convinced that competition was the only really effective way to keep prices down.

Expressing the hope that the House would agree that government had been right in bringing in a rent Control Act but would be guilty of wasting money and effort on an attempt to improve price controls, he left his reply in its hands.

COMPLAINT

Mr. Frederick Wade (P.L.P.) rose to complain that at a previous meeting between the Government and the Opposition over procedure, at no time had it been suggested that the petition and Mr. Sharpe's reply would not be debated in committee.

Since this would stifle free debate, his party would show its disapproval by abstaining from debate. To cries of "Are the facts too much for you?" Mr. Wade and other P.L.P. members rose one by one and left the chamber, leaving only three of their members still seated.

Mr. Fernance Perry (U.B.P.) said that the Member for Finance had told the House time and time again that food importers in Bermuda were faced with increases that were beyond their control, and yet some members of the House and the public seemed incapable of accepting this fact. "Some have not got even enough interest to find out," he said stating that he had kept quiet on the matter of food prices in the past because of his personal interest in a supermarket. Mr. Perry said that he was going to speak out now because the matter had reached a stage where it was essential that the public be put right.

None of the Opposition had taken him up on his invitation to visit his store and have all the information on markups supplied to them, so he had to come out in public and give it to them straight from the shoulder.

ACCUSATION

"I cannot remain silent any longer. I and other merchants have been accused of milking the public and other accusations which are just contemptible," he said. The petition he found insulting not only to the merchants, who worked hard to give the public the high standard of service and variety they deserved, but also to the public themselves, who were very sensitive to prices and would go a mile to save a penny. The petition made them appear stupid.

"Price controls," he said, "could be the worst thing that could happen in Bermuda. Deprived of incentive, merchants would give up stocking essential items because they could not afford to tie up money in…goods when they could get seven percent on it elsewhere."

He too was presently surprised to see the price comparisons that Mister Sharpe had obtained. These showed that Bermuda was in a pretty fair position, despite the extra expenses it had to pay. Mr. Perry then took up the matter of gross and net profits, which he felt the man in the street misunderstood.

In simple terms gross profit was what was left after the expense of importing a product had been met. Net was what remained after local operating costs and expenses had been absorbed. For example, on average local food merchants spend 80 cents in every dollar on bringing an item into the island. This left a gross profit of 20 cents from which many things still remained to be deducted.

"Such as cheap wages?" asked an Opposition member.

"Cheap wages can be very expensive when balanced with productivity," countered the speaker, amid laughter.

TAXES

Returning to his 20 percent gross profit, Mr. Perry said that from this had to come incorporation taxes, land taxes, legal fees, corporation taxes, parish vestry taxes, capital depreciation, building depreciation, purchasing of equipment, buildings, freezers, fixtures, etc.

"This still leaves your day-to-day operating expenses," he said, "of which wages are the biggest." Then you have electricity, wrapping supplies, warehousing, and many other expensive commitments. The balance after all these things were paid for was called a net profit (or loss if you were unfortunate) and in the third business it was a good year if this represented four percent, or just four cents from that original dollar.

In the United States tax was paid on this net profit, and not on the gross profit, so what had appeared recently in a letter to the morning newspaper was quite inaccurate. "What I am telling you is the truth," went on Mr. Perry, "Last year our gross profit (at the Piggly Wiggly) was 20.6 percent, and our net profit was four percent and here are the figures to prove it."

At this point the member produced an audited statement of his firm's affairs and offered them to any member of the House to inspect. He continued that it was essential for a firm to retain earnings, because it had to have something to back up its operation so that it could expand, if necessary, maintain its standards and replace worn out equipment.

"Do intelligent people begrudge us our profit," he asked. "Don't they want to see a healthy business, able to search the world for the best prices and to provide the community with quality foods and the working population with the source of employment? Would they rather see a failing business, which they will end up paying for in the long run?"

NAILED TO CROSS

"The merchant is always being nailed to the cross and crucified, he is never given credit for adding to the economy of the country." Mr. Perry then came to the defence of the middleman, the commission agent, who was paid five percent by the manufacturer for promoting his product. It would bc impossible for the Colony to maintain its price structure without him, said the speaker because he was the key to volume buying. Col. J. Brownlow Tucker (U.B.P.) revealed that the recent wage agreement signed with dock workers had increased their wage from $2.52 an hour to $3, an increase of about 19 percent.

Couple that with the 10 to 30 percent freight increases just put into effect for Eastern seaboard freight runs to Bermuda and the effect of the 45 percent pay increase awarded longshoremen there and one could see what importers meant by increases beyond their control. New methods, such as containerization, had helped keep operating costs down over the last three years, but the shipping companies had now found it impossible to hold the line. Devaluation and wage increases will probably completely absorb the freight rate increases and he was sorry that Dr. Barbara Ball (P.L.P.) was not in the Chamber to hear the figures.

Mr. Marshall revealed that the Board of Agriculture and Fisheries had voted, although not unanimously, to ask for the duty on milk to be abolished, in an effort to help steady the cost of living. He felt that the Government had bent over backwards to get the petition considered, and he was disappointed that the Opposition refused to discuss it over a mere technicality.

SPEAKERS VIEW

The speaker commented that he had attended the meeting referred to by Mr. Wade and there had been no mention made of having the House go into committee. If there had been, he would have advised against it since such a step would have been most unseemly, in his opinion.

Mr. Harry Viera applauded Government for its tolerance over the petition, which he felt projected the narrow view of a pressure group since it ignored many other ingredients, such as vandalism, shoplifting, pilfering, incompetent management, etc. He felt the unions could be more helpful in hitting at the rising costs but at the same time people had come to expect so much more.

He understood 25,000 Bermudians have been abroad, almost half the population. That there were five to 7,000 boats in the Colony and 10,000 motor vehicles. Many homes he visited had sophisticated electronic equipment, and local people made-up a healthy proportion of every nightclub audience. "We have to learn we all cannot live like millionaires," said Mr. Viera, advocating tighter hire purchase laws and spot checks on merchants who were suspected of fleecing the community.

The Hon. James E. Pearman said there was no other parliament in the world that would have accepted a petition of this nature and debated it, and no other Member of Finance would have paid the petitioners the courtesy of meeting with them and preparing a far-reaching report.

OTHERS RIGHT

He was now convinced by what he had heard that other parliaments were right, and Bermuda had been wrong. It had proved to be neither appropriate nor desirable for the petition from this small group to have been debated. Instead, he suggested it should have been laid on the table, as the speaker had in fact recommended. How the petitioners could say they had not been treated properly was quite beyond him. Mr. Quinton Edness (U.B.P.) was sorry that there had been the suggestion that the petitioners were politically motivated since it was of the greatest importance to the Colony that employers and unions, Government and Opposition work together on this common problem.

At this point the two remaining P.L.P. members rose in turn to comment. Mr. Austin Thomas hit back strongly at the "stupid" suggestion that the group were politically motivated or that the P.L.P., was linked with them. The problem did indeed transcend politics and he was sure his party was prepared to help find the solutions. He felt that the problem was bigger than just the grocery businesses, and that it spread throughout the many facets of the Colony's economy.

"It isn't the P.L.P. that you need to convince, it's the public that needs to be convinced," he said. "The public are never going to get to understand what is going on, because it is they from whom information is being withheld." He was concerned that the U.B.P. had moved quickly to, he alleged, stifle debate on a critical matter, an action that the newly enfranchised electorate might misunderstand.

QUESTION

Mr. Reginald Burrows felt that food prices in Bermuda were comparable with many other countries, but he wondered if the figures given on Mr. Sharpe's list referred to the lowest prices to be found throughout Bermuda or if they came from one store, as in the case of the U.S. figures. Mr. William Cox (U.B.P.) was pleased that members of the P.L.P. had decided to ignore their leader's boycott of the debate, since the petition did focus on the attention of the House on a matter of importance and the debate had been valuable.

He criticized Mr. Wade for his stand and for suggesting there have been "political chicanery." He felt that for the P.L.P. member, to opt out on the basis of a procedural point was itself an example of petty party politics at its lowest level.

Mr. Sharpe, rounding off the debate, said he, too, was disappointed that the P.L.P. had shunned the debate and he praised the three members who had stayed behind to listen and to contribute. Answering Mr. Burrows, he said that the Bermuda prices on his list came from a large Hamilton supermarket and were in Bermuda dollars. The Bahamas prices had been discounted by five percent to bring them in line with our currency, while the U.S. and the Canadian prices were in their dollars. The reply, which in essence rejects the petition's call for price controls, was then adopted unanimously.

There is a great deal to reflect on in the prior account, but what struck me was that the Bermudians for Reconciliation were in fact a great thorn in the side of the ruling party. Rev. Dees was considered a foreigner, and his presence was not appreciated. How dare they ask to meet with the government minister and then have the audacity to suggest a venue such as Vernon Temple A.M.E. Church as a meeting place. To be fair, the honorable member said they suggested three venues, as if they could not make up their minds.

Record Budget Ups Tax on Liquor, Cigarettes

Additionally, in the Saturday, February 26, 1972, issue of *The Royal Gazette,* the following article dealing with taxation, titled "Record Budget Ups Tax on Liquor, Cigarettes" was presented.

> Another record year in the advance of the Colony's economy was foreseen as the Hon. Jack Sharpe, Member for Finance, presented the estimates to the House of Assembly in a 40-minute Budget speech yesterday.
>
> "I am satisfied that this year's Budget proves a good basis for another record year in the advance of the Bermuda economy on which we all depend for the fulfillment of our personal and community goals," he said he told the house. In handing down the record $48,393.205 budget, Mr. Sharpe said: "It has been possible to achieve a financially strong and responsible budgetary position without premature ventures into new taxation before we can be satisfied about all the consequences."
>
> "This has been done by making overdue adjustments in the existing structure of fees and taxes, which bring them more into line with the current costs in the economy generally." However, he pointed out in conclusion that the Government is considering changes in the existing tax structure.
>
> The Government believe that the thorough study of a tax system now underway will enable the Government to propose changes in the existing structure in ways which can strengthen Bermuda's

economy, ensure fairness and encourage fuller participation by Bermudians in their own economy.

The good financial position of the Government resulting from this Budget will ensure that changes to this end can be made free from undue immediate pressures and in the light of the best long-term interests of Bermuda and all Bermudians.

Among the increases in customs duties was that on alcohol such as brandy, vodka, liqueurs and cordials, other alcoholic beverage of 70 percent under proof gallon for the preferential rates and from $15.30 to $17.00 per proof gallon for the preferential rates and from $15.57 to $17.30 for the general rates.

The duty on whiskey is to be raised from $14.40 to $16 per proof gallon for the preferential rate and from $14.64 to $16.25 for the general rate. Duties on rum and gin are to be raised from $9.00 per proof gallon for the preferential rate and from $9.15 to $12.20 for the general rate.

Duty on all types of beer is also to be raised from 54 cents to 62 cents per gallon for the preferential rate and from 56 cents to 64 cents for the general rate.

The duty on cigarettes is also to be raised from $1.86 to $2.42 per pound for the preferential rate and from $1.92 per pound to $2.50 for the general rate.

These increases are expected to increase revenue by an estimated amount of $1 million. Per bottle or package, the increases are modest and per drink relatively inconsequential. They will continue to be a bargain when compared with the prices in the United Kingdom, the United States or Canada.

On the land tax the Member said: "As members will be aware, the new land valuations will become effective in the second half of this year. Hence, I have had to consider what adjustments, if any, should be made to the present land tax rates and the present sliding scale or taper by which the majority of the residential properties pay less than the full rate of tax."

I have had to bear in mind the increased need for Government revenue, the abolition of Part II of the tax which I have just revealed, and in controvertible fact that the increases in land valuations reflect the large increases in rents, in property values and indirectly in the incomes generally, which have occurred over the past five years.

For these reasons I have decided to maintain the present tax rate at 10 percent. This will continue to apply to all commercial properties and should yield an increase in revenue from such properties of approximately $1,100.00 to a new total in a full year of about $2,100.00.

The taper for residential properties will be adjusted in two ways. First, I have accepted the principle used by the former Parish Vestry taxes that all properties should bear a tax liability, however small.

There will therefore be no exemptions from the land tax: however over 6,000 properties will pay at a rate of only 1 percent—probably less than they pay previously in the Parish taxes. Secondly, I have adjusted the whole taper upwards by an average appreciation of 50 percent so that those with new annual rental values over $3,240 will pay the full rate of 10 percent.

Under this scale only some 2,000 properties out of a total of over 16,000 residential properties will be liable for the full rate of tax. Nevertheless, this group will pay over half of the total bill on residential properties. It is estimated that the revenues for residential properties will amount to about 1.4 million in full year, an increase of about $700,000 over the present yield.

It may soon cost $1.60 more to leave the Colony, according to Mr. Sharpe. "I decided that if an increase in this tax (passenger ticket tax) was appropriate at this time, as I consider it was, it was only sensible to set a level at which it could stay for a reasonable period."

On this basis, I propose an increase of $4.00 effective from 1st of April 1972, which it is estimated will raise $800,000 additional revenue in the coming year.

I am also considering whether this tax might be more appropriately collected in a different manner than at present but have reached no final conclusion.

"The retail price index rose just over 9 percent during the last calendar year," Mr. Sharpe said. This was about the same as the United Kingdom but rather more than experienced by other supplying countries.

However, I think there is reason for guarded optimism as the rate of acceleration may be slowing he said. The member also said that $400,000 necessary to complete the Prospect scheme was allocated in the budget and a further $1 million is being requested for the commencement of two new—the construction of 32 two-bedroom apartments, probably in the area of Saint Brendan's and a housing development in St. George's.

On the subject of company fees, Mr. Sharpe proposed that both the annual fee for exempt companies and exempted partnerships be increased to $1,000 commencing on July 1st with a provision for the Member of Finance to reduce the amount of the fee to not less than $600 in respect to classes of companies and for periods of time designed by the Member. "It was contemplated that only those companies which utilize the whole assets for families or their trusts could, the benefits of individual farther effect filed with the Registrar of Companies at the time of making payment of the annual fee, obtain a reduction to the lower prescribed amount," he said.

We intend to set this lower amount at $600 for such companies. He also said that he was intending to introduce legislation to increase the initial and annual fees paid by non-resident corporate bodies (accept non-resident insurance undertakings) to $1,200.

A higher contribution to Government is appropriate for such companies, commonly known as permit companies, because unlike other exempted or local companies, they do not pay stamp duties or incorporation and on increases in their authorized capital.

The number of international companies registered here rose from 1,922 at the end of 1970 to 2,281 at the end of 1971.

Mr. Sharpe also said that the new refuge disposal plant should be almost completed by the end of the year and that the first phase of integrating the Transportation Department with the Examination center, for the convenience of both staff and public will be undertaken.

"Funds are provided to study pollutions and for additional beach cleaning equipment," he said. "Just short of $100,000 is requested to continue the existing and important work being done in the development of freshwater supplies in the optimistic expectation that freshwater needs in the future are underground."

"Further funds are provided to combat drug abuse and to do other medical surveys in the interest of the community's health," Mr. Sharpe said.

As last year the King Edward the VII Memorial Hospital will require a substantial operational grant—not anticipated when the hospital insurance plan was introduced but made necessary by both increased wages and increased staff.

Assemblymen Debate Role of Church ...

On April 25, 1972, the headline in *The Royal Gazette* read, "Assemblymen debate role of the church in political affairs." The account is as follows:

> Mentioned recently by a United Bermuda Party of Assemblyman of clergymen—by inference Ministers of the A.M.E. Church—was taken a step further yesterday in the House by the Progressive Labour Party. Mr. Stanley Morton noted that the Hon. Lancelot Swan had been quoted in *The Royal Gazette* last week as saying at a meeting that the church should not intervene in government matters.
>
> "We should charge Ministers to stay out of Government affairs and do their duty of changing people to live a Christian life," it had been stated in the paper. Said Mr. Morton, "I find these remarks very strange, coming from the member who was responsible for Youth. One would have thought that he would have loved to see the church involved in public matters and also to give some sense of direction to Government."

The opposition member considered that if anyone wanted guidance, he should look to ministers and to the church. I think they should be in a position to give us the best guideline, in particular when it comes to behaviour.

For me, it was both amusing and disheartening, but not surprising, that the members of the Bermuda House of Assembly felt it necessary to debate the role of the church in politics, especially when the two pastors in question were Americans who were civil rights activists. If Rev. Dees nor Rev. Brandon (both men would have been very young) did not participate in the Selma Montgomery nonviolence march with Dr. Martin Luther King, Jr. in 1965, the two ministers who arrived in Bermuda only a few years after would have nevertheless been influenced by the success of peaceful demonstrations and the need for them. When injustice is exposed, both pastors perhaps believed that people would then do what they know is right. When Dr. King called all who were against the treatment of the downtrodden to march with them, Black and white clergy stepped forward. Yet, in Bermuda the need for the clergy to get involved in politics was questioned, or the fact that these two *foreign* pastors confronted the injustices in Bermuda that affected their congregations was not wanted.

I must interject here that after the Bermuda general election, held on February 18, 2025, Rev. Dr. Emily Gail Dill, my friend for many years and wife of Bermuda's Presiding Elder, Rev. Howard H.L. Dill, became the first A.M.E. woman elected to serve in Bermuda's parliament.

The Royal Gazette article continues:

> **SILENT VIGIL**
>
> Mr. Morton observed that the Rev. John Brandon and the Rev. Lloyd Dee—both A.M.E. ministers—were once more keeping their silent vigil outside the house in protest about the high cost of living, especially food, rents and houses. This was a peaceful demonstration noted Mr. Morton, "and I think it is an indication of the type of leadership ministers can give."
>
> When Christians are the line of demarcation between ministers or Christians. If a man professes to be a Christian, then he can serve in the same capacity as a minister.
>
> "In the past churches had been used for the convenience of governments here and throughout the world, and some people had even posed as ministers. But if people are genuinely interested in the welfare of human beings and prepare to sacrifice their own time to the welfare of the community, I think this is commendable," said Mr. Morton.
>
> Mr. Swan (U.B.P.) said he would make no apologies for his speech, "but I do think it was taken out of context." He felt that the church was one of the few institutions in the existence for nearly 2,000 years. During this time, there had been all kinds of political parties and economic situations. These had faded away, "and the church alone remained, as a guiding star to everyone."
>
> But I do say that the moment the church goes too far from its mission of saving souls, and gets so completely immersed in the

political affairs, it changes, and where there should be peace and harmony, there is dissension that is what I said in my speech.

He also said that actual changes should be made by political parties and other such bodies, pointing out that the church would "sing out loud and clear" if Government tried to interfere with the internal functions of the church.

GUIDING STAR

Mr. Swan thought in this day and age, youngsters needed a guiding star to hang on to, since there was unrest everywhere they went, caused by dissension. The church should be free of this; should be the sanctuary, where you go for peace, and this would be good for youth and the whole community.

Opposition leader Mrs. Lois Brown-Evans pointed out that if Archbishop Makarios had not come out of his pulpit and did what he could for the people of Cyprus, there wouldn't be the tranquillity there is today.

"He nearly got shot the other day," and interpolated the Hon. David Wilkinson (U.B.P.) causing laughter. Mrs. Brown-Evans reminded Mr. Swan that the A.M.E. Church to which he belonged, had been borne out of protest. As for the ministers conducting their vigil outside the House of Assembly, she suggested that Mister Swan should "give them his help and join them for a few minutes in their walk, because there is nothing that is more peaceful than ministers keeping vigil."

The late Rev. Martin Luther King (Jr.) had wanted a better mankind and that's what Rev. Dees and Rev. Brandon were trying to do, and she saw nothing wrong with that.

"They are foreigners—we don't want them here," quipped Mr. Wilkinson.

> **WHITE MINISTERS**
>
> The opposition leader said she had known of white ministers who came to Bermuda "and meddled in politics." The chairman of the Race Relations committee was the Reverend George Buchanan and even his sermons published in *The Royal Gazette* had political overtones. Mrs. Brown-Evans could see no difference between the two A.M.E. ministers outside the house, protesting against the high cost of living, and another minister and followers sitting on the steps of the Cathedral recently at the start of Christian Aid week to help combat poverty and hunger throughout the world.
>
> She felt it was "lamentable that no Bermudian pastor had had the courage and foresight to make a demonstration in this day and age, when a personal demonstration is demanded. You have to act in this day and age." With obvious emotion Mrs. Brown-Evans said that the two A.M.E. ministers were outside.

I found this article interesting and asked Rev. Trevor Woolridge, a past pastor of Mount Zion A.M.E. Church in Bermuda, now pastor of Washington Chapel A.M.E. Church in Tuskegee, Alabama, to reflect. He sent me his thoughts on what he called, "The Call to Serve Beyond the Four Walls of the Church" and noted that: "In 1968, the late Dame Lois Browne-Evans, who was light years ahead of her time, sought young people to become involved with the Bermuda Progressive Labour Party. I was twelve years old when I joined the Youth Wing of the P.L.P. Even at that age, I knew there was a calling on my life for the preaching ministry. However, the life and leadership of the Rev. Lloyd E. Dees, then pastor of Bethel A.M.E. Church, Shelly Bay, in Hamilton Parish, Bermuda was the inspiration that a preacher could do more than just preach and pray to improve the lives of people."

The Royal Gazette article continues:

The Rev. Lloyd E. Dees and the Rev. John Brandon pastors of Bethel and Vernon Temple A.M.E. Churches, respectively, provided much needed leadership to the church and community in Bermuda. Rev. Dees was often the voice of the voiceless in Bermuda. Major white business leaders in the country were also elected Members of Colonial Parliament. That kind of power required the likes of the Rev. Lloyd E. Dees to raise concerns about unfair practices that were prevalent. The

African Methodist Episcopal in Bermuda and around the world, and their pastors, have provided similar leadership as Rev. Lloyd E. Dees and Rev. John Brandon. Bermuda owes a debt of gratitude to these pastors for the valuable contribution spiritually and politically they provided.

It was easy for me to decide to serve my country as a clergyman politically. The honor and privilege to be the first clergyman to serve in the Bermuda Senate (1989-1993) and the first clergyman to serve as an elected Member of Parliament (1993-1997) is a cherished time of my life in public service. For those publications and persons that argue against clergy serving in elected or appointed offices are without merit. All persons offering themselves for public service should be committed to serving with integrity and transparency regardless of the chosen profession. How much easier it was for those who came after me to make their contributions: The Rev. Cindy Trimm, The Rev. Leonard Santucci, The Rev. Wilbur M. (Larry) Lowe, Jr. Bermuda is better for those who serve with God as the priority in their lives.

Bermudians for Reconciliation Reply to Members' Reply

The Saturday, February 26, 1972 edition of *The Royal Gazette* captioned Bermudians for Reconciliation replies to Members' speech continued on page 7 and read as follows:

> The Bermudians for Reconciliation Organization are not satisfied with the reply which the Member for Finance the Hon. Jack Sharpe M.C.P., gave in the House of Assembly last week concerning their petition on the cost of living.
>
> In a statement issued yesterday, the organization takes issue with the Member on several points, and declares it is very easy to detect the reports evasiveness of the real issue on high prices, and failure to understand the economic position of the consumer. Full text of the statement is:
>
> After having studied Mr. Sharpe's reply to our petition to the House of Assembly, as given in the daily paper, we find that the Government has not itself made any concrete steps toward curbing the ever-increasing cost of living in the Colony and has given no possibility of relief to the consumer from the present situation.

> "Since Mr. Sharpe thought it necessary to mention in his reply that government took a decision in September, well before the petition was presented—to control rent increases…" it must be pointed out that Bermudians for Reconciliation started the petition September 3, 1971. It is interesting to note also, that on February 25, 1971, the Chamber of Commerce asked that Government state publicly "advising that unfair profits are not being made."

As you may recall, the name of Mr. Phil Perinchief was first referenced in *The Royal Gazette* newspaper as he was a Black Beret and had attended at least one meeting with Rev. Dees and Rev. Brandon. I approached Mr. Perinchief and asked him to reflect on that time period. He is a lawyer and has been on numerous recent talk shows (including *The Need to Lead*) in Bermuda discussing the concerns of the rising cost of living. I take this opportunity to thank him profusely for taking the time to send me a great deal of in-depth material, especially as his son passed in November 2024.

PRICE PROTEST GETS 'GOOD RESPONSE'

The Royal Gazette, October 1970

To introduce him, I have summarized his very lengthy resume:

> Mr. Phil Perinchief is a distinguished legal professional and economist with extensive academic credentials and over four decades of diverse experience in law, economics, and public policy. A graduate of Dalhousie University, York University, Osgoode Hall Law School, the University of Leiden, Tulane University, and the University of Malta, he holds multiple degrees, including a Master of Arts in Economics, a Bachelor of Education, and several advanced law degrees specializing in areas such as civil litigation, maritime law, aerospace law (aviation and space law), and international relations.
>
> Called to the bar in Ontario and Bermuda in 1985, Mr. Phil Perinchief has served in significant roles within the legal and government spheres, including as Attorney General of Bermuda and Principal Crown Counsel. He has led legal teams, managed substantial operational budgets, and provided advisory services on constitutional, administrative, and international law matters to high-level government officials.
>
> Mr. Perinchief's professional journey also includes founding his own law practice PJP Consultants, where he advises clients in satellite communications, shipping, and aviation. His involvement with various government boards and committees reflects his commitment to public service, including as Chairman of the Marine Resources Board, the Regulatory Authority, Director of the Bermuda Shipping and Maritime Authority, and Director on the Bermuda Civil Aviation Authority. As a legal consultant, he has offered expertise in civil, corporate, and employment law to numerous organizations and individuals, consistently demonstrating a dedication to advancing legal excellence and regulatory reform.

What follows is Mr. Perinchief's account of the significance of self-identity, the Black Berets, and the cost of living in Bermuda, then and now:

Meetings with the Reverends

Although it wasn't a well-known fact at the time, except of course between the Reverends and clergy of the various churches (mostly A.M.E.) and the Black Beret Cadre (BBC) members themselves, there was a very close and respectful bond between these "soldiers" in the struggle for equality, fairness and justice for everyone, not just the wealthy and/or white in Bermuda.

To be true, and it must be said, the BBC had the closest bond with the Reverends of the A.M.E. Church and the "Black Muslims" located then on Court Street, Hamilton. Reverends Dees, Foster and Brandon, apart from, alone, and together with the Black Muslims, were social activists and put their "feet in the street" when the occasion demanded on any and every issue negatively impacting the Black community. These Reverends, often despite of or even against the very real tension and strain this caused amongst the more conservative hierarchy under whose command they ultimately were, nevertheless showed up singularly or as a group, to address the then current issues negatively impacting the Black community and Bermudian society generally. The BBC were always ready, willing and able to back at any level needed these righteous brothers, should such an eventuality arise.

In full transparency, from a purely personal level, and largely as a function of the nature and reality of the "cell" system under which the BBC operated, my direct association with Rev. Dees was more tangential. My direct association and interaction with A.M.E. Reverends had more to do with Revs. Foster and Brandon. Rev. Dees was assigned to another member of the BBC who worked more closely with him and reported, as we all did, the progress or status of that association in a subsequent "debriefing session."

In all candor, and for a time even amongst the rank and file of the BBC and the "laity'" of the A.M.E. Church and other denominations, the symbiotic relationship between these religious organizations and the BBC was for a very considerable time simply unclear to them. They could not see, nor understand, the synergy flowing between the two entities, especially since many of them had been inundated and indoctrinated with negative propaganda which pejoratively shaped their perceptions of the stories they had read and were attributed to the BBC. The majority of these stories were mainly of a "violent" nature. The BBC attempted, successfully or otherwise, to disabuse these folks of the falsehoods deliberately spread by the "propaganda media" of the status quo. The status quo, we argued, in many violent ways, emotionally, psychologically and physically via its legislative, prosecutorial, judicial and penal systems, all in service of the interests of "white supremacy," capitalism and colonialism, sought to denigrate the BBC and to forever consign our people to a life of servitude at one level or another.

History was rife with such examples which we abundantly provided. Reversing such a state of affairs required more than only showing up for "candlelight vigils," passing into law legislative mandates which are routinely ignored, and organizing "peace" rallies. Where and when necessary, the Berets took the view that it may at times require a more "direct and forceful" confrontation to physically and permanently remove unjust obstacles or barriers to our progress, even when those obstacles etc., like apartheid, have lawfully been implemented and brutally upheld by the State and its supporters. Nelson Mandela and the A.N.C. understood that. The Revs. at the A.M.E. Church understood that too, even though their doctrines and discipline taught them that they had to abide by the laws of the day, which they always did.

However, why are we as a people on a whole, having such a hard time understanding that unjust laws must be removed, oft times by any appropriate means necessary? Berets were no longer prepared to ask the oppressor "why do you have your foot on our neck?" Perhaps, just perhaps, the simple, honest and straightforward answer to why many of our people never resisted the "foot on the neck" is that "many of us wish one day to be precisely like those people who have their foot on our neck, and who some of us are trying to remove." The BBC too, was very much aware of that fact which has materialized today across the socio-politico-economic spectrum. I often see such types in the shadowy hierarchy of the "big company," sitting on the local and international Boards from time to time, replete with a sheepish grin on their faces. Again, it appears that Revs. Dees, Foster, Brandon and the BBC were far too successful in bringing about this state of affairs, only to have too many of us believe they "made it" entirely on their own. These folks have rapidly developed selective amnesia and completely forgotten the "rest of us."

That outcome, of course, does not diminish the fact that the BBC and the A.M.E. Revs. nevertheless, saw merit in, and found it necessary at the time, to join together to primarily serve the true needs of the majority of our people in our unique ways. Revs. Dees, Foster and Brandon "walked their talk" as well as preached from the pulpit and the "street corner" soapbox with equal alacrity. The BBC will not let those prodigious contributions on the part of these courageous warriors go unnoticed or unacknowledged.

The BBC were keenly aware of the fact as well, that these Revs. faced at times bitter criticism from both their clergy and certain conservative segments of their respective congregations for their association with that allegedly violent and radical band in the BBC. They wondered aloud as to why would these Revs. join up with this group even if it was for a laudable cause such as protesting high prices for goods and services, homelessness or discrimination of one kind or the other throughout the community?

In partial response to their inquiries, the Revs. invited certain members of the BBC to speak at the Vernon Temple, A.M.E. Church in Southampton in October of 1970. I do not remember all of the Black Berets present, however, I do remember that Eliyatsoor (Mel Saltus, a righteous brother who passed away on Friday, October 25, 2024 in the U.K.) spoke and so did I.

Eliyatsoor's remarks were primarily an insight of the BBC's position on the U.K.'s sale of weapons to apartheid South Africa which were used to slaughter Black people. Those remarks included the BBC's further position on how we intended to respond to authorities, locally or abroad, who aggressed our people anywhere in the world including Bermuda. His remark that "we are willing to die" was to illustrate that many of us, in the cause of global freedom for Black people, were willing in self-defense and liberty, to kill and die for that cause. We meant that. It was a well-known fact to the authorities here in Bermuda that every member of the BBC hierarchy never expected nor particularly desired at the time to live past 35 years of age. The cause of liberty and freedom meant more to us than life itself. We were not prepared to "live on our knees" any further in an oppressive imperialist, capitalist, colonial and white supremacist world or society wherever we lived. Certainly we were not prepared to do so at least without a daily struggle to remove these pernicious forms of degradation, exploitation, and violation of human rights of the less well-to-do, poor and vulnerable persons amongst us.

Notwithstanding that position, the BBC recognized the genuine and earnest efforts of Revs. Dees, Foster, and Brandon to right the wrongs being perpetrated against the Black and poor congregants and population of Bermuda during their activist times in our community. In that light, these Revs. were the BBC's kindred spirits. There was much mutual respect amongst both groups.

As mentioned, I spoke that evening as well in October 1970. Rather than my exact words, I more accurately recall the themes shared with the audience that evening. I broadly spoke of 1.) the BBC and what it stands for in its quest to provide necessities of life to the poor and vulnerable in our society, and to move Bermuda to Sovereignty, 2.) the Church as an institution and how I viewed its activities or mission in the Black community and 3.) unbridled capitalism being the root cause of high prices in particular, and the high cost of living generally, in Bermuda.

I explained to the incredulous ones that the A.M.E. Church and the BBC only differed in the methodology or methods of achieving our mutual and similar goals. We understood and did not criticize our respective boundaries or approaches as to how to solve the shared problems before us or our respective ideologies or philosophies. Our aims were largely the same. We "merged and converged" when needed, on secular issues devastating Black people at the time, which fifty+ years later, are ironically hardly distinguishable at their root, then current challenges today to the Black community. It's easily arguable that today's calamitous circumstances are even worse. The more things "change," the more they remain the same as the saying goes.

In response to those who repeatedly asked the BBC for its' rationale or justification for the use of violence to achieve its goals, the answer was generally along the following lines.

The BBC would not, and did not, initiate nor instigate physical violence. However, if provoked, or the BBC had to act in self-defense, or to achieve, or not be unjustly prohibited from attaining, its' rightful goals, then without further reservation the BBC will proceed against any and all obstacles to those rightful goals using any means necessary to effect those goals.

The BBC generally viewed the use of physical "violence" in chronological and proportionate terms. It should be patently obvious to the least discerning that if a people, any people, have endured slavery, discrimination, abuse of every kind imaginable, and general exclusion from the necessities for acquiring a decent and human existence for centuries; that one day those same people having endured those many years of "psychological violence," will eventually react by way of "physical violence" to free themselves from such torment and tyranny. The BBC therefore took the position that "enough was enough." We took the view that we will not endure any more of the oppressors' "psychological violence" and we were prepared to use "physical violence" if all else failed to end the madness. The Zionist Jews in Israel have taken, rightly or wrongly, that position, seemingly with the armaments, the blessing and the encouragement of the U.K., the U.S.A. and the Western European nations as well. Where is the world-wide outcry against the Zionist Jews' excessive use of physical violence in Gaza, Lebanon and the Middle East?

The BBC's position was: "There will be peace for everyone, or peace for no one." Hence our motto: "Peace, if possible, compromise (of principles) never, freedom by any means necessary."

It was against this backdrop that the BBC worked tirelessly with these Reverends, to ameliorate the harm and damage wrought physically, emotionally and psychologically upon our people every day, week, month, year and throughout their entire lives in some cases.

Those Reverends need to be "canonized," not ostracized, in any manner was our firm position.

We would like to think that was what precisely happened.

Mr. Phil Perinchief continues:

Another Perspective

On The Budget Specifically:

My comments in respect to the preparation and financing of the budget for Bermuda in October 2024, are not very much different in substance than they were in 1970 with the possible exception of these current remarks being even more scathing and damning.

Unless and until we have a properly designed and equitably administered progressive, proportionate and graduated income tax system employed and deployed in the relevant sectors of our economy in Bermuda; then we are going to continue to wrestle with and experience the maldistribution of the true financial and economic wealth of Bermuda. Doing "financial sleight of hand" and alleged "zero-budgeting" magical tricks simply just does not "cut it," I'm afraid. Nothing of fundamental substance and lasting progress has been achieved with such "smoke and mirror" chicanery.

Further, until we deploy such a taxation system as suggested, we will not be in a position to underwrite with relative ease, the approximately $3 to $4 billion annual budget allocations required to service our social and financial aid programs etc., build, replace and maintain our infrastructure, and meet our national and international debt obligations.

What is required is that we, in addition to the Global 15% Minimum Tax (GMT) regime imposed on us by the European Economic Commission (EEC), must insist on, and successfully negotiate, 1.) that this 15% GMT be applied to international companies who earn revenue or profits, say between $500 million and above instead of $805 million and above annually, and siphon off the difference to the "host countries" administrations such as

Bermuda, to underwrite their "annual budgets," or 2.) locally apply a graduated tax, say from 1% to 3%, on all international and local companies, such as Belco, Digicel and the larger banks and financial insurance institutions making annually say $101 million and above up to $804 million.

In all other respects, and in the initial phase(s), there should be no tax, corporate or personal, on residents of Bermuda and Bermudians earning $100 million or less. All other regressive taxes such as payroll, property, estate etc., and levies, wharfage charges, fees and tariffs etc., are to be abolished. The latter move will lower the prices of goods and services, and therefore generally reduce the "cost of living" and put more money in people's pockets and savings accounts. With this overall "increase in wealth" people will tend to spend more, Bermuda will concomitantly, and because of the capitalist economic law of "supply and demand," spend more and the "multiplier effect" will "kick in" and grow the economy via investments etc., thus generally giving rise ultimately to increased employment. This will start the cycle again for increased wealth in Bermuda which will be equitably distributed or allocated where and when this wealth should be so distributed or allocated by the reformed taxation system. I would not rule out "price controls" being applied on staple goods and medications, for example, for cancer and other life-threatening ailments, also on foods and other essential items not otherwise available to people of limited means at a cost-effective or attainable level.

Accordingly, and in the round, I have no appetite for "tinkering around" with an inequitable regressive taxation system which only results, no matter how many ways the manipulators "move the itemized chairs around the budgetary Titanic;" in the continuance of shifting the "heaviest tax burdens" upon those who can afford it the least, that is, the middle class and those of meagre and/or fixed incomes. The current taxation system was deliberately put into place by the white aristocracy and merchants in Bermuda centuries ago, to economically exploit the wider population, largely the poor indentured servants and the newly freed landless slaves or Black people. It's past due time that we remove such an historically oppressive, controlling and unfair system, which today is tantamount to "economic apartheid."

Sadly, the P.L.P administration of "today" appear to see no reason for dismantling this pernicious and exploitative system, notwithstanding its' deleterious and devastating effect on its' extremely vulnerable "voters" base who are largely working and low-income classes.

As with the current antiquated political, parliamentary and electoral models, the P.L.P appear to be content to fundamentally continue to employ the exploitative economic and financial "model," mold and mechanisms of their former "centuries old," colonial and merchant class masters and mentors. It is of some further and considerable concern that before we make any fundamental changes in our taxation system, the P.L.P, OBA and FDM seem to deem it necessary to first turn to be vetted and approved by the International Business (IB) sector who have thoroughly, unfortunately, succeeded in full "state capture" of these Party organizations and individuals and likely governments. The IB sector are the final arbiters of our economic and financial destiny. Make no mistake about it.

Bermuda, and Bermudians who deserve it most, are in a most difficult position currently.

It remains to be seen what, or who, will free us from this diabolical dilemma.

Note: The P.L.P is the Progressive Labour Party, the OBA is the One Bermuda Alliance and the FDM is the Free Democratic Movement.

As we can see, Mr. Perinchief has stated the reasons that Rev. Dees, Brandon and, additionally, Rev. Foster listened to all members of society with a view to righting wrongs. They, like Dr. Martin Luther King, Jr. did not prescribe to violence, but in their own way stood up for justice. The rising cost of living and those ills that plague our society were cause for their active participation, and all these years later injustices still exist. They did what they could. The questions become *what still needs to be done?* and *who will do it?*

This information raises important questions about pricing and the lack of controls in Bermuda today. We see the efforts of Rev. Lloyd Dees and Rev. Brandon in the past, but what is being done now?

Listeners of talk radio, particularly on Bermuda's Magic 102.7 with Mr. Anthony Richardson and Dr. Llewellyn Simmons, frequently highlight the severe impact of the cost of living on the people of Bermuda. Undeniably, people are struggling—not just here, but globally. However, Bermuda seems to be one of the most expensive places in the world. So, what is being done? What can be done? More importantly, what is the church doing?

Christ didn't remain in the temple, merely praying—He went out into the community, and I believe He expects us to do the same. As He said in Matthew 25:40:

> "Truly I tell you, whatever you did for the least of these my brethren,
> you did for me."

Can our churches do more? Can we do more? How can we demonstrate greater compassion and kindness to those in need?

I must commend Bethel A.M.E. Church in Lansdowne, Philadelphia, where Pastor Rev. Lois Wilkerson and her husband, Evangelist Michael, led an inspiring initiative Christmas of 2024. This small yet generous congregation adopted six families in need. They covered one family's rent for a month, provided a Christmas tree and gifts for another family with many children, and assisted a family who lost everything in a fire by furnishing their home with dressers, tables, a couch—even a large-screen TV. They invited these families to church, provided meals, and distributed food vouchers to every church member, as well as gifts to visitors, as an expression of God's love.

I've been told that Rev. Wilkerson has carried out this mission for years, at every church she pastored. Their congregation also runs a weekly food drive to support those in need. While I recognize that other churches give as well, I still ask, "Can our churches do more?"

Not long ago, while driving to the radio station to host my show (*The Need to Lead*), I tuned in to *Medical Radio* hosted by Dr. Henry Dowling, affectionately known as "Doctor D." That morning, a caller brought up the pressing issue of Bermuda's high cost of living. They claimed that a significant number of residents (estimated at around 6,000, the majority believed to be Black) have relocated to the United Kingdom because they simply cannot afford to live in Bermuda any longer.

The conversation also touched on the steady influx of foreign workers, spanning both high-end professionals and those in lower-wage roles. This led to pointed questions: Do Bermudians expect too much? Are we, perhaps, living beyond our means?

Unfortunately, I've observed a more layered and complex reality.

It is true that expatriates, especially those at the lower job scale, live and work in Bermuda for years, often decades, making immense personal sacrifices. They may only see their families once a year, yet they consistently send money home, saving for their eventual retirement so that they can return to enjoy the fruits of their labour.

By contrast, many Bermudians, especially Blacks who leave the island, face a very different reality. For them, visiting home even once a year can be financially difficult, and over time, for some, the dream of returning to Bermuda becomes an increasingly distant and unreachable goal.

This contrast weighs heavily on my heart and forces me to look beyond the surface and ask: What kind of Bermuda are we building? What are we willing to sacrifice to stay connected to the place we call home? These aren't just policy questions—they're deeply personal ones. As we navigate rising costs, changing demographics, and evolving dreams, I hope we can work together—across generations and backgrounds—to create a Bermuda that not only welcomes us back but makes it possible for us to stay, to belong, and to flourish.

Beyond charity, what can be done about price control? Who is truly advocating for change? Who really cares?

After reflecting on that radio show, I reached out to Mr. Chris Furbert, President of the Bermuda Industrial Union, and he graciously provided me with two significant reports issued by his organization: one, issued on September 26, 2028, titled "BIU Report on a 'Living Wage'" and the other, written in October 2022, titled, "Bermuda's Cost of Living." I also thank Mr. Furbert for the following contribution on this subject:

> Over the years, numerous studies have shown that the cost of living in Bermuda has risen to unsustainable levels. Today, the average Bermudian struggles to maintain a reasonable quality of life due to the steady erosion of disposable income. This decline has severely impacted the purchasing power of nearly every Bermudian over the past fifty years.
>
> Common concerns about the cost of living in Bermuda are not new. In March 1971, more than 54 years ago, the Bermuda Ministerial Association submitted a report outlining these very issues. This effort began in November 1970 with the formation of the Committee on Social Concerns, which was tasked with examining the cost of living in Bermuda, particularly in relation to:
>
> - Consumer expenditures for food and rent.
> - Wages and income, including income of pensioners.
>
> Since then, many others have produced similar reports, all pointing to the same concerns. However, these efforts were often hampered by several challenges, including:
>
> - Reluctance from government officials and business representatives to provide or be quoted on the data.
> - Difficulty obtaining information on retailer markups for specific food items.
> - An inadequate Cost-of-Living index.
> - Incomplete statistics on wages and salaries.
> - Lack of data on poverty levels.
>
> The Committee on Social Concerns produced a report with 13 key recommendations aimed at reducing the cost of living in Bermuda.

One critical recommendation was for the government to ensure that wage levels are aligned with the cost of living, so that a single, full-time job can adequately support the average family. The need for multiple incomes within a household should not be a determining factor in what constitutes a fair or livable wage.

Perhaps the most powerful tool the government holds is the ability to reform the tax structure. Unfortunately, successive administrations have been reluctant to take bold action in this area. Addressing this issue will require open, inclusive dialogue involving all stakeholders. Only through such engagement can we build a sustainable path forward that offers Bermudians a viable quality of life.

We must take a serious look at closing the widening gap in income inequality and creating a fairer, more equitable Bermuda. The challenges we face today are not beyond our control. The laws, policies, and financial systems we live under were created by us, for the common good of all Bermudians. If those systems no longer serve that purpose and instead contribute to growing inequity, then they must be changed.

The government has the authority and responsibility to reshape these structures. The real question is whether we have the courage and the collective will to create policies that meet our goals, reverse the outward migration of Bermudians, and restore hope and opportunity for all.

Live to Make a Difference is more than a book about Rev. Dees legacy—it's an imperative. Rev. Dees made a profound difference in social, spiritual, and political areas during his eras and now it's our turn.

Chapter Three

Overview of *The Protest* Magazine

In addition to all Rev. Dees and Rev. Brandon attempted to do through their activities headlined in the local newspapers noting that great changes were required for Bermuda, both pastors found the time to produce *The Protest* magazines. These astute men were determined that Bermudians, especially their parishioners, were kept abreast not only of the workings of the church, but of the issues of the day. I think that many people will find these magazines interesting and enlightening.

I had heard about the magazines from my mother, who was an avid supporter of the efforts of Rev. Dees. The issues were produced quarterly. The first issue in my possession is dated November 1969. I have no idea how many issues were produced before or after, but I do have five copies. The bold title of the magazine, *The Protest*, demonstrates that the pastors were not satisfied with the status quo. The magazines were sold to the community and the cost varied. The November 1969 issue sold for a nominal 75 cents and the sender address was c/o Rev. Lloyd E. Dees, Shelly Bay, Bermuda.

The opening statements informed the reader that these magazines were "An earnest endeavour on the part of the editors to speak to the issues of the A.M.E. Church and in the society." It sought to "constructively criticize many of the outmoded and antiquated procedures of the A.M.E. Church which actually hinder the church in performing its duties as Christ would have it in the world today." The introduction also stated that the magazine "does not attempt to make a false dichotomy between the spiritual on the one hand and the social on the other, but tries to state very realistically that man is a whole and the spiritual cannot be stressed successfully over that of the social, psychological, or political."

The Protest magazine introduced the authors Rev. Dees and Rev. Brandon. Although I began this project with the resumé information that Rev. Dees had given me, the magazines afforded me additional details and insights. For instance, in the first edition I learned that Rev. Dees was born in Camden, Alabama, but had spent most of his adult life in New York City. Also, as previously stated, he spent some months in Berlin, and he spent two years in the United States Army.

It also revealed that while at Interdenominational Theological Center (I.T.C.) in Atlanta, Georgia, he had been a member of the International Society of Theta Phi for excellence in scholarship. He was also the recipient of the Sammye F. Coan Memorial Award for high academic achievement during his seminary career and received the Henry McNeil Turner Memorial Preaching Award for outstanding achievement in homiletics. Obviously, he was a brilliant scholar and after reading this information, my respect for him was only amplified.

The information concerning his co-editor Rev. John E. Brandon was also documented as follows:

> Rev. John E. Brandon is the pastor of Allen Temple A.M.E. Church. He is a native of Louisiana where he received his early education. Rev. Brandon received his (A.A.) Associate of Arts degree in Education from Jackson Mississippi; (B.A.) Bachelor of Arts Degree from Morris Brown College in Psychology and Sociology, Atlanta, Georgia; and the (Th.M.) Master of Theology Degree in Ecumenics, Missions and World Religions from Boston University School of Theology, Boston, Mass. Rev. Brandon served on the Executive Board of the United Christian Youth Movement in Georgia (Georgia Council of Churches); he worked for two summers (1965-1966) with the Philadelphia Council of Churches in the Migrant Ministry; served as the Co-Chairman of the Consultation on the Black Church; a member of the National Committee of Black Churchmen; and is a member of a number of honour organizations and societies.

I was amazed to read in the magazine the *puissance* (my Toastmaster's word) wielded by bishops and the article questioned how pastoral appointments in the A.M.E. Church were made. I also wondered about the repercussions—I imagine that he was cautioned about the content. When I mentioned this to one A.M.E. pastor in 2023, a staunch supporter of the current bishop, he responded, "What they wrote in those magazines was their opinion." I guess that, even today, some do not take kindly to the stance these pastors took, what they believed, or what they said, particularly in reference to the A.M.E. Church and the bishops. It is up to the reader to decide if what was written was relevant, considering the times.

At the time of this writing, I am a current member of the Bermuda Annual Conference, having served as the Church School Superintendent since around 2011. Having attended numerous conferences over the decades, I am aware that congregations often wait with bated breath to see if their respective pastor will be returned to them, although sometimes praying that they will be removed. Certainly, dissatisfied congregants have written to the bishop to express displeasure with clergy. At the seat of the annual conference, crowds gather to see if the bishop will honour their requests.

Many pastors go out of their way to please the bishop, perhaps trying to secure their appointment or enhance the prospect of receiving an even greater charge. I've seen this first-hand. Years after returning to Bermuda, while I was the A.M.E. Director of Drama, we traveled to Philadelphia to stage a performance of my play, *The Songbirds*. The pastor who was responsible for helping to acquire the props abruptly left because he had forgotten his gift of ginger beer for the bishop. He rushed to meet another pastor at the airport who was bringing the ginger beer. I was left in an unfortunate position because the actors needed to rehearse with the props since the production was to take place very soon. I had to scramble!

One necessary prop was a bookcase which, after locating one, my sister Shelby and I had to drag it through the streets of Philadelphia. Luckily, my brother-in-law Melvin Jackson used his connections with another church to secure the other required props. We did not appreciate being left high and dry by that overly ambitious pastor.

I am noting here that of the vast number of bishops in the A.M.E conferences, one of them was a Bermudian by the name of Vinton Randolph Anderson. He was the author of a book called *My Soul Shouts,* and he too understood the value of the arts as his book includes a few poems written by his wife Vivienne L. Anderson.

The Protest magazines also held wonderful vignettes, and of course this pleased me tremendously. I love stories, poetry, plays, all literature. I wrote my first full-length play, *Battle for Freedom*, which documented the history of the A.M.E. Church. This was at the request of Mr. Lionel Phillips and his wife Marva, who gave me the notes surrounding the history of the church. The event was attended by over six thousand people and was held in the Bermuda Botanical Gardens.

The Bermuda Musical and Dramatic Association provided me with white actresses and actors for the roles of slave masters. One great actress of that era was Mrs. Connie Dey. Proceeds from the play were to provide all eleven A.M.E. Churches with new hymn books. I was told that the name of the play and my name would be inscribed inside. The play focused on the emancipation for Blacks and was attended by both political parties of the day, including the Governor. The regiment band played and all eleven churches formed a mass choir, directed by Mrs. Doris Corbin.

Every year, I wrote and directed many plays for the church to help boost the coffers and in one case, to ensure that a church's mortgage was paid. Perhaps it's now more apparent why I was so thrilled to discover again the power of drama and the high regard these pastors held for the theatre. I absolutely loved the conversation between the two fictional characters "Charley" and "Pete" in *The Protest.* It reminded me of Langston Hughes' character, "Simple" (introduced to me by Rev. Dees).

At North Carolina Agricultural & Technical State University (N.C. A&T), I had studied drama under the renown Dr. John Marshall Kilimanjaro. Dr. Kilimanjaro was the head of the theatre department at N.C. A&T and someone who became another mentor and friend. He was also the owner of *The Carolina Peacemaker,* a newspaper that printed an article about me after I graduated. When I read the vignettes, I wished I could have shared them with my former professor as I am convinced that Dr. Kilimanjaro would have loved the conversations between Charley and Pete centered on church issues. It seemed that there had been a rumor circulating that a bishop had threatened to resign. I am sure that this was an issue at the time that many were unaware of, and the two ministers used the dramatic discussion between these two fictional characters to highlight the situation and enlighten their readers.

Rev. Dees and Rev. Brandon used a great deal of drama and poetry in these magazines to communicate their views. The characters Charley and Pete voiced their concerns about the church in a humorous and informative way. I recall Judge Arthur Hodgson, a member of Parliament and another Bermudian icon who passed in 2023, extolling the importance of drama. He said that the facts were the facts, but people *remember* the facts when they were dramatized. He wanted me to write plays about the history of Bailey's Bay so that people of the parish in Bermuda would better appreciate who they were. His church had been recently renovated and had lights, a stage, sound etc., and he thought the facility could be better used to engage the community.

I'd like to share a little about how this vignette between Charley and Pete in *The Protest* played out. First, the pastor was awakened at 8:30 a.m. on a Monday by a zealous parishioner. This pastor explained that after a hectic Sunday teaching Sunday School class, preaching two services, and then making hospital visits, he should have lost five pounds. When Pete tells the pastor that he had been up all night thinking about the A.M.E. Church and the topics for discussion at the next church meeting, the pastor's reply, although humorous, cynically hints at the debacle at the previous general conference held in Philadelphia. The play on names is a nice dramatic device that adds to the humor of a serious story. As the parishioner leaves, the audience may accept that the reason for the pastor's cryptic revelations was that he was awakened too early.

To give you a sense of these historically important magazines, following are examples and excerpts. I encourage you to view the full text and more information in Part II of this book.

The Protest Magazine, 1969

The Protest magazine of 1969 incorporates a piece written by Rev. Brandon asking, "Is the A.M.E Church Really Serious?" In this selection, the issues surrounding worship between Black and white congregations were not avoided, but alas, the point that Black denominations must "make a greater effort to unite in order to talk from a stronger base of power" was established. The submission highlighted that the A.M.E. Church and other Black denominations could not fully participate in the Consultation on Church Union (COCU), and the pastors thought that thc A.M.E. Church should be fully informed about the COCU and what it stood for. This piece noted that "we must keep in mind the historical situation of Black and white relationships in the church and the present conditions of those relationships today."

Churches participating in this initiative were The African Methodist Episcopal Church, The African Methodist Episcopal Zion Church, The Christian Church (Disciples of Christ), The Christian Methodist Episcopal Church, The Episcopal Church, The International Council of Community Churches, The Presbyterian Church (U.S.A.), The United Church of Christ, and the United Methodist Church.

Here's a little background: the idea of forming a united body of believers came from a sermon preached by Dr. Eugene Carson Blake on December 4, 1960, "A Proposal Toward the Reunion of Christ's Church." Dr. Blake wanted his church to enter discussions with the United Church of Christ to unite them in a "truly catholic, truly evangelical and truly reformed" entity. He envisioned a union of churches of different theological and historic traditions. Bishop Jordan, he noted, stated that "white Christians don't really believe in the black religious experiences."

It seems that no matter where we go, or what we do, race remains an issue. Rev. Brandon reminded us of the importance of dealing with racial issues. Although the church talks about unity, he questioned if the players were serious about resolving this age-old conflict. The COCU cannot deal effectively and honestly with their own Black parishioners and therefore it is a relevant question to ask how they can unify if they do not deal with their own internal conflict. Additionally, the A.M.E. Church and other Blacks needed to come together so that they could talk from a position of power. This reoccurring theme is still present in Bermuda today and may answer the question as to why Bermuda remains a British Colony. But that's perhaps a story for another time.

The 1969 edition of *The Protest* magazine went on to state that sometimes people pretend that racism doesn't exist or doesn't impact procedures. I believe also that when Blacks speak of solidarity, this is often mistaken for reversed racial discrimination. I recall advocating for Bermudians to wake up and prepare for a future where they can participate in the upper echelons of our society, only to be called racist. If people cannot come together and meet their own needs, resentment occurs, and unity becomes an impossible ideal. Ecumenism will remain only an ideal if people do not first appreciate themselves, then one another.

The five original *Protest* documents I now have are "gold" and I vaguely recall doing my small part to distribute them in the community. Years later, I am impressed by the audacity of these two young preachers and their commitment to inform the public, present questions for parishioners and community members, and raise the consciousness of the community through these publications. I know they worked with conscious deliberation and put in a great deal of time to research, write, edit, and distribute these magazines as they sought to meet the needs of the people.

The Protest Magazine, January - March 1970

In this second magazine I noted that subscription rates in Bermuda were $2 per year, outside Bermuda, $2.50 per year, and a single copy sold for 65 cents. This lets me know that the magazine was not intended only for the people of Bermuda, although the subscribers outside Bermuda must have found the information as riveting for them as it was for the Bermudian readers.

In this issue, the Table of Contents revealed the topics for discussion as: No Vision, No People; Speaking about the Church (Charley and Pete) another dramatic vignette; An Urgent Call for Action; Expressions; and A New Thing (a sermon).

The first article, "No Vision, No People," is written by Rev. John Brandon. I will reiterate here that I have no intention of trying to share the entire magazine, but will highlight those parts that struck me. The full *Protest* magazine can be read in Part II, and I encourage the reader to do so and draw their own conclusions. Rev. Brandon asked in this article if an institution or nation could survive without vision. He, being a pastor, related the importance of having a vision to the discontented Israelites who suffered the consequences of their own poor spiritual vision because they could not "see" the Promised Land. He speaks here about two kinds of vision, *physical* and *spiritual*. He noted that vision is one of the purest forms of reporting upon an immediate awareness of the will of God. As a Christian, I had to reflect on my vision and my immediate priority seems to be the publication of this work that I hope will enlighten, encourage, and show that these men were men of substance—men who did not shirk their responsibility to enlighten the world and bring glory to God.

Rev. Brandon stated that we ought not worry about trivialities when immensities face us—racism, injustice, and undemocratic processes. These things still plague us today and I ask the reader what part they can play in righting wrongs. What are our priorities? Can we just go about our daily lives, unconcerned about the suffering of others? What can we do to help improve our world? How can we make a difference? He urges the A.M.E. Church to consider its priorities.

According to Rev. Brandon, the church must do much more than "pass resolutions and print smooth sounding words and phrases in the discipline. It must constantly plan on a national and international basis from a central point of operation." He says that he is not talking about each district with its own "planned – pre-planned" planning council, but rather, of a "massive examination and thorough ongoing look at the present structure of the A.M.E. Church." His words ask us to examine ourselves and remember that we should not miss out on an opportunity to meet the needs of our changing world.

I must state here that the priorities he expresses are valid and his ideas are not ones I simply accept; I acknowledge that his concerns are expressed with deep passion. Rev. Brandon thought that the church might better use school funds for scholarship aid for students who might not otherwise be able to attend college which certainly made me think. I know that A.M.E. pastors today will say that they are working to assist their communities. He notes that we have a few schools that are barely surviving and there is a need to strengthen other schools. I wondered, why do our Black institutions seem to struggle? Are there not enough members to pledge funds to these schools? Why can't we solicit corporations to assist? What I want to demonstrate here is that reading his words evoked other thoughts and questions that serve to enhance opportunities for action.

The three other points made here are that the A.M.E. Church should seek union with other churches, such as the Methodist Episcopal Zion Church, as we basically have the same liturgy and doctrine. He notes that perhaps the lack of vision hinders the expansion of the Interdenominational Theological Center in Atlanta, Georgia. And he then asks if it is the vision or lack of it to divide small conferences into such small districts throughout the A.M.E. Church for the sake of only creating jobs—what else? Certainly Rev. Brandon was not afraid to question the running of the church and I imagine that he stepped on many toes.

A statement that stood out to me was, "My concern at this point is for the people who have to suffer the consequences of 'episcopal vision.' Sometimes 'episcopal vision' is what Shakespeare called in 'Measure for Measure'; Proud man dressed in a little brief authority…plays such fantastic tricks before high heaven…the angels weep." Although this made me laugh, it also made me think about what we are prepared to do when things bother us. Finally, he said, "The church needs more than the few progressive bishops it now has. They must be joined by others, because time marches on and waits on no one." Good heavens! I agree that "our 'vision' in the church must extend beyond mere symptoms."

Rev. Brandon cites what James H. Cone wrote in his book, *Black Theology and Black Power*, asking if the church has "lost its zeal for freedom in the midst of the alluring white power structure." He concludes the article by reminding the church that they have the capacity of foresight and the manpower to deal with "the needs of our times." So, is this happening today? That's my question.

I have discussed the value of drama and once again, the vignette, "Speaking about the Church" in *The Protest* emphasizes its importance. The discussion between Charley and Pete is not only witty but thought-provoking. Many people do not want to hear the opinion of others, especially if it opposes what we believe, or want to believe. Charley tells Pete that every time they get together, he has to listen to his faulty ideas about the church—the A.M.E. Church to be specific. There are those in the A.M.E. congregation who simply "go along to get along." They do not question or want to question—they are simply sycophants. Charley tells Pete a parable that demonstrates what happens when some in the church are cared for and others are not. The reader can infer here what they wish, but this article reinforced for me the importance of doing what is right to benefit everyone, not just bishops, or certain pastors, or those in the community who look out for themselves with little concern for the well-being of others. The vignette spoke to me about what I can do instead of simply "go with the flow." The question for the reader would be, *what can you do?* The result of only looking out for oneself is that when you disregard the needs of others, they will turn on you, and you will be left with nothing. I implore the reader to read the vignette to enjoy and digest the inspirational drama.

What follows is an interesting article by Rev. Dees titled, "An Urgent Call for Action." I, like many parishioners, was unaware that an Office of Urban Ministries and Ecumenical Relations has been in existence since the General Conference of 1968. As a way of enlightening the members of the church, this article explained what the office does. Rev. Dees noted that the new discipline had not yet been circulated and used the magazine as another way to filter information to the members. He noted that an informed church is a better church and that "we should at least give some thought to what the department is, the reason for its existence, and what it intends to accomplish." He explained the office "was set up to deal with pressing social problems and reconciliation among the churches. Therefore, this Agency has been given a tremendous responsibility."

I am sure that the readers of the magazine gained better insight into the workings of the A.M.E. Church. Church members should be informed about any organization they join, and the reasons for its existence, if they are to be serious members. He noted that many members had their own ideas for the existence of the above office, one being to curb the power of the bishops in the church. Yikes! Or that another substantive reason that the office was established was because of the genuine need for change in the adverse social conditions and aha…the strained relationships that seemed to be widespread among the different religious denominations. Perhaps, he states, the reason for the creation of such an office was because the church understood that a greater concern for world issues and the total life of the individual is important, and he admits that "somewhere in these diverse thoughts the truth can be found."

The article goes on to address what the office intended to accomplish and cites page 649 of the *1968 Book of Discipline of the African Methodist Episcopal (A.M.E.) Church*. He gave two reasons, noting that "separately and in cooperation with other agencies, it shall promote and conduct Seminars and Institutes for both ministers and laymen. It shall develop curricula, prepare and distribute study material, and other information." His documentation presents the ideals of the office as praiseworthy, if not lofty, but the readers of the day (and today) may be interested in the duties fundamental to the existence of such an office. He explained that to fulfill the purpose of such an office implies dealing with the issues, especially for Black people, of inadequate education, and unemployment. When the church addresses "these elements in our society which tend towards its disorganization and dissolution, it is fulfilling its reconciling role in the world."

Rev. Dees noted the article was written at a time of unusual political, social, economic, moral, and religious and spiritual strain, which rings true for me today. He also said that "it is the privilege, duty and challenge of the Church of Jesus Christ to now renew its early vows and engage itself in this higher calling of salvation for our generation." He also noted that this is also an expression of the Bishops of the Church which should give these ideals more relevancy, and urgency. He also pointed out the sad truth that during the "past eighteen months, little or nothing has been done to put these noble ideas into practice." I am certain that these sentiments were not always appreciated, but as a man who stood for justice and equality, he did not refrain from making statements to help people understand what was, in his opinion, needed. Like the vignette between Charley and Pete, many wanted to bury their heads in the sand without questioning the objectives and not live and act upon the reality. The end result, he noted, will be tragedy.

Finally, he said that the call to the A.M.E. Church is for action—NOW! The question for me is, how relevant is the call for action today, and what part can we play in meeting the objectives?

What follows are wonderful poems, written (I believe) by the magazine's authors/publishers. The poems speak of our obligations to our brothers and sisters and the importance of religion. My heart was filled with appreciation again for their acknowledgment that the creative arts can be utilized to bring expression and relevancy to their readers and the world.

In the last article in this issue, Rev. Dees presents a sermon, "A New Thing." In another poetic way, he presents his ideas accompanied by Biblical references. He employs us to be quiet and listen concerning the new thing that God is doing for mankind: "Behold, I am doing a new thing. I create new heavens and a new earth. If anyone is in Christ, he is a new creation. I saw a new heaven and a new earth…the former things have passed away, new wine is put in new wineskins."

"The mighty hammer is striking. And with each stroke the intensity is increasing. It is shattering the OLD; And the echo is; NEW! NEW! NEW!"

I know this magazine was God-inspired. It has motivated me to listen more carefully to the voice of God. It further encouraged me to use the gifts God has given me to do a new thing in my life. I am encouraged to fulfill my life's purpose and reach out to the world to draw others to Him. Rev. Dees and Rev. Brandon set a fine example for all of us. We can choose to let their lives inspire us to *live to make a difference*. They availed themselves to be used by God to fight injustice, to speak on behalf of the people, to use their voices and impart the word and they, all these years later, inspire me to do likewise. Make a difference!

Finally, the magazine concludes with information to the readers that a meeting concerning *Consultation on the Black Church and Social Issues* was to be held at Allen Temple African Methodist Episcopal Church, Somerset, Bermuda, March 1-7, 1970. It noted that "Outstanding persons from Bermuda and the United States will be participating in the consultation. The opening service will be on Sunday, March 1, 1970, at 4:00 p.m. at the Allen Temple Community Centre." Registration was free, and for $3.00, refreshments would be served. Topics to be addressed at that time were:

- The Black Church in the Midst of Political, Economic and Social Change in Bermuda
- The A.M.E. Church and the Black Press
- The Black Church and Politics
- The Black Church and Black Power
- Black Youth and Revolution
- The Implications of the Cancellation for Further Action

So, you can see that these pastors moved around the community and were not chained to their pulpits to deliver lofty sermons on Sunday mornings and attend their own worship services. They did not simply attend prayer meetings and conduct a variety of church meetings for their members. No, they went into the world. They listened to the people. They worked for the people… all of God's people.

The Protest Magazine, October - December 1970

The Protest magazine dated October-December 1970 featured what the authors called, "A Contemporary Look at Bermuda and African Methodism." This issue included an article titled, "Lest We Forget," and, like other issues, included poetry. Rev. Brandon gives a description of the island, noting that its proximity to the United States ensures that it is afflicted by the same problems. It has been said that, "if America sneezes, Bermudians catch a cold." Rev. Brandon, however, emphasizes that although Bermuda is a small island (21 square miles), it cannot distance itself from the issues of the world. He reminds the church that it has a great role to play as the A.M.E. Churches are found in various parts of the world.

As Bermuda was and still is a British commonwealth country, Rev. Brandon records that at the time of his writing Bermuda was preparing for the arrival of a British Monarch, His Royal Highness, The Prince of Wales. He records the sentiments of the Opposition Progressive Labour Party, who stated that they did not plan to attend any of the events for the occasion. Blacks, he noted, were conscious of their identity and the image this visit portrayed.

The A.M.E. Church is one of the largest institutions owned, operated, and supported by Blacks, and that even if the church was not in agreement with any of the political views expressed, it had to acknowledge the mood of the people. He also noted the mood of the young Blacks and understood why they were perhaps suspicious of the Christian beliefs based on years of indoctrination (as discussed by Rev. Dees in the April-June 1970 issue issue of *The Protest*). You may notice that I do not have a copy of this issue, but this article validates its existence. He implored the A.M.E. Church to play a more important role in the Bermuda community and while he acknowledged that a Social Action Committee exists in the Bermuda Annual Conference, it is bound by "bureaucratic procedure" which causes it to be ineffective at crucial times.

He urged the church to not alienate who they may consider young radicals and questioning minds. The reader may recall that these pastors met with Bermuda's young people, the Black Berets included, and were criticized by the local newspapers for doing so. He wrote, "...the inability to act when it really counts is an intentional reflection of a problem that permeates the whole of African Methodism." He also boldly asks a number of provocative questions, including, "Would the bishop, over a short period of time, lose his effectiveness by being in the forefront of issues in the community?" He then poses the idea that the A.M.E. Church might be more effective if the bishop came to the island more frequently and for longer periods. He acknowledged that the statement produces even more questions, but the fact remains that the church must respond constantly to social change. The church members must be less confined to the service of the altar and to look upon the ministrations of worship.

Rev. Brandon emphasized that all churches should follow the mandates of our Lord and Saviour. Jesus did not just walk the earth and preach to sinners, He met the needs of the people and as Maslow reminds us, we must deal with people where they are. We must first meet their basic needs before they can reach self-actualization. For many people, we are often the first introduction to Jesus and we must care and love them before we can reach their souls.

There are numerous gems in this magazine edition. The "Pressure Point" section asks the question, "The Minister's Wife: Person or Position?" We sometimes forget that pastors have wives who are people in their own right.

The poems listed under "Expressions" were all written by Rev. Lloyd E. Dees. I absolutely love the poem called "Momentum," where he challenges Black people to strive and keep awake. If you are a lover of poetry, perhaps you too will be enamoured with the cadence with which the poems are written, and the sentiments expressed.

The final poem in this section is "For My People," which reminds me of the poem by the same title by Margaret Walker, which I read during high school. Our Black Studies teacher, Mrs. Sharon Parris, introduced it to us through the book *Black Voices.* This poem touched me tremendously as I realized that Rev. Dees—touched by the infirmaries of his people—like Jesus, wept. I now imagine him up at night, unable to sleep, considering ways that he could help right the injustices for his people. How he, like Jesus, was criticized, misunderstood, even hated. He noted that he did not always smile, but when he did, it was for his people. He shared that he went without food...didn't Jesus fast? He talked about his protesting for his people and being misunderstood—I felt his loneliness as I read this poem—I felt his pain as he noted that he lives for and will someday die for his people, and I wondered, as he must have, if all of his efforts were in vain.

In the final article that you can read in Part II, Rev. Dees reminds us of the past, especially the Black man's struggle, in his piece, "Lest we Forget." He reviews our history with stories including how the Supreme Court's decision of 1954 met difficulties in execution while it provided stability for the Civil Rights Movement. He details the Supreme Court's decision in Brown v. Board of Education, the 1955 episode with Rosa Parks, and how on September 4, 1957, Elizabeth Eckford and eight other African-American students were unsuccessful in their attempt to enter Little Rock High School (in Arkansas) to secure a better education, and the effect this event had on Black people to "keep striving."

Rev. Dees also discussed the 1960 efforts of the three Black girls at the Woolworth store who sat down to eat at the lunch counter and encountered such hostility that it ignited the movement. He discussed how the sit-ins gave birth to the Student Nonviolent Coordinating Committee. He relates their complete statement of purpose. He described the 1963 "March on Washington" by thousands of people, including Asa Philip Randolph (then 75 years old), who had proposed such an initiative 20 years earlier. Additionally, he records how in 1966 a young man named James Meredith was inspired to walk from Memphis, Tennessee, to Jackson, Mississippi. Then James, escorted by officials, entered the University of Mississippi by federal force. In the article he interjects the writing of Langston Hughes, "Lest we forget!"

And it doesn't end there—Rev. Dees must have taken many hours, if not days to provide us with the vital information concerning our history. He notes the contributions of Martin Luther King, Jr., Whitney Young, Roy Wilkins, Floyd McKissick, and Stokely Carmichael. He records the comments of Vice President Humphrey and President Lyndon Johnson as well as the language of Roy Wilkins in his denunciation with words such as "separatism, wicked fanaticism and black death." Here he makes references to the idea that perhaps the words Black power are an affirmation of positive potentials.

And while I live in Bermuda, this is my history too. After all, I am now a product of N.C. A&T University, which gave me a great foundation. The article captures the spirit of a downtrodden people to overcome adversity. It certainly justifies the reason that *The Protest* magazine was created: to educate, enlighten, and inspire us all to continue to "Stand Tall for Justice." All these years later, I reflect on what he recorded in this riveting article. Perhaps I use this word a great deal to describe these writings, but as I reread these works, I felt such admiration, deep respect, and immense gratitude for all that Rev. Dees and Rev. Brandon did for people.

The Protest Magazine, March 1971

The sixth-edition magazine, titled, *A Special Issue on Bermuda*, underscored that these magazines were distributed far and wide. Bermuda is considered the First District of the A.M.E. Church and there are twenty districts, each with its own bishop who oversees the organization. Thirteen districts are situated in the United States, mostly in the South, and seven are based in Africa. There are approximately 7,000 churches in this enormous A.M.E. Network with a global membership reported of around 2.5 million.

For those who don't know, the first district is comprised of Delaware, New Jersey, New York, Western New York, New England, Philadelphia, and Bermuda. The second district includes Baltimore, Maryland, North Carolina, Washington, D.C., Western North Carolina, and Virginia. The third district includes Ohio, West Philadelphia, and West Virginia. The fourth includes Nova Scotia, Ontario, Quebec, Illinois, Indiana, Iowa, Michigan, Minnesota, North Dakota, South Dakota, Wisconsin, and India.

I have no idea how widely *The Protest* magazines were distributed, but I do know that both Rev. Dees and Rev. Brandon had the ear of many people, so just what did this issue say about Bermuda? I do note here that as of the printing of this magazine, Rev. Dees had left Bermuda and was the Director of the United Christian Ministry at N.C. A&T in Greensboro, North Carolina.

This issue begins with editorial comments, extending thanks for the work of the late Bishop George Wilbur Baber (1898-1970) as he had headed the first Episcopal district from 1956-1964. It then gives Rev. Dees' and Rev. Brandon's perspective on the assignments of pastors in the Bermuda Annual Conference, which they state needed immediate attention. It highlighted the plight of foreign-born pastors assigned to Bermuda, a practice which carried a number of problems. While the problems of foreign-born pastors could also occur in the United States, Bermuda, being a British colony and isolated from the "mainland" territory, carried its own set of problems that needed to be rectified as the foreign pastors had to make numerous sacrifices to serve in Bermuda.

One sentence gave me pause: "A pastor should not be assigned to Bermuda simply because there is an opening, or because Bermuda is for 'upstarts' only." Exactly what did this mean? Could this be an acknowledgment that Rev. Dees and Rev. Brandon suspected that this was how they were viewed? We know how they were viewed by the Bermuda press as they fought in Bermuda to rectify injustices. The pastors noted that the congregations to which pastors were to be assigned should know who they were getting so that their expectations would be, using my word, realistic. I can only surmise that some congregants were not completely satisfied with the work they did. Perhaps some expected that they would simply preach the Sunday sermons, conduct prayer meetings and oversee the general administrative duties of the church without being concerned about what happened outside of the walls of the church. These members would be completely "taken aback" with their work in the community, especially with their seeming support for young "troublemakers." This special issue was perhaps an embarrassment for some, but the topics they addressed affected other districts as well. The small island of Bermuda had two districts which had caused some confusion. Many held the perception that when there was one district, people worked together, while with two districts there was conflict.

Rev. Brandon then asked, "Who is writing Bermuda's history?" When he was pastor, about a year prior to this writing, he had a Black female pastor come to Bermuda as the Women's Day Speaker and, as she had searched for information about the country, she was disappointed with what she found—or more specifically, did not find. While she discovered brochures about Bermuda as a vacation destination, she found little about the Black man's struggle in a British colony.

Rev. Brandon noted the importance of people knowing their history so that they can chart their course for the future. While he acknowledged Dr. Eva Hodgson's contribution to Bermuda's history, he noted that this work only covered a span of ten years, from 1953-1963. In this work, he discussed at length her historical record of the importance of Cup Match and its value to Bermudians.

While he reflected on the importance of Cup Match to Bermuda, he asked if the Black churches history in Bermuda would be lost. It was feared that the A.M.E. Church's vigour was questioned by some, including the Black Beret Cadre. In their position paper it explained that the Black church had set itself apart from the problems that afflict the Black community. He also noted that the people of Bermuda held a sense of pride for the work on their behalf by Dr. Edgar Fitzgerald Gordon. He continued this discourse questioning what art form could be claimed as Bermudian. Ouch! Certainly, as he impresses, "It is too easy to become lost in the crowd. A nation, a colony, an individual must seek and find its own unique identity if each is to survive very long as such and make a positive contribution."

The article noted that while "Bermuda's history is rich, the African Methodist Episcopal Church's history in Bermuda is also rich. So, there is a history within history, yet there is only one history. May this history not be lost in practice or in written word so that generations to come will be able to chart their course well. May the artists do their part and the historians do theirs."

Rev. Dees pointed out what *The Bermuda Recorder* (January 9, 1971) stated in their editorial about the difficulty of finding an outfit for the Miss Universe competition when the contestants were to dress in their native attire! And what do you think that was?

This magazine then related the importance of art. This certainly thrilled me. It made me think and it revealed that there is still much more that artists can do. As a N.C. A&T graduate of The Arts, and later the Officer for the Arts for the Department of Education in Bermuda, I have spent much of my life recording Bermuda's history in plays and poetry. My first book of poems and plays, *Battle for Freedom* (published in 1994 by Dale Butler with the University of Toronto Press), is but one example. In fact, I was asked to change the title of the book and simply call it *Bermuda Poetry and Drama*. The fact was that the play in the book called *Battle for Freedom* was a play that recorded the history of the A.M.E. Church in Bermuda. It was written specifically for Bermuda's conference Lay Organization at the request of Mr. Lionel Phillips, a great Bermuda Lay President. Perhaps more books could have been sold if the title was changed, but many of my works also depict the struggle of Bermudian people and I felt that the title was fitting.

I also wrote a play called "Mazumbo" that attracted a tremendous audience. I wrote this play after being captivated by the book written by Mr. Ira Phillip on the life of Dr. Edgar Fitzgerald Gordon. When I was a high school teacher, I used Mr. Phillip's book in my communication classes as a way to help Bermudian students better appreciate who they are and what they can do to contribute to society.

The Protest magazine demonstrated what should be important in our lives and I was thrilled that Rev. Dees highlighted my high school art teacher, Mr. Charles Lloyd Tucker. He was an outstanding artist and I discovered that it was Mr. Tucker who had designed the cover of *The Protest* magazine! Thanks to Mr. Tucker, I got a distinction in my Art General Certificate of Education (G.C.E.). He told my mother that I needed to focus more on my visual art talent, and after his death, his wife allowed me to use his studio.

Charles Lloyd Tucker died suddenly of a heart attack on Monday, January 11, 1971. I vividly recall the school assembly where the announcement was made. The student body was stunned as our principal, Fredrick Shirley Furbert, revealed his last conversation with Mr. Tucker. He said that Mr. Tucker asked him, "Are all the children in?" The principal said that Mr. Tucker was concerned about us even on his death bed. Yes, he certainly impacted my life as he did so many others. I remember him as a colourful dresser and very personable.

Mr. Tucker had told Rev. Dees that the A.M.E. Church played a very important role in his life. He also attended Bethel A.M.E. Church, which was a very short walk from his house, and Rev. Dees served as his pastor. Rev. Dees noted that Mr. Tucker's artwork was outstanding, as his works were shown in galleries around the world. In an interview he talked with Rev. Dees about one of his latest paintings called *I Have a Dream*, a work symbolizing the Black youth in Bermuda who wanted to be somebody and who were being "frustrated in the process." He also discussed his painting, "Let my People Go." Reading the account of the interview impacted me enough to question why I paint, for whom, and the impact of my work. Certainly, I fall far short. I never thought of naming any of my paintings.

The Protest magazine was a treasure trove of information. One interesting note is how St. Philip A.M.E. Church, once situated in Tucker's Town, "an exclusive domain" for white people, was purchased by the Bermuda Government and moved to Harrington Sound.

I learned more about the history of my Alma Mater, the Berkeley Institute. The magazine gave an account of what was called "an interesting meeting, which was held in the Town Hall, Hamilton." It placed before the public the twelfth annual report, and at this meeting the financial state concerning the real estate holdings, investments, and balance of the budget was revealed. One of the objectives of the Berkeley Education Society was to create a high school for the Colony. The officers were listed for interested readers. Additionally, included was a letter written by W. Berkeley Dowling asking why the governing body should be limited to "one sect and colour?"

A short dramatic sketch about a student interview with a pastor was one of the more creative articles in the issue. The student questioned the pastor about biblical teachings and noted that so-called "Christians" seemed to deny the relevancy of the teachings of Christ. I believe this sketch attempted to help people (especially Christians) understand why Rev. Dees and Rev. Brandon worked so diligently to rectify injustice. In the fictional interview, it emphasized to the student that Jesus cast His lot with the poor and denied Himself the comforts of the world. Many Christians fail to do this. Not everyone who calls themselves a Christian is a committed follower of Jesus Christ. I chuckled as I read the drama. The student questioned how Bermuda could raise funds for an overseas cause (in Pakistan), yet disassociate itself from the islands to the South in need of funds. The very deliberate response was that the great philanthropists who could afford to help would get greater recognition and honours from the Queen while they pretended that the longstanding problems in Bermuda did not exist. The student, changing the topic, asked what the Bible said about revolution. The preacher responded with a quote by Dr. James Cone: "The Christian man is obligated by a freedom grounded in the Creator to break all laws which contradict human dignity."

The Protest Magazine, September 1971

The eighth-edition of *The Protest*, September 1971, dealt with the following subjects: a prologue concerning the voices of Black churchmen; a consultation on church union; the kingdom, and the power, and the infamy as well as the usual, dramatic/poetic expressions.

The first article, "The Voice of Black Churchmen," is gleaned from the thesis of Rev. Brandon while at Boston University, 1969, titled "Black Churchmen—A New Challenge to True Ecumenism." You may agree that this article is another way that this magazine captured ideas that were important for consideration, not just back then, but even today. The quotes selected as a precursor to the article itself were thought-provoking. It seems that the matter concerning unionism within the church was at issue and that for Blacks, especially the A.M.E. members under Richard Allen who walked out of the Methodist church to create their own, wished the matter of race within the church be addressed as the matter of identity was and perhaps still is an issue. The COCU, designed to unify all churches and promote that Blacks and whites work together in love, could not escape the injustices of the past and Black members asked that the church not simply acknowledge the need to unify, but address the race problem directly. They also asked that the church provide compensatory treatment for those who had been poorly treated in the past.

Rev. Brandon noted in this thesis that men will always be obsessed with power and although we see the value in working together in love, race still is a matter of concern. The statement by the United Church of Christ Ministries which reads in part that "we are morally obligated to confront ourselves and our white brothers..." helps us understand that the issues around unity were of great concern, even for whites. I believe they felt it was imperative for whites to not just acknowledge the injustices endured by Blacks, but to redress what was done in the past. My question is, "What is the best way to do this, and can it be done?"

The quote from A. Cecil Williams struck me as rather poignant; that "black men are organizing for the power to determine their own future in the church. Once the masses of blacks know they count, then we can move to reconciliation." The question was then raised: who should reconcile?

I will be the first to admit that the writings are profound. Here I attempt to give a snapshot of the article, "Consultation on Church Union," and I believe there is something here that resonates with everyone—congregations, pastors, and bishops as well. The Consultation on Church Union, which Rev. Brandon says was organized in April of 1962 as a response to a sermon, "A Proposal Toward the Reunion of Christ's Church," preached by Dr. Eugene Carson Blake (December 4, 1960), was comprised of the nine denominations listed in the article. The stated objective of the COCU was to "begin anew." It noted that the union had to deal with very touchy, yet important subjects with the challenge to make dramatic changes to the structure. The statement that if structural changes were not addressed, the death of both Black and white churches would be the result as the churches must take seriously God's demand for justice and righteousness.

I can only imagine the amount of work and thought that went into presenting this information to the readers. Rev. Brandon's references are numerous, and I am aware that this is a work produced for his thesis, so it is scholarly in content. He referenced and quoted people such as Mr. E.U. Essien-Udon from his book, *Black Nationalism*; Dr. Gayraud S. Wilmore, *The Case for a New Black Church Style*, Church in Metropolis, No. 18, 1968; Mr. Ian Henderson in his book, *Power Without Glory - A Study in Ecumenical Politics* (Hutchinson of London, 1967) and Douglas Jones in his book, *Instruments of Peace—Biblical Principles of Christian Unity* (Hodder & Stoughton, London, 1965), and others.

The statement that "we need only to look at a few pages of history in order to note the kind of unfortunate situation that forced black people out of white churches" includes a rather lengthy letter which was written in the form of a petition in 1867 and presented to the white members of the Fairfield Baptist Church by 38 Black members of the congregation. This letter, says Rev. Brandon, taken from Dr. Harry V. Richardson's book, *Dark Glory* (Nashville, 1947), discusses how the members of Fairfield Baptist Church appealed to the Elder to think about the need to preserve the identity of the Baptist Church in any new relationship that was to be established. The argument seemed to be that any relationship with others of another faith needed to ensure the peace and harmony characterized by "those of the same faith", especially since Blacks had left white churches in order to serve as they wished. The letter writer emphasized that a separate church organization may be the best way forward to preserve the privileges of church organization, meetings, order of service, and the like.

Of course, this letter emphasizes the challenges that confront us as a people and no less as a Christian people, for even in Christian duty the question of identity continues. It seems though that the letter made an impact, and the request was unanimously granted. Two white members donated small plots of land for a temporary place of worship and the situation of white church structures remained the same. The article concludes with the unanswered question concerning the type of union required and the needs of Blacks and minorities on this race question.

This article and the issue of race resonated with me, for I recalled an incident around 1990 when I was the church school Superintendent at Bethel A.M.E. Church. My assistant Mr. Richard Warner and I attempted to have our church school students join with a white denomination so that our students could appreciate the value of worshiping and fellowshipping together. We had joined with other Black churches in Bermuda when it dawned on me that we had made no attempt to have our children worship with white children. As a result, we wrote to the pastor and were both astonished to receive a reply from the pastor stating that while the idea had value, he felt it better that we meet together in the sweet by and by!

The next article in the eighth magazine is called, "The Kingdom, and The Power, and the Infamy." Rev. Dees relates information about the events that occurred in November of 1946, when the church held its first "extra session of the General Conference." It had been decided that the affairs of the New York Annual Conference had not been properly handled by the bishop. The Bishop's Council then relieved the bishop of his duties. It seems that as a result, the bishops were divided, and a number of them were expelled. As Bermuda is part of the First District, it would have been important for Bermudians to know that their bishop was expelled with a vote of 999 to 35! The bishop later filed a lawsuit.

In relating the events, Rev. Dees asked the readers to consider the three points made by the judge in rendering his decision and gave lengthy explanations. He noted that the judge also made mention of the power afforded bishops. Rev. Dees shared that this was well known but rarely stated. He then related a story of a pastor who had lost favor with a bishop, which emphasized the power bishops held over thousands of pastors. He said that from the time of appointment until the time of his death a pastor is never allowed to forget "who feeds him."

The story he related, however, is a rather disappointing one that shows that, as it is often said, "power corrupts and absolute power corrupts absolutely." What he wrote was that a pastor at an annual conference asked a bishop for forgiveness. The bishop told the pastor, "Get down on your knees, my brother, get down on your knees." This was in front of the entire assembly. Rev. Dees said that "this was no joke" since "one way or another, a pastor is always down on his knees." I am certain that Rev. Dees' information, documented for all to read, did not sit well with bishops, their supporters, and others for many reasons. He felt that what is done in the dark should be brought to light.

Although Rev. Dees spoke out concerning misguided bishops, we know that there are bishops who do their jobs without attempting to abuse their power. Bermuda was proud to have Rev. Vinton Anderson, an elected bishop. Although we were proud of him, I am sure that there were decisions he made that were not perfect. After all, we are all human.

Rev. Dees continued the article by recalling how ten years after the first extra session of the annual conference a major "storm" arose in the General Conference held in Miami, Florida. The storm that began there in 1956 increased and caused a disruption at the General Conference in Los Angeles, California in 1960. It seems another bishop was put out of the church until the convening of the General Conference of 1968. The money spent on the court case was difficult to account for, and he questioned if the bishops were killing the church. It seems that in the 1970s the A.M.E. Church was on the verge of another extra session of the General Conference. If more bishops were expelled, confusion would continue to reign and he offered this biblical admonition from Galatians 5:15: "...if you bite and devour one another, take heed lest you are consumed by one another."

The final edition of the magazine included expressions by Rev. Lloyd Dees. He offered a poem called "Sympathy," and another one, "Advice." Also he wrote and published his poem, "A King" in that final magazine. I found them all creatively enlightening. Again, I appreciated how he used poetry to convey meaning symbolically.

Chapter Four

Beyond Bermuda

Rev. Dees in North Carolina

(North Carolina Agricultural & Technical State University)

After Rev. Dees left Bethel A.M.E. Church, he became the Director of the United Campus Christian Ministry at North Carolina Agricultural & Technical State University (N.C. A&T) in Greensboro, North Carolina. Rev. Dees and my mother worked together on my college application and both were instrumental in my ultimate attendance. This was a great achievement, as I had just turned sixteen and was one of the first from my high school to go off to University. As I was one of the youngest students on the college campus, an article was written about me in the school's newspaper highlighting my youth and that I was from Bermuda.

I recall my mother asking me what I wanted to study. I wasn't sure, but thought I might focus on Art or English, as I had obtained my G.C.E. (General Certificate of Education in English) in year four with excellent results. I also had received a distinction in Visual Art. I told my mother that I wanted to study English, and she replied that I could study drama and teach English with a dramatic flair, which would make me stand out among the "zillion English teachers." She then sent me to talk with her friend, Mr. Calvin Smith, who at the time was Bermuda's first Black statistician, to ask about the benefits of having a Speech and Drama degree in Bermuda. He told me that the world of the arts would soon be flourishing, which solidified the idea that studying in that area would be a great choice.

That summer, at age fifteen, I received an acceptance letter. Mr. Fredrick Shirley Furbert, the school principal, had put together my transcript which stated that I had four years of high school courses. So, when I returned to The Berkeley Institute for my final year (year five), I informed a group of students who were stressed about studying for their G.C.E.'s that I'd been accepted to a university. One student told everyone that I was delusional and stated, "She didn't even say a 'college'…she said she is attending 'University.'" Quite honestly, at the time, I didn't know the difference between the two.

In hindsight, it is probable that by helping me attend the university, Rev. Dees was trying to show how Bermudians could use their gifts and efforts and achieve success. As is still true today, Bermuda is a British colony and at that time many Bermudians were told that they needed to attain five G.C.Es. That certification is a British designation, and many students attended schools in the U.K. or Canada.

My mother recalls that when it was announced that I had obtained a teacher training scholarship, one of our teacher relatives unknowingly asked if I would then transfer to an accredited school. My mother was livid that anyone would think she would send her daughter to an unaccredited university. N.C. A&T University was a Black school and not a place that Bermudians sent their students, especially if they had attended The Berkeley Institute. At that time, The Berkeley Institute was recognized as one the best schools for higher education, especially for Black students.

All of my siblings attended The Berkeley Institute and N.C. A&T University, as my mother felt that we should all be grounded in our own identity. My siblings and I went on to attend schools such as Temple University; Howard University; The University of North Carolina at Greensboro, Miami University, Oxford, Ohio; St. John's University; Webster University, and my brother, Rev. Danny, graduated with his second Master's from Payne Theological Seminary in Ohio with top marks.

My sister Donna, while at Howard University, received a research award for her discovery of the P gene for *vitiligo* (an autoimmune disorder). After leaving Howard University, Dr. Donna Durham-Pierre worked at Fox Chase Laboratories. She later taught at Winston Salem State University where she was Dean of the Science Department and a tenured professor until her retirement.

At N.C. A&T, I studied Speech and Theater/Speech Pathology and minored in English. My youngest sister, Shelby Durham-Jackson, followed in my footsteps, but hated the late nights in the theatre and decided to pursue a career in Speech Pathology. She later opened a Health Care Agency in Philadelphia and, because of a work program that she and her husband Melvin Jackson had instituted, was invited to the White House by President Bill Clinton. Because of her work in health care, she was awarded a key to the city of Philadelphia.

God certainly had a plan for our lives and Rev. Dees' initial help to ensure that I obtained a college education had a domino effect. In *The 21 Irrefutable Laws of Leadership*, John Maxwell teaches in the "Law of the Picture:" "People Do What People See." Not only were my siblings impacted, but my peers were as well. One schoolmate, Dr. Kathy Ann White, told me years later that she went abroad to study in America because, as she said, "If you could go to college in America, I believed that I could too."

Rev. Dees had encouraged me to use my gifts and talents to glorify God. As a result of God's grace, I realized that as a teacher, I, too, could make a difference. I know that we are all put on this earth with gifts and potential to be used for God's glory. It's something I think is important to remember and I use this conviction in my introduction to my weekly radio show, *The Need to Lead.*

I gave my life to Christ at age eleven, and as a result of my gift for public speaking, reciting poetry, etc. (in the church initially), God has been glorified. As an adult, when I was asked to deliver a speech for Bethel A.M.E.'s congregation, the then pastor, Rev. Malcolm Eve, who later became a Presiding Elder in the A.M.E. Church, pulled a paper from his Bible and gave it to me in the pulpit. It was a piece that I had written when I was eleven years old, titled, "Why I am a Christian." He said he'd kept it in his Bible all those years—I was overcome. I recall that I had been asked to read that selection in churches throughout the island to encourage other young people to follow Christ. It was also perhaps because of that writing that I was selected as Bethel A.M.E.'s youth delegate to The Christian Education Congress in Dover, Delaware.

So, Rev. Dees was the conduit who ensured I stayed connected to God. His impact made a huge difference in my life which directly resulted in my ability to help others. As we remember Rev. Dees with admiration, we must also appreciate that "the ripple effect" of his life well-lived is still making a difference, and I imagine it will continue through countless generations.

Allow me to elaborate a bit more about how Rev. Dees impacted me while I was at A&T.

My first introduction to North Carolina was quite an experience. Honestly, I had no idea where I was going. When my aunt, a graduate of Ottawa Teachers' College in Canada, asked why I had chosen to attend school in the South, I replied with complete innocence, "Oh no. I'm going to North Carolina."

On the flight there, my mother and I attempted to find our seats on the plane. When she asked the flight attendant for assistance, the flight attendant sharply responded that "she should be able to read." My mother—never one to let a moment slide—fired back, "If you'd done better in school—in reading, math, and otherwise—you might be more than a glorified waitress."

We landed in Greensboro to what felt like another world. The airport was filled with white people, many wearing denim overalls, giving the impression of a deeply rural, farming community. A few years later, I would come face-to-face with the region's darker legacy. Alongside a group of Bermudian and other college students, I attended a Ku Klux Klan march in downtown Greensboro. I still remember the repulsive flyers they handed out—graphic depictions of large, menacing Black men chasing thin white women with flowing blonde hair. On another trip, as I took a Greyhound bus to visit my godmother Pat Coston at Fort Bragg, I saw a chilling sign that read something like, "Welcome to Klan Country."

At N.C. A&T, Rev. Dees—a kind and steady presence—took it upon himself to help us acclimate. He drove us around the sprawling campus, pointing out landmarks, and must have been amused when we expressed concern at the many wreaths displayed. We thought people had died. He chuckled and explained they were symbols of sororities and fraternities—something I had never heard of.

He also proudly pointed out bullet holes in several buildings, explaining they were remnants of the 1969 civil unrest when the National Guard was deployed to campus. He spoke with reverence about the Greensboro Four—Joseph McNeil, Franklin McCain, Ezell Blair, Jr., and David Richmond—freshmen from N.C. A&T who, on February 1, 1960, staged a now-famous sit-in at a segregated Woolworth's lunch counter. Refusing to leave or accept takeout, even when police arrived, their quiet courage sparked a movement that spread across 55 cities in 13 states. Rev. Dees was visibly proud of their nonviolent resistance.

He also took us to meet Chancellor Dowdy, an experience few students could claim. The Chancellor's first question was whether I knew Mrs. Lois Browne-Evans, Bermuda's opposition leader at the time. Apparently, she had visited him just weeks before.

After my mother returned home, I became deeply homesick. I cried every day and longed to return. Someone once explained to another student that I was a "foreigner," as though that justified the tears. My dormitory, Vanstory Hall, overlooked a parking lot and rows of brick buildings. I was too young to drive, and nothing felt familiar. Kind-hearted Rev. Dees visited me at least four times a week. Each time, he would take me to McDonald's. Even though a hamburger, fries, and a drink cost less than $1.75, it felt like a feast on a student budget. Yet even this kindness couldn't stem the tears. Eventually, he asked if I could just try to stay until Homecoming. Little did I know that I would be crowned the Homecoming Foreign Student Queen, just like both of my sisters after me.

What helped most, though, was my dorm's location—right across the street from Bethel A.M.E. Church. Rev. Dees took me there, introduced me to the pastor, and before I knew it, I was teaching the teenage Sunday school class. This was August of 1972, and I had just turned sixteen. My students were seventeen and eighteen. As a theatre major with access to many parties and events, I became selective about what I attended, careful to maintain the image of a church schoolteacher—thanks to Rev. Dees's early influence.

Although he worked in Christian Ministry at A&T, I never quite knew what his official role entailed. He never pressured me to join his programs or initiatives. In hindsight, I feel a bit embarrassed that I didn't take more interest in his work. Years later, I learned that campus ministers are responsible for leading worship, hosting retreats and discussion groups, offering spiritual guidance, and counseling students. If nothing else, I definitely helped him fulfill the "counseling" part—Rev. Dees spent many hours supporting me through my homesickness.

Rev. Dees had recently become a United Methodist minister, though he had come from an A.M.E. background like mine. I now realize he may have been careful not to confuse me in my faith and chose instead to entrust me to the care of Bethel Church.

Just days into my first semester, excitement buzzed around campus—Jesse Jackson was scheduled to speak. I rushed to the quad with hundreds of other students. I was proud to learn that he had graduated from A&T with a degree in sociology in 1964 and had been a quarterback and student body president during his time as an Aggie. I had heard of him in Bermuda and recognized him as a powerful African American icon.

A&T impacted me in profound ways. I remember attending my first football game. I didn't understand the sport—then or now—but the halftime performance and the singing of the Black National Anthem moved me deeply. I wrote to my friend Ianthia Simmons back in Bermuda and insisted she attend a Black university. Ironically, I didn't even realize I was supposed to be at A&T for four years; I thought it was a short-term study program.

During my first year, I occasionally babysat for Rev. and Mrs. Dees, but the family moved the following year to West Virginia. By then, his work with me was complete. I was no longer homesick. I had friends, a boyfriend to return to after Christmas, and a growing sense of purpose.

Rev. Dees played a pivotal role in shaping my early journey at A&T. His quiet, consistent support helped me find my footing. By the time I graduated, I knew that I was meant to use my gifts to help others. In 1976, I returned to Bermuda and became a public school teacher, as well as a Sunday school teacher at Bethel A.M.E.—just as my mother instructed.

Rev. Dees in West Virginia (Human Rights Director)

After one year at N.C. A&T, Rev. Dees accepted a pastoral position at Simpson A.M.E. Church in West Virginia. During that time, he also became the Director of the Wheeling Human Rights Commission in 1973. Rev. Dees did not force his beliefs on others. He was solution-oriented, but he never hid his Christian principles and beliefs. He always showed others the utmost respect. He thought that each of us should have a voice and encouraged everyone to examine themselves and look for solutions. This was his way of bringing people together and encouraging them to *live to make a difference.*

People soon began to hear about Rev. Dees and his work, as evidenced by the following *Intelligencer* news article from sometime in 1973, captioned, "Simpson U.M. Pastor is Wheeling Human Rights Director." The article read as follows:

> The pastor of Simpson United Methodist Church, Wheeling, is also the Human Rights Director for the city. The Rev. Lloyd E. Dees assumed his dual role in March of this year.
>
> A native of Alabama, Rev. Dees joined the Commission following several years of social and theological work in the South.

He said he believes the city ordinance outlining the goals of the Commission will be effective in bringing people in the community together.

The two basic purposes of the Commission according to Rev. Dees, are the enforcement of civil liberties and the reconciliation of persons divided by disagreement.

"The focus of the Commission will be devising the means of bringing people in the community together for the purpose of better understanding," he said. The Commission will not seek to be problem-oriented, he said, even though a great many problems will arise and will hopefully be solved.

The Commission will "not force people" to come to mutual understandings but will "encourage people" to do so. It is the commission's desire for "people to consent, voluntarily," to a better understanding between people.

Problems the Commission will seek to alleviate are the 'problems that keep people… all people…divided and misunderstood," Rev. Dees said…

Simpson U. M. Pastor Is Wheeling Human Rights Director

Rev. Lloyd E. Dees

The pastor of Simpson United Methodist Church, Wheeling, is also the Human Rights Director for the city. Rev. Lloyd E. Dees assumed this dual role in March of this year.

A native of Alabama, Rev. Dees joined the commission following several years of social and theological work in the South. He said he believes the city ordinance outlining the goals of the commission will be effective in bringing people in the community together.

The two basic purposes of the commission according to Rev. Dees, are the enforcement of civil liberties and the reconciliation of persons divided by disagreement.

"The focus of the commission (will be) devising the means of bringing people in the community together for the purpose of better understanding," he said. The commission will not seek to be problem-oriented, he said, even though a great many problems will arise and will hopefully be solved.

The commission will "not force people" to come to mutual understandings, but will "encourage people" to do so. It is the commision's desire for "people to consent, voluntarily," to a better understanding between people.

Problems the commission will seek to alleviate are the "problems that keep people . . . all people . . . divided and misunderstood," Rev. Dees said.

Prior to coming to Wheeling, Reverend Dees served as the director of the campus Christian ministry at A and T State University in Greensboro, N. C. He, his wife and son, live in North Park, Wheeling.

Page 7

Intelligencer, 1973

Not one to turn a blind eye to challenging issues, Rev. Dees was soon involved in a situation concerning unfair hiring practices for minorities in West Virginia. In his role as Executive Director for the Wheeling Human Rights Commission, I know he worked tirelessly to right injustices through education and training in his quiet, dignified manner. What follows are two articles which appeared in the Wheeling newspaper, *Intelligencer.* One article written by Andy Leheny verifies that Rev. Dees was dedicated to the causes of the downtrodden. He was never one to "not get involved" where injustice was concerned. Rev. Dees seemed to seek opportunities for involvement and his work was appreciated by many, as evidenced by the article below, which read in part as follows:

> Members of the Wheeling Human Rights Commission said Wednesday they are still awaiting a reply from the United States Office of Civil Rights Compliance concerning the minority hiring practices of the city's police and fire departments. According to the Rev. Lloyd Dees, director, a letter was sent over two weeks ago to the federal office informing them of a possible conflict in recommendations made by the federal office and by the Commission concerning minority hiring practices.
>
> Rev. Dees said recommendations for changes in the hiring practices were made by the federal office last August but were never implemented by the police and fire departments. He said the Commission does not want to recommend any changes until it learned why the federal recommendations were not implemented. He said the letter asked if any steps would be taken to implement the recommendations. Group members voted to send another letter to the office. They said if a reply is not received by March 20, the Commission will take whatever steps it feels necessary concerning the matter.
>
> Wheeling Police Chief Harry Bruno has informed the Commission that he was unaware of the letter from the Office of the Civil Rights Compliance. However, Bruno said he will secure a copy of the letter. The Commission discussed plans for a two-evening program on "Justice in the Community" and endorsed the establishment of "Diversionary methods" to help stem juvenile delinquency.
>
> Rev. Dees said the two-evening affair would be scheduled in April or May as part of the Commission's community education

> program. He said the group will select an individual to speak on "Justice in the Community" one evening and a seminar on the subject would be held the following night.
>
> Members praised a meeting concerning the need for a juvenile rehabilitation center in the county which was held Monday. The meeting was attended by educators, law enforcement officials and citizens. Ohio County intermediate Court Judge George Spillers recommended at the meeting that "Divisionary methods" be established to reduce youngsters from…

Another article from the *Intelligencer* was captioned, "Human Rights Director Resigns," and stated:

> The Rev. Lloyd E. Dees, executive director of the Wheeling Human Rights Commission, has submitted his resignation from the post effective June 20, City Manager Charles C. Steele said Thursday.
>
> Steel said Dees is resigning because he has accepted an appointment in Charleston as pastor for a congregation. In addition to his part-time duties with the Human Rights Commission, Dees is pastor of Simpson Methodist Church in Wheeling. Dees has worked with the Human Rights Commission since March 1973. He is the only person to hold the post since the Commission was reorganized and a new human rights ordinance for Wheeling was adopted by council in 1972.
>
> Steele said he has discussed the executive director's resignation with the Rev. David Birch, Chairman of the commission. Steele said the Commission expects to launch an immediate recruitment drive to find a new part-time executive director. The Commission chairperson said members of the group have all expressed "deep regret" regarding Dees' departure from Wheeling. He said Rev. Dees is a "capable man" who has done an "admirable piece of work" helping

> the Commission get organized and establishing guidelines that will be the basis for its future work.
>
> Rev. Birch said Dees' "main function" as an executive director is "investigative." He said the executive director has gathered facts and data on which the Commissions decisions have been made in a quiet and efficient manner.
>
> The chairman said the Commission as a whole will meet next June 5. Steps already have been taken to advertise for candidates for the post, and officers of the Commission will meet next week to discuss procedure for selecting a new executive director, he added. "Lloyd will be a hard man to replace," the chairman said. Rev. Dees is a native of Camden, Alabama, and was a minister in Greensboro, N.C., prior to his arrival in Wheeling. He is a graduate of Shelton College and the Interdenominational Theological Center and has attended Princeton Theological Seminary. His background includes employment with the New York City Department of Social Services, as a youth counsellor and as a probate probation officer in Atlanta, Georgia.

Rev. Dees was respected by his community and people knew that he did not shirk responsibility. I believe, if we follow the example set by Rev. Dees, who followed the example of Jesus Christ, we, too, should look to use our gifts and talents to benefit others, for "we are our brother's keeper!"

Rev. Dees in White Plains, N.Y. (Standing Up for Firefighters)

Another news article written in 1977 by staff writer Bill Falk, "Fireman Tells of Biased Treatment," demonstrates, once again, that Rev. Lloyd E. Dees worked as a champion for justice. He was sought out to assist others as he was widely respected and had become well-known as an effective orator. This article noted that Rev. Dees could deliver his message confidently and emphatically. I know that although he spoke passionately, his delivery was without hate or malice, and came through with a reasoned heartfelt insistence that justice must not be denied. I am only including part of the article here, as the original document had frayed over time and was illegible. The beginning of the article is as follows:

One of the two blacks in the White Plains fire department testified Wednesday that he asked for a new job five years ago because he "was tired of riding on the back step" of the fire truck. And the pastor of a White Plains church said in the same, racially divided Manhattan courtroom that "blacks feel they need not apply" to the city's "racist" fire department.

In a testimony in U.S. District Court, White Plains firefighter Shearin O. Higgs said he volunteered to leave active fire duty five years ago to become an inspector in the department's fire prevention bureau. Higgs said in the eight years he had served "on the line" he was always assigned to ride on the back of the truck. And when the truck arrived at the destination, Higgs said, he "usually was the person closest to the fire." Higgs, a member of the Vulcan Society of Westchester, testified on behalf of that black firefighter's group's claim that a high school education is not needed to perform a fireman's tasks. The Volcans and the U.S. Justice Department contend that current diploma requirements of White Plains and New Rochelle illegally screen out blacks and Hispanics.

Higgs said under questioning by an attorney for White Plains, he did complete high school and later took some college courses. But, Higgs said, that education "was meaningless because I wasn't afforded the opportunity to use the knowledge…I was a back-step man." Higgs' testimony came during the eighth day of an unusually, non-jury trial on the diploma issue before Federal Court Judge Abraham Sofaer. White Plains and New Rochelle are trying to convince Sofaer their diploma requirement is not illegal and provides some assurance candidates are qualified to perform a fireman's tasks.

Also on Wednesday, four leaders of Westchester's black community asked Sofaer to eliminate "racist" practices in the fire departments. A fifth minority leader proposed a compromise to the dispute over the high school diploma. But a sixth Westchester resident, a fire captain in the Hartsdale fire department, warned against lowering standards in the fire departments.

Those comments were submitted to Sofaer during a hearing on the out-of-court agreement that recently ended the Vulcan's discrimination lawsuit against White Plains, New Rochelle and Mount Vernon.

The agreement includes a number of provisions designed to increase the number of blacks, Hispanics and women on the city's fire departments. It was approved earlier this year by the city's legislatures. But White Plains and New Rochelle refused to go along with the demand they eliminate their diploma requirements, forcing the ongoing trial. The rest of the settlement—which also ended in a parallel discrimination suit by the Justice Department—will be implemented in the three cities when Sofaer gives his approval, which is expected soon.

Yonkers, also named in the two lawsuits, refused to approve the settlement terms and will have to fight the discrimination charges in a separate trial.

Of the six persons submitting statements on the settlement Wednesday, only one delivered his orally—Lloyd E. Dees, pastor of the Trinity Methodist Church in White Plains. In a stinging oratory delivered with the cadence and conviction of a sermon, Dees, who is black, said "the conclusion the majority of blacks in White Plains have drawn is that the fire department is racist—racist in its composition and racist in its intent."

Dees spoke in front of a crowded courtroom in which whites uniformly sat on one side of the aisle and blacks on the other. On one side, five rows deep, members of the Vulcans and Westchester's black community, on the other were White Plains Fire Chief William J. McMahon and five rows of the fire unions members from the three cities, who have vehemently opposed the settlements.

> Dees urged Sofaer to give the black community "some relief" by both approving the settlements and striking down the city's diploma requirement. Dees said that despite a black population in White Plains of about 16%, only two of the 170 current firefighters are black and no more than four blacks have been employed at any one time by the department in the last 20 years.
>
> "Blacks feel that they need not apply," Dees said. If current policies are not halted, Dees said "the fire department of the city of White Plains will be 100 percent white in the very near future."

Rev. Lloyd Dees certainly availed himself to help everyone he could. He did not accept the status quo, but used his time on earth to give his best service to others. On Friday, July 12, 1996, Susan Harris of *The New York Times* took a photograph of Rev. Dees and two others, and under their picture was the following: The Rev. Luther Evans of the Community Memorial Baptist Church in Yonkers, left, and the Rev. Lloyd E. Dees of the Trinity United Methodist Church in White Plains, right, hug the Rev....

(I am hesitant to reveal the name of the pastor here, as he was tried and found innocent.) The photo's caption stated: "Minister is Released in Child-Abuse Case."

The article was written by David Stout and read, in part:

> "BEACON, N.Y. July 11—after 10 years behind bars for child abuse crimes he swears never happened, the Rev. walked out of prison today and into bright sunshine and the bear hugs of friends."

The Rev. Luther Evans of the Community Memorial Baptist Church in Yonkers, left, and the Rev. Lloyd E. Dees of the Trinity United Methodist Church in White Plains, right, hug

Minister Is Released in Child-Abuse Case

By DAVID STOUT

We will win the appeal. No question," ... was convicted by a ... ents about "a robber" who would

The New York Times, July 12, 1996

Yes, Rev. Dees was a friend to all, and I am sure he believed in the innocence of his fellow colleague of the cloth. I do not know how much time he spent on this case, but I am certain that once he had committed to working to clear an injustice, he worked methodically and deliberately.

Rev. Dees in Georgia (A Lifetime of Advocacy)

Because Rev. Dees worked tirelessly for others, he was recognized in news articles and in magazines such as the March/April 2013 issue of the monthly publication, *The Pelican Brief,* from the Coastal Regional Commission of Georgia. The article was titled "A Lifetime of Advocacy," by Dionne Lovett, Aging Services Director, and demonstrated why he should be recognized and awarded. It read as follows:

> Coastal Area Agency on Aging has nominated Rev. Lloyd Dees for the "Martha Eaves Advocacy for Positive Change Award." This award, sponsored by the Georgia Council on Aging, recognizes adults, (60 and above) from across the State who have devoted time and energy advocating for positive change at the local, state or federal level. By creating this award and recognizing role models for local involvement, it is hoped that others will be encouraged to become advocates for issues concerning older adults in their own communities. Rev. Dees is among five recipients who will be honored at the April 25 Coalition of Advocates for Georgia's elderly (CO-AGE) meeting in Athens, GA.
>
> Rev. Lloyd Dees has served as a member of the Coastal Advisory Council for more than eight years. But more than that, he has been a staunch advocate for human and civil rights throughout his lifetime. Rev. Dees is a native of Alabama, is married to Dolores Mills Dees of New York. He is retired and currently resides in Rincon, GA (Effingham County.) Having lived and served as a human rights activist in New York, New Jersey, Bermuda, West Virginia, North Carolina, and now coastal Georgia, Rev. Dees is no stranger to hard work and grassroots organizational efforts for positive change. Rev. Dees graduated with honors, from the Interdenominational Theological Center in Atlanta and has done further study at the

Princeton Theological Seminary in Princeton, New Jersey and Union Seminary in New York City. After 17 years in the A.M.E. Church and pastoring churches in New Jersey and Bermuda, he became a member of the United Methodist Church in 1972.

In North Carolina, he was a Campus Minister at North Carolina State University in Greensboro for several years. He then moved to Wheeling, West Virginia where he was the first Executive Director of the Commission on Human Rights for the city. In New York, where he pastored mostly transitional churches, he was a member of the Board of Ordained Ministers for eight years and a member of its executive committee for six years. He served as a member of the Commission on Equitable Compensations for six years and chairperson for four years.

Rev. Dees has a keen interest in civil affairs as well as secondary and higher education. He was a member of the Superintendent of Schools Advisory Committee in Lawrence and White Plains, New York, as well as a member of the Task Force on Graduation Standards for the White Plains Board of Education. During his pastorate in Freeport, New York, he was a founding member on the Board of Directors of Habitat for Humanity, Nassau County and served as chairperson of Public Relations and Fund Raising. While pastoring in Bermuda, he co-founded Bermudians for Reconciliation, as a means to create a better economic and social environment for people on the island.

Although retired from his professional careers, Rev. Dees is still advocating for positive change affecting seniors in the Coastal Region of Georgia. He makes a point to request opportunities to speak at the local county commissioners' meetings to educate members and residents of senior issues and insists that more resources be made available for senior services within the county. Effingham County has vowed to let no senior go hungry; and there is never a waiting list for meals in this county. Rev. Dees has also made himself available

> to the Coastal Regional Commission Council meetings, speaking at these meetings to educate members regarding the importance of senior issues within our region.
>
> Rev. Dees keeps abreast of senior issues and opportunities for advocacy. In November 2012, he was one of fifteen enrollees in the First Annual Coastal Advocacy Academy held in Savannah, GA. He attends the annual Senior Week at the Capitol in Atlanta event each year to have a chance to speak to elected officials. Not only does he attend, he like many others across the state, reaches out to elected officials to inform (and sometimes educate) them on issues relevant to seniors in our communities. Rev. Dees has voiced concerns to State Senator Jack Hill, U.S. Senator Johnny Isakson, and Congressman John Barrow, just to name a few. At nearly 80 years old, Rev. Dees continues to advocate for issues and continues to make sure he provides a voice for those in need.

What a fine tribute to this man of God!

A Lasting Voice

In 2013, another article titled "A Lasting Voice" appeared in the spring edition of *The Effingham Living Magazine* (pages 52-53). It includes a wonderful picture of Rev. Dees. That article read as follows:

> For more than four decades Lloyd Dees' strong voice and faith graced the pulpit and the altar. Now he's a retired minister; but Dees continues to preach for senior citizens' rights.
>
> Dees is one of the members of the Effingham County's delegation on the Coastal Regional Commission's Aging Services Advisory Committee, and he's been a faithful participant—even at the age of 82.
>
> "I have had concerns with seniors and all kinds of citizens," he said. "Somebody asked me if I wanted to do this."

He served as a chairperson of the Aging Services Advisory Committee for two years and is one of three Effingham representatives on its board. After spending a lifetime spreading the word of God, he's now spreading the word on the issues facing older citizens.

Still in Service, Preaching for Seniors

Dees served as a pastor in the United Methodist Church for 40 years, spending much of his time in and around New York City. He also spent a couple of years in Bermuda.

When he retired in 1999, he and his wife moved to Rincon. His mother-in-law lived there, until she passed away a year and a half ago at the age of 96.

Dees celebrated his 82nd birthday on 12/12/12—that's right, December 12, 2012. He was born in Alabama and left there at age 23 in 1951. He was drafted into the army that year, and stayed in for two years.

"I was stationed at a base in New Jersey near New York City, and I liked it," he recalled.

It was there that he met his wife, Dolores, and they were married in 1957. They celebrated 55 years of wedded bliss last September.

Dees and his wife have two children, Jason and Janet. He graduated from the Interdenominational Theological Seminary in Atlanta and also studied at the Union Theological Seminary in New York City and the Princeton Theological Seminary in New Jersey. He served churches in New Jersey, New York City, Long Island and in the New York City suburb of Westchester County.

"I've been a lot of places and seen a lot of things," Dees said with a smile.

Dees sang in his high school choir and in the glee club. His great joy, however, was singing church hymns, leading the congregation in worship.

Blessed with a rich, deep singing voice, Dees continues to sing. He has been a part of the "Chimes of Hope" with violinist Dr. Anne Yarrow, performing at New Covenant Church and historic Trinity United Methodist Church in Savannah and in Bermuda.

Preserving Services for Seniors

Dees still sings, and now his voice is used to champion for senior citizens.

"We're pushing hard to maintain an overall quality of life," he said. "We're really pushing hard to keep Social Security, Medicaid and Medicare. They are essential to the health and well-being of many senior citizens, not only in this county, but throughout the nation."

Each year, senior citizen advocates gather at the state Capitol for Senior Week, making sure state officials, particularly elected officials, understand the concerns facing the state's older population.

With the help of the Coastal Regional Commission, aging services advocates composed a resolution on behalf of senior citizens a couple of years ago and "sent it to the representatives from North to South and in between," Dees remarked. "This year seems to be a critical year in respect of budgeting. The needs we had a couple of years ago, we still have. Whatever pressure we can bring to bear, we're going to try to do that."

Dees is hoping to enlist the help of more than just other seniors' representatives in pushing for help.

"We want the public at large to join with us in contacting our representatives, local, state and national, so we can help provide the services our seniors need," he urged. "We welcome the help, wherever it comes, to meet some of these needs."

Ensuring the future, near-term and long-term, of safety net programs such as Medicare and Social Security, is a pressing issue for Dees.

"Radio, TV, newspapers, you've been saturated with whether Social Security is going to be able to keep going, because it's too expensive to maintain," lamented Dees.

"We don't want to let that happen," Dees said. "We're going to strive as hard as we can to keep that from happening."

Senior citizen advocates will continue to press the issue with state and federal lawmakers, Dees added, and even make their concerns to their local elected officials. "We try to get them involved and stay aware of the needs," he said.

To Dees, the government can find ways to continue to make Social Security viable and enduring—given what other areas receive funding.

"Our federal government subsidizes all kinds of things," he said. "I really get perturbed when I think of all the money we spend on all kinds of things. But when it comes to taking care of our people when they get old and get in need, we can't find the money to do that."

Dees does put credence into what Mahatma Gandhi once said: "A nation's greatness is measured by how it treats its weakest members." And to Dees, society can do more, much more, in its treatment of the elderly.

I fully believe in that. I hear a lot of talk about it, from people in different leadership positions. But in some ways, there is a distance from what they say and how they really vote.

"I'm a great fan of going to the moon. But I don't see any senior citizens going up there," he said.

Population of Seniors Booming

The members of the Aging Services Advisory Council use their vast experience and knowledge to assist the Area Agency for Aging. The Coastal Regional Commission Area Agency for Aging oversees services for senior citizens in the 10-country region stretching from Screven to Camden County.

Dees, along with Effingham's other two representatives, Linda Wright and Linda Mercer, are on the 28-person council.

If the council was at full force, "We would have 1,900 years of living, all kinds of experience and made contributions to our nation by living that long," Dees noted. "It's amazing, people coming together from all different kinds of experiences, and we gather in a room and still have concern about helping our brothers and sisters."

The AAA also has the Aging and Disabilities Resource Center, which connects clients with needed services.

"We do want them to be aware of the services the agency provides," Dees explained to fellow seniors. "A lot of them are free. What we have found is that there are needs that can't be met because of budget cuts. We were faced last time and we're faced again with budgets that are being cut from the state and federal level."

"So we've got a waiting list. People who want services can't get it because we don't have the money."

And those services are expected to have exponentially more demands to meet in the coming years. Coastal Georgia is the second fastest-growing region in the state. Its population is expected to jump 51 percent by 2030. Coastal Georgia's senior population is projected to soar to more than 200,000 by 2030, up from its 210 level of 75,260.

"The senior population is going to be increasing," Dees said. "It already is. They are going to keep coming. These are people moving from other states to coastal Georgia. If we can do a little planning ahead for that, that would be wise."

That means those fighting on behalf of senior citizens, such as Rev. Dees, will have to push for more resources devoted to the area's aging population. Dees commended Effingham County for what it does to provide for seniors. Meals are delivered to shut ins, and the senior center in Springfield provides congregate meals.

"Our county does well in providing meals for senior citizens. We have a very nice little center in Springfield," Dees added.

Dees also gladly welcomed the CRC's Coastal Regional Coaches. The system works on demand and on advanced reservations, and all vehicles are wheelchair accessible.

"After having pleaded and begged for more public transportation in our area, we did get that. I rejoiced every day I see the buses going down the road to take people," he said. "That's a wonderful thing. We really appreciate that, and many people appreciate that."

He also expressed his gratitude toward Effingham Health Systems dedicated Alzheimer's wing.

"That's commendable, and you can tell them I said, 'thank you,'" Dee said.

And it's not just care for the elderly and assuring their services and life lines are left intact that are priorities for Dees—extended care and specialized care, especially that required by those suffering from Alzheimer's, is another matter for those pushing seniors causes.

"That's becoming a critical problem," Dees said. Long-term care for seniors is another worry, particularly those who face moving into a nursing home.

Protection of Seniors

Dees gave praise to state Sen. Jack Hill, the chairman of the Senate Appropriations Committee for being "a staunch supporter" of seniors. He also said former State Rep. Ann Purcell was a friend to seniors, as is State Rep. Jon Burns.

He also wants to see the state do something for seniors who are put in positions their pensions or retirement funds were never designed to do—provide for the care of children placed in their care.

"A lot of seniors are taking care of their grandchildren," he said. "Some of them are using the pennies they have. We have tried over the years to get some kind of stipend for grandparents who are taking care of their grandchildren. It's more loving, and it's cheaper than putting them in a foster home."

For some senior citizens, getting enough to eat and having a warm place to live is "tough for a lot of people," Dees said. While massive meal preparations around the holidays are nice, "two days later people forget about them," he added. "Even veterans, in our streets, I advocate for them, too."

Seniors' issues include protection from crime. The elderly are particularly vulnerable to scam artists and to brutal home invasions.

"There is a lot of violence being perpetuated upon old people, breaking into their homes and beating them up and taking what they have," Dees explained. "A lot of seniors live by themselves. The rip-offs of old people is horrible. I guess they found out I'm old, he said wryly, because they're always calling me."

A Voice That Lasts

When it comes to singing, Dees did not have any formal training. "I had 40 years of leading the congregation in hymns," he pointed out. "I just love it. I can't do all the notes like people would

For more than four decades Lloyd Dees strong voice and faith graced the pulpit and the altar. Now, he's a retired minister but Dees continues to preach for senior citizens rights.

Dees is one of the members of Effingham County's delegation on the Coastal Regional Commission's Aging Services Advisory Committee and he's been a faithful participant — even at the age of 82.

"I have had concerns for seniors and all kinds of citizens," he said. "Somebody asked me if I wanted to do this."

He served as chairperson of the Aging Services Advisory Committee for two years and is one of three Effingham representatives on its board. After spending a lifetime spreading the word of God, he's now spreading the word on the issues facing older citizens.

Still in Service, Still Preaching for Seniors

Dees served as a pastor in the United Methodist Church for 40 years, spending much of his time in and around New York City. He also spent a couple of years on Bermuda.

When he retired in 1999, he and his wife moved to Rincon. His mother-in-law lived here, until she passed away a year and a half ago at the age of 96.

Dees celebrated his 82nd birthday on 12/12/12 — that's right, December 12, 2012. He was born in Alabama and left there at 23 in 1951. He was drafted into the Army that year and stayed in for two years.

"I was stationed at a base in New Jersey near New York City, and I liked it," he recalled.

It was there he met his wife, Delores, and they were married in 1957. They celebrated 55 years of wedded bliss last September.

Dees and his wife have two children, Jason and Janet. He graduated from the Interdenominational Theological Seminary in Atlanta and also studied at the Union Theological Seminary in New York City and the Princeton Theological Seminary in New Jersey. He served churches in New Jersey, New York City, Long Island and in the New York City suburb of Westchester County.

"I've been a lot of places and seen a lot of things," Dees said with a smile.

Dees sang in his high school choir and in the glee club. His great joy, however, was singing church hymns, leading the congregation in worship.

Blessed with a rich, deep singing voice, Dees continues to sing. He has been a part of the "Chimes of Hope," with violinist Dr. Anne Yarrow, performing at New Covenant Church and historic Trinity United Methodist Church in Savannah and on Bermuda.

52 • effinghamLIVING

Preserving Services for Seniors

Dees still sings, and now his voice is used to champion for senior citizens.

"We're pushing hard to maintain an overall quality of life," he said. "We're really pushing hard to keep Social Security, Medicaid and Medicare. They are essential to the health and well-being of many senior citizens, not only in this county but throughout the nation."

Each year, senior citizens advocates gather at the state Capitol for Senior Week, making sure state officials, particularly elected officials, understand the concerns facing the state's older population.

With the help of the Coastal Regional Commission, aging services advocates composed a resolution on behalf of senior citizens a couple of years ago and "sent it to representatives from north to south and in between," Dees remarked. "This year seems to be a critical year in respect to budgeting. The needs we had a couple of years ago, we still have them. Whatever pressure we can bring to bear, we're going to try to do that."

Dees is hoping to enlist the help of more than just other seniors representatives in pushing for help.

"We want the public at-large to join with us in contacting our representatives, local, state and national, so we can help provide the services our seniors needs," he urged. "We welcome the help, wherever it comes, to meet some of these needs."

Ensuring the future, near-term and long-term, of safety net programs such as Medicare and Social Security, is a pressing issue for Dees.

"Radio, TV, newspapers, you're being saturated with whether Social Security is going to be able to keep going, because it's too expensive to maintain," lamented Dees.

"We don't want to let that happen," Dees said. "We're going to strive as hard as we can to keep that from happening."

Senior citizens advocates will continue to press the issue with state and federal lawmakers, Dees added, and even make their concerns to their local elected officials. "We try to get them involved and stay aware of the needs," he said.

To Dees, the government can find ways to continue to make Social Security viable and enduring — given what other areas receive funding.

"Our federal government subsidizes all kinds of things," he said. "I really get perturbed when I think of all the money we spend on all kinds of things. But when it comes to taking care of our people when they get old and get in need, we can't find

...eaper than putting them in a ...home."

...ome senior citizens, getting ...gh to eat and having a warm ... to live is "tough for a lot of ...le," Dees said. While massive ... preparations around the holi... are nice, "two days later, people ...t about them," he added. "Even ...ons, in our streets, I advocate for ... too."

...rs issues include protection ... crime. The elderly are particu... vulnerable to scam artists and to ... home invasions.

...e's a lot of violence being per...ted upon old people, breaking ... their homes and beating them ...d taking what they have," Dees ...ned. "A lot of seniors live by ...selves. The rip-offs of old people ...rible. I guess they found out I'm ...he said wryly, "because they're ...s calling me."

A Voice that Lasts

...it comes to singing, Dees did ...ave any formal training. "I had ...ars of leading the congregation ...mns," he pointed out. "I just love ...an't do all the notes like people ...d want me to do. I sing a cap... because I improvise sometimes ...nes out pretty good."

...g in and around New York City ...ded him the opportunity to hear ...mber of musicians and artists, ...d trumpeter Wynton Marsalis ...ed in outdoor venues, for free. Dees heard him often.

...s tempted to go see Elton John," ... added, "but when they said 'the ... seats we have are $75,' I said, ...k you very much.'"

Dees looks forward to continue ...g a voice for fellow senior citi... those who have reached that ...now and those who will one day.

...2, you would think I would want ...t my feet up in a hammock and ...g back and forth," he said. "That ...d be nice. But it's always some... to know you have to keep go-

A Lasting Voice, 2023

In this issue:

- *A Lifetime of Advocacy*
- *Highlights from CRC Council Meetings*
- *What am I Doing on the Planning Commission?*
- *Seniors and Law Enforcement Together*
- *Job Position Available at CRC*
- *Community Incentive Programs*

The Pelican Brief March/April 2013

Coastal Regional Commission

1181 Coastal Drive | Darien, GA | 31305

912.437.0800 | http://crc.ga.gov

March /April 2013

The Pelican Brief

A Monthly Publication of the Coastal Regional Commission

A Lifetime of Advocacy

Coastal Area Agency on Aging has nominated Rev. Lloyd Dees for the "Martha Eaves Advocating for Positive Change" Award. This award, sponsored by the Georgia Council on Aging, recognizes adults, (60 and above) from across the State who have devoted time and energy advocating for positive change at the local, state or federal level. By creating this award and recognizing role models for local involvement, it is hoped that others will be encouraged to become advocates for issues concerning older adults in their own communities. Rev. Dees is among five recipients who will be honored at the April 25th Coalition of Advocates for Georgia's Elderly (CO-AGE) meeting in Athens, Ga.

Rev. Lloyd E. Dees has served as a member of the Coastal AAA Advisory Council for more than eight years. But more than that, he has been a staunch advocate for human and civil rights throughout his lifetime. Rev. Dees is a native of Alabama, is married to Delores Mills Dees of New York. He is retired and currently resides in Rincon, GA (Effingham County.) Having lived and served as a human rights activist in New York, New Jersey, Bermuda, West Virginia, North Carolina, and now coastal Georgia, Rev. Dees is no stranger to hard work and grass-roots organizational efforts for positive change. Rev. Dees graduated with honors, from the Interdenominational Theological Center in Atlanta and has done further study at the Princeton Theological Seminary in Princeton, New Jersey and Union Seminary in New York City. After 17 years in the AME Church and pastoring churches in New Jersey and Bermuda, he became a member of the United Methodist Church in 1972.

In North Carolina, he was a Campus Minister at North Carolina State University in Greensboro for several years.

(continued on page 5)

> want me to do. I sing a cappella because I improvise sometimes. It comes out pretty good."
>
> Living in and around New York City afforded him the opportunity to hear a number of musicians and artists. Famed trumpeter Wynton Marsalis played in outdoor venues, for free, and Dees heard him often.
>
> "I was tempted to go to see Elton John," Dees added, "but when they said the only seats we have are $75," I said, 'thank you very much.'"
>
> Yet Dees looks forward to continuing to be a voice for fellow senior citizens, those who have reached that age now and those who will one day.
>
> "At 82, you would think I would want to put my feet up in a hammock and swing back and forth," he said. "That would be nice. But it's always something to know you have to keep going as long as you can. That's what I try to do."

Anyone can see that Rev. Lloyd E. Dees, a respected, outspoken, assertive man of God, came into the world to spread the gospel of love. I believe that this is a great way to end this particular chapter of his life as he reminds us in his speech to the NAACP, that the work is ongoing. Using history he educated and reminded us of the work still to be done

Below is part of the speech Rev. Dees gave to the NAACP in 2013, as reported by the *Intelligencer* newspaper:

> **Black Man's Struggle Not Over**
>
> The black man's struggle for equality in America is not over despite the past victories in significant battles waged by the National Association for the Advancement of Colored People (NAACP), according to the Rev. Lloyd Dees, Director of the Wheeling Human Rights Commission.

Reverend Dees, who is also pastor of the Simpson United Methodist Church of Wheeling, was the main speaker at Friday's annual membership dinner of the Wheeling Chapter NAACP. The theme of the event was "Lest We Forget."

According to Reverend Dees, the NAACP has been in the forefront of major achievements in the civil rights struggle throughout its 63 years of existence.

"And the road to justice was long and hard. The struggle brought suffering, torture, and even death to many noble members of the cause," he said. Reverend Dees traced the history of the black civil rights struggle since the signing of the Declaration of Independence in 1776 until present times.

"The fact is, that while some people were talking freedom... and writing 'all men are created equal'...Some people were in chains," he said.

He described the practice of slavery in America as brutalizing...despicable. Some signers of the Declaration of Independence, according to Reverend Dees, "were slave owners themselves." Their words were mockeries of their beliefs. According to Reverend Dees, the selection of the theme for Friday's event was significant in its meaning to black people today.

"Lest we forget...the road ahead is still hard. Some brothers and sisters are still denied access to schools; some leading institutions still deny loans to our people; some employers will not hire or promote black employees; and some employers will not give equal pay for the same amount of labor done by others," he said.

"The task of today's NAACP members is to keep the torch of freedom burning, and to pass it to their children if they should die before full equality is won," Reverend Dees said.

Other speakers at Friday's banquet included Clark Gordon, president of the Wheeling Chapter of NAACP; The Rev. Lee Wright, pastor of the Macedonia Baptist Church and past president of the Wheeling Chapter; and the Rev. John K. Frazier, pastor of the Wayman A.M.E. Church. Marvillis Webb was Master of Ceremonies.

Rev. Dees Speaks to NAACP

Blacks' Struggle Not Over

By MICHAEL K. ZASTUDIL
The Intelligencer Staff

The black man's struggle for equality in merica is not over despite the past ictories in significant battles waged by e National Association for the dvancement of Colored People NAACP), according to the Rev. Lloyd ees, director of the Wheeling Human ights Commission.

Reverend Dees, who is also pastor of e Simpson United Methodist Church of heeling, was main speaker at Friday's nual membership dinner of the heeling Chapter NAACP.

The theme of the event was "Lest We orget."

According to Reverend Dees, the AACP has been in the forefront of major achievements in the civil rights struggle throughout its 63 years of existence.

"And the road to justice was long and hard. The struggle brought suffering, torture, and even death to many noble leaders of the cause," he said.

Reverend Dees traced the history of the black civil rights struggle since the signing of the Declaration of Independence in 1776 until present times.

"The fact is, that while some people were talking freedom... and writing 'all men are created equal'... some people were in chains," he said.

He described the practice of slavery in America as "brutalizing... despicable."

Some signers of the Declaration of Independence, according to Reverend Dees, "were slave owners themselves. Their words were mockeries of their beliefs."

According to Reverend Dees, the selection of the theme for Friday's event was significant in its meaning to black people of today.

"Lest we forget... the road ahead is still hard. Some brothers and sisters are still denied access to schools; some lending institutions still deny loans to our people; some employers will not hire or promote black employes; and some employers will not give equal pay for the same amount of labor done by others," he said.

The task of today's NAACP members is to keep the torch of freedom burning, and to pass it to their children if they should die before full equality is won, Reverend Dees said.

Other speakers at Friday's banquet included Clark Gordon, president of the Wheeling Chapter of NAACP; the Rev. Lee Wright, pastor of the Macedonia Baptist Church and past president of the Wheeling Chapter; and the Rev. John K. Frazier, pastor of the Wayman A.M.E. Church.

Marvillis Webb was master of

The Intelligencer, date unknown

Chapter Five

A Forever Bond with Bermuda

Although Rev. Dees left Bermuda and continued his work abroad, Bermuda was never far from his mind and heart. He remained connected with the island, its people, and its events and certainly, he was never far from the minds of Bermudians either, as he was still held in high regard by them.

This was evident by the letter sent to him in care of St. Marks United Methodist Church in Brooklyn, N.Y., on May 2, 1983, by Mrs. Lovette Brangman, then the Secretary General for the Progressive Labour Party. The letter stated that the officers of the Progressive Labour Party were delighted to have him accept their invitation to be the Father's Day speaker that year, as this would give them the opportunity to reacquaint and reunite with old friends. She noted that the time of his arrival in Bermuda should be no later than June 17, and that they would provide accommodations, airfare, and a small renumeration for his services. She thanked him for his promptness in dispatching his resume for use in advertising the event.

On June 19, 1983, Rev. Dees delivered the keynote speech, "In Honour of our Fathers," for the Progressive Labour Party Father's Day event. Rev. Dees liked to interject our history into his presentations to help educate some and remind others of our past so that we can "move forward." I believe that what he said on this occasion will resonate with many, as it did with me.

In Honor of Our Fathers

Mrs. Lois Browne-Evans, the distinguished leader of our party, other Honourable members of Parliament, officers, and members of the Progressive Labour Party, ladies and gentlemen, sisters and brothers: I express deep appreciation to you for inviting me to share with you in this great collaboration. I really look upon this as a kind of homecoming for me. I have some very fond memories of the time that I spent with you several years ago. Indeed, I have a daily reminder! My son was born in King Edward's hospital. So, I'm doubly happy to be present.

We have gathered today to pay homage to our fathers, both living and dead. I must say, however, that for us who are present, there is in our hearts abiding honor and devotion for our mothers, our wives, and all women of Bermuda. So, we want the record to show that on Father's Day, June 19, 1983, the fathers and men of Bermuda embrace the mothers, and women of Bermuda with love and deep affection.

Much has happened to us and for us since we were last together; some for good and some for ill. But in it all, and through it all, profound lessons have been learned. So, I believe that it is good for us to remind ourselves of the distance we have come, and the achievements we have wrought, lest we be overwhelmed by what some persons perceive to be our non-accomplishments. This is our vantage point: we can look back with hope. Indeed, we must look forward! I believe that it is important for us to see and to understand that we have been given a great deal by and through our fathers who have gone on before us. Let us cherish what they have done and embrace that which they cherished. The nobleness of their deeds should affect our character. The courage which they possessed should give birth to a greater resolve within us. The goals which they sought should provide a stimulus for us to pursue our goals with faith and fortitude.

We are heirs of a great legacy. Our fathers had a great sense of what was fundamental for them, for their children, and for those of us who were to follow. Many of our fathers cannot be mentioned by name. But, as I look back, with due consideration for the times and circumstances in which they lived, I heap praise upon them for their courage, for their foresight, and for their vision. Separately, and together, they were possessed, and in some cases, they were obsessed with a burning desire and a consuming hope for complete liberation for their people.

I have deep and profound admiration for the keen intellect, and the abiding commitment of Dr. Eustace Cann. My soul comes alive when I ponder the blazing zeal of Dr. E.F. Gordon. And, my course in life is made more steady when I muse the "strength of character," the "integrity of purpose," of the Honorable W.L. Tucker. All of these "fathers" were travelling in the same direction on "liberation highway." Such men deserve to have an appropriate monument erected to them, that will be visible in the marketplaces of the people of Bermuda. This expression of Jesus must surely apply to them: "Well done you good and faithful servants."

On the 28th day of August 1963, the Honorable W.L. Tucker M.C.P., C.B.E., breathed his last breath. The newspaper headlines of that day read: "The Father of the Franchise Bill Dies Peacefully at Home." It was just three months earlier that universal franchise was realized in Bermuda. It is evident that the Honourable W.L. Tucker did much to make this franchise a reality. But he was aided by persons whose names do not appear in the written record.

Dr. Eva Hodgson, in her informative book, *Second Class Citizens, First Class Men*, makes this perspective statement: "The Parliamentary Election Act of 1963 gave to the Negro the most important political opportunity to achieve first-class citizenship through constitutional means in his 100 years of freedom." But she goes on to say that, "May 1963 was not just the beginning of a new phase of political awareness on the part of the Negro, but it was also the end of that decade which has seen increasingly collective, through sporadic protests on the part of coloured people. Although black men in Bermuda have protested in one way or another from the time of their enslavement, the preceding decade has laid the foundation for 1963. The protests were against injustices that were not only political and economic but were also a matter of the mind as well. Coloured people are most often conscious of injustices wrought by their economic and political powerlessness. In actual fact, their greatest handicap, although about which they protested least, is the one which has been inflicted on their mind and their spirit."

No man, no woman, no boy or girl is free until the mind is free. This is our present task, this is our noble opportunity, this is our calling. We must pursue, we must achieve freedom of our minds and spirits. We are enslaved by fear. We are enslaved by doubt. We are enslaved by notions of inferiority. We fathers and mothers must teach our children to have wholesome and healthy concepts of themselves. We must live by high standards of ethics and morality, and challenge our children to do the same. We must encourage them to test the waters of life before they conclude that they cannot swim.

In this struggle for the freedom of our minds, we must combine all of our resources. Preachers must be informed by politicians, and politicians must be inspired by preachers. Mothers and fathers must go to grammar school, and young people must go to Sunday School. Young men must find their way back home, and fathers must remain healthy and strong. Our goal is set. Our path leads onward and upward. But, we shall have to clear the way as we go. But we shall go on! We shall go on until, in the words of the prophet Isaiah: "Every valley shall be exalted, every mountain and

> hill shall be made low, the crooked shall be made straight and the rough places plain." That will be the day when the "glory of the Lord shall be revealed" in us, "and all flesh shall see it together."
>
> This is our calling! This is our task! This is our struggle! Today we rejoice in our hope, but tomorrow, we shall rejoice in all our possession!

As I reread his speech, I am aware that as a people, we still, even now, have much to do, but hope springs eternal. We must only remember to *live to make a difference!*

Retirement Celebration

Rev. Dees retired from the Ministry in 1997. On that occasion, my mother and I flew to New York where we were pleased and proud to be a part of the celebration. At that time, we met Rev. Dees' huge family. I wrote and recited for him the following poem, created to celebrate my mentor's forty years in the ministry along with his forty years of marriage. The poem is titled "Stand Tall for Justice" and is now published in my 2022 book, *Poetry from the Heart*.

Stand Tall for Justice

by Shangri-La Durham-Thompson

I remember the time…1970
The place: A tiny isle
Land of the could be, should be free
Citizens lacking nourishment
Hungry for justice
A repressed, suppressed, depressed people
Living in another world
Merchant legislators proclaimed
"Mark Ups Essential"
And justice to them meant 'just us'
In other places people march
Protest, yes and even die
They express dissatisfaction for their plight
But in my land of people crying
Frustrated, but not trying...to change their world
They just…accept their fate

But my God sees all and He knows all
He controls all
And unfolds all
And when He is ready and according to His plan
To my very curious Nation, God sent a most effective man
Armed with righteousness, prepared for battle, armed with truth
Born in Alabama
A male child, a child of ten
Husband to Dolores
A father now and my friend
He came to us as God commanded
Transversed, to set God's people free
And he carried out God's mandate
Willingly

Quietly on Sunday mornings
He spoke poignantly of justice
From his pulpit he extolled respect for all mankind
He loved his fellow people
And that love, like the river Nile
Rejuvenated weary hearts and souls and minds
About democracy he was emphatic
And economic transformation too
And without recrimination planted seeds of hope
The people heard
I think they listened
They just simply could not act
For on their own behalf, the people could not stand
While food costs rose
And pay checks didn't
They pointed fingers to place blame
But no one stood
No one cried out
Silence reigned

I watched Rev. Dees in silent protest
Grow thin from lack of food
Requested economic sanctions fell on deaf ears
Yet, he stood tall for truth and justice
He stood for what he knew was right
For what was just
For what was true
For what was good

The Recorder pictured in its paper
Rev. Dees and Rev. Brandon
Two lonely pastors on the battlefield for truth
With placards waving
They and few others
Stood for justice all alone
But they stood tall

And determined in the fight
Parliamentarians discussed them, while in the House up on the hill
But peering through opaque windows
They could not see
For when your heart's not for the people
When your service is not for God
Then you never see what it is you ought to see

Bermudians for Reconciliation
Was the sprout he left behind
The Consumer Affairs Bureau
Is what it has grown to be
Poet and past contributor to *The Protest*
My mentor still lives to do God's work
Pastor now at Trinity United Methodist Church
With his bride of forty years
He celebrates forty years of pastoring too
And has worked in top positions in your land
But his cause is not yet over
For great disparity persists
And his "raison d'être" still remains the same
I have learned from Rev. Lloyd Dees
You, Sir have taught me to stand for truth
And I will stand until that day of reckoning dawns
I'll not grow weary of well doing
I will stand tall for justice, just like you
I'll serve our God
I'll do my part
Friends…what will you do?

Return Visits to Bermuda

As Rev. Dees felt a strong connection with Bermuda, he telephoned me often concerning what was happening in our community. Through the years, he returned to Bermuda periodically. On one occasion, my husband and I purchased an airline ticket for him and his wife, and they stayed with us. I recall that my sons were young and although I don't cook, I tried to prepare a meal for everyone. I vividly remember Mrs. Dees diplomatically informing me about the importance of eliminating sodium from our diets—I guess I'd used too much salt!

Rev. Brandon often accompanied Rev. Dees when he returned for a visit to the island. I thoroughly enjoyed driving them around to visit friends, and I listened intently as they talked about so many local topics of interest. We always made sure to visit Randolph Hayward, who often stayed with Rev. Dees and Rev. Brandon at their homes when he traveled to the U.S. When those three gentlemen got together, there was certainly lots of laughter, as Mr. Hayward loved to joke and laugh.

It was not surprising that they would return to Bermuda for the historic victory of the Progressive Labour Party in 1998. They were elated to come and celebrate with their friend, Jennifer Smith, who later became Dame Jennifer. The fact that Rev. Dees had not been successful in encouraging me to run in that election did not lessen his elation. He was aware that Mrs. LaVerne Furbert had called me to discuss how the polls in Hamilton Parish showed that I could win. Mr. Horton, who was interested in running in that constituency and who had been my past principal when I taught at Warwick Secondary School, called to tell me that he would step aside if I wanted to run.

I also vividly recall the phone call received from Rev. Dees while a few of us were sequestered at the Bermuda College to discuss the 1998 election. Alex Scott, now also a past premier, Mr. Calvin Smith, Bermuda's first Black statistician and Jennifer Smith all spoke with him to try and convince me to run. They then called my mother, as they knew that I usually would follow her advice. Perhaps because years prior my mother had been approached to run in the same constituency, she did not try to pressure me to become a candidate and left the decision to me. Without the added pressure, I safely declined. My sister though, Mrs. Shelby Durham-Jackson, was chosen to be the speaker for the gala banquet held at the Southampton Princess Hotel just prior to the election and my mother made sure that the place was packed.

I will note here that my sister Shelby and her husband, Melvin Jackson, held a reception on a ship in Philadelphia for Jennifer Smith, who was accompanied by her good friend, Rev. Trevor Woolridge. At that time, Shelby was a member of Philadelphia's Chamber of Commerce. Previously, Shelby, my sister Donna, and I had been featured in a half-page article in Bermuda's *Royal Gazette* newspaper, under the headline, "Shangri-La and Her Sisters, Island Too Small for All of Them." Allow me to interject here that I was most upset with the editor who had assured me that they would feature my brother as well. This was important, as Black men in Bermuda are often overlooked for their accomplishments. At the time, my brother was the superintendent of roads in Bermuda. He obtained a second Masters in Divinity from Payne Theological Seminary and his thesis was "Systemic Racism and its Negative Impact on the Educational Advancement of Black Youth in Bermuda." Another interesting tidbit is that the same editor told me that the P.L.P. won the election because he felt it was time for them to do so!!

The WORKERS VOICE
Vol. 23. No. 11. Friday, January 15, 1999 Price: 25¢

Reverends Brandon and Dees make presentation to Premier Jennifer Smith

REV. JOHN BRANDON

REV. LLOYD DEES

TWO PASTORS, who made their mark on the Bermuda landscape over twenty years ago, were in Bermuda last week to join with the Progressive Labour Party and the people of Bermuda in celebrating the PLP's election victory. And while here, the two gentlemen made a presentation to Premier Jennifer Smith.

Having served in the A.M.E. Church here in Bermuda in the turbulent 1960s and 1970s where they were active in the Bermudians for Reconciliation group, the Reverends John Brandon (Vernon Temple) and

Continued on page 12

The Workers Voice, January 15, 1999

Shelby and her husband brought an abundance of buttons to Bermuda with the slogan, "Make it Happen, Vote P.L.P." Our mother made sure they were distributed at the P.L.P. banquet. There was no way that Rev. Dees or Rev. Brandon would have missed this historic victory. Their return did not go unnoticed by the newspaper.

On Friday, January 15, 1999, the Bermuda Industrial Union (BIU) *The Worker's Voice* (Vol. 23, No. 11) featured an article, "Reverends Brandon and Dees make presentation to Premier Jennifer Smith." Here is an excerpt from the article:

> Two pastors who made their mark on the Bermuda landscape over twenty years ago where in Bermuda last week to join with the Progressive Labour Party and the people of Bermuda in celebrating the P.L.P.'s election victory. And while here, the two gentlemen made a presentation to Premier Jennifer Smith.

The Worker's Voice also included a copy of the poem "Ode for the Premier." The Reverends John Brandon and Lloyd Dees presented this poem to Premier Jennifer Smith on January 4, 1999, printed on parchment paper and framed. It is as follows:

An Ode for the Honourable Jennifer M. Smith, JP, MP, upon becoming Premier of Bermuda

Our souls speak with joy to you, old living God. For in the magnificent unfolding of history you have played a mighty part.

For 30 years, the people of Bermuda have been coming this way, and now their eyes behold a beautiful and glorious day. It is a day of brilliant light, emerging from the darkness of a long deep night.

So let the trumpets sound, and the organ chime. Let the people sing and the church bells ring. For today is a many splendored thing. It is a day of human souls embracing, with the effulgence of joy in their faces. It is a day in which a Premiere is born—beautiful, gentle, wise, and strong. Ever pleasant in the sight, the object of people's delight.

May her reign be peaceful and true, and may her deeds be fruitful too. May she hold her people in her heart, and from there never part.

May her words be like showers of blessing and her acts like the morning dew. May she be loved by all her people—the old, the young and the children too.

May the blossoms of her flowers never touch the ground, and may her sun never go down.

So, that all this may come true, O Living God, we humbly and reverently commend her and the people to you.

The article noted that these pastors served in the A.M.E. Church in Bermuda in the turbulent 1960s and 1970s, where they were active in the Bermudians for Reconciliation Group, the Rev. John Brandon (Vernon Temple) and the Rev. Lloyd E. Dees (Bethel).

Prior to this on January 8, 1999, on page 2, *The Mid Ocean News* featured an article, "A Holiday to Remember." This was written by another Bermudian icon, my special friend Mr. Ira Philip and is also in his *Island Notebook*. It read as follows:

> Ladies and Gentlemen, please, one more round of applause for our new Government and the New Bermuda!
>
> That simple exhortation from the master of ceremonies on the podium of City Hall went straight to the heart of what Monday's sunrise-to-sunset celebration of the Progressive Labour Party's historic victory in the November 9 General Election was all about.
>
> And that was all that the massive crowd who were taking full advantage of the government-appointed holiday needed to explode into a crescendo that almost shook City Hall from its foundations.
>
> Moments before, Premiere Jennifer Smith gave a stirring thank-you speech, where she gave the crowd what amounted to her "permission to exhale." She said, "Rejoice, enjoy it [the official holiday], be jubilant, the victory is ours. We have done it!'"
>
> Government wanted the youth to know that it was their day, and Miss Smith told them that there was nothing that they could not aspire to or achieve, and there was no mountain they could not climb. Preachers and poets played a key role in etching the new day ceremonies into the hearts and minds of the thousands attending Monday's celebrations; leading the way was Bermuda's first lady of poetry, Shangri-La Durham-Thompson, reciting at the Clearwater Beach service her composition, "Dawn of a New Day." Her lines went like this:

In the midnight of our lives /when darkness like a pervasive covering
blanketed our minds / Bermuda really was another world /
paradise for those selected / hell perhaps for those neglected /
and those who toiled became dejected / by life's view /the darkness
whispered in showing division / and the people without vision / closed their
eyes. They closed their hearts and they closed their minds…

At City Hall was former P.L.P. Assemblyman, the Rev. Trevor Woolridge, who was invited to come home from his Philadelphia-based church especially to introduce Premier Smith. In the staccato style of the old southern Black preachers, at which he is most adept, he captivated his audience, likening Smith's having become Premier to Jesus' parable in Matthew 21, verse 42. She was like the stone the builders rejected, which became the cornerstone of the building. She became a rolling stone, having been rejected each time in her five separate attempts to get elected in her St. Georges North constituency. "Then the Lord said, 'Enough is enough.' What we see today is the Lord's doing and it is marvelous in our eyes," thundered the former politician.

Rev. John Brandon and Rev. Lloyd Dees made their contribution at City Hall. They came to Bermuda from their respective churches in New York to recite an *Ode for the Premier,* which they composed especially for the occasion. The Ode was in fact addressed to God, reverently commanding her and the people of Bermuda to him. Its opening lines state:

Our souls speak with joy to you, O living God:
for in the magnificent unfolding of history, you have played
a mighty part. For 30 long years, the people of Bermuda
have been coming this way, and now their eyes behold a
beautiful and glorious day. It is a day of brilliant light,
emerging from the darkness of a long deep night…
It is a day in which a Premier is born, beautiful, gentle,

> *wise and strong; Ever pleasant to the sight, the object of the people's delight. May her reign be peaceful and true, and may her deeds be fruitful too. May she hold her people in her heart, and from them never part.*

Mr. Ira Philip's article noted that, "As pastors in Bermuda in the late sixties and seventies, Mr. Dees and Mr. Brandon were active in the sociopolitical activities of the island during the early days of the two-party system, and at the time of the Black Power conference and civil unrest. They helped organize and develop the Bermudians for Reconciliation organization, which in turn led to the Government setting up the Consumer Affairs Bureau because of their focus on economic issues, like the cost of living and fairness in pricing, which touched on ethical concerns underlying the structure and system of the economic enterprise in Bermuda. Mr. Brandon gave the invocation at City Hall. He said later that Bermudians who wanted the best for their country, who believed all people were equal in the sight of God, would support the new Government in its bid to advance the cause of good."

The next visit that Rev. Dees made to the island, that I am aware of, occurred in 2003. At that time, I took him to the Sunday morning worship service at Bethel A.M.E. Church in Shelly Bay, the church where he had been the pastor. He was accompanied by my family members and the Premier, The Hon. Jennifer Smith.

The Dees Benevolent Society, a group established in his honour after he left Bermuda and who provided help to people in the church and community, was in attendance and everyone, especially the older members, were excited to greet him. The members of The Dees Benevolent Society are recorded as follows: Sis. Marina Ottley, Sis. Rebecca Trott, Sis. Winfred Trott, Sis. Elizabeth Trott, Sis. Francella Blyden, Sis. Cynthia Ming, Sis. Edna Dill, Sis. Lena Mae Brangman, Bro. Eric Whitter and Sis. Pat Whitter. After the service, I took him to the Hamilton Princess Hotel for brunch where he met with other members of parliament.

The next day, I took him to visit one of Bermuda's most senior residents, my cousin Ms. Hilda Marie Smith. "Aunt Hilda" was a retired schoolteacher, a staunch churchgoer, and a lover of Jesus Christ. She used her gift of playing the piano for the glory of God up until the time of her death. Every Sunday, she played at a church service, at Bible studies, and prayer meetings. She also prayed aloud for hours, asking God for forgiveness. I never understood this as she always lived as an example of Christian values. She read her Bible every day and knew it well. When I told her that since 1997, I read the entire Bible every year, she advised that I read different versions. When I wrote plays as the Director of Drama for the A.M.E. Church, and before the existence of the internet, she was a valuable resource to me when I needed bible verses to substantiate my writings.

When Queen Elizabeth visited Bermuda in 2009, Aunt Hilda played the piano for her at the Clock Tower in Somerset and was featured on the BBC and other stations in Bermuda and around the world. Rev. Dees enjoyed his time with her, and I'm sure his personal visit made her feel special. I can visualize them now in heaven—Aunt Hilda playing the piano and Rev. Lloyd Dees singing in his baritone voice.

Visit to House of Assembly

According to Rev. Dees' wife, Dolores, a highlight for Rev. Dees was when I took him to the House of Assembly while it was in session in 2003. She said he spoke of the visit with great fondness, and I was happy to have played a part. Rev. Dees had visited the House of Assembly on many occasions. He had, as noted in Chapter 1, marched around it to protest the rising cost of living and sat in the House of Assembly listening to the budget debates. During one of his interviews, he mentioned how the painting I gave him of the House of Assembly hung proudly in his home, as a reminder of the past challenges.

Before taking Rev. Dees to the House of Assembly, I wanted to see if it was possible for him to be recognized and acknowledged during the visit. I sent a message to Mr. Randolph Horton, a member of Parliament who had been my past principal when I taught at Warwick Secondary School. The message included information about past accomplishments of Rev. Dees to help Mr. Horton understand why I wanted him recognized.

Rev. Dees and I were both delighted when Mr. Horton called for a break in the proceedings of the House of Assembly to acknowledge that Rev. Dees was in attendance. He spoke glowingly of Rev. Dees' contributions to Bermuda while he was the pastor at Bethel A.M.E. Church. I remember Rev. Dees' wide smile as he stood tall as they recognized him for his contributions to our country. Everyone applauded. This contrasted greatly with his prior engagements with the House of Assembly when he was described as a "trouble maker" and "foreign element." In retrospect, he made good trouble.

I am grateful to Mr. Horton for such a significant and public recognition of Rev. Dees. I will always have great regard for him, as he recommended me for a principalship. However, Mr.

Horton denied me once; he failed to release me from the school when I gave him my application to teach at Bermuda College because, he said, "These children need you."

As Rev. Dees and I left the House of Assembly, I spotted Rev. Nicholas Genevieve Tweed, a new pastor to Bermuda, who was in charge of the mother church, St. Paul A.M.E. Church, the largest A.M.E. Church on the island. This church housed Centennial Hall, a huge venue where I held many of my dramatic performances. I was just getting to know him personally and as time went on, I realized that he and Rev. Dees were cut from the same cloth. Ironically, Rev. Tweed, along with others in the community like Mr. Chris Furbert, then head of the Bermuda Industrial Union (BIU), started what was called "The People's Movement." They worked with intense dedication to right the injustices on the island, just as Rev. Dees and Rev. Brandon had done, including giving great attention to the rising cost of living.

The Bermuda Industrial Union (BIU)

After leaving the House of Assembly, I took Rev. Dees to visit the Bermuda Industrial Union where we met with its President, Mr. Chris Furbert. Rev. Dees was pleased that Mr. Furbert remembered articles written about him over the years that had appeared in the *Worker's Voice*, the BIU newspaper. Also present was Mr. Furbert's right-hand man, Mr. Colin Simmons. (Mr. Simmons actually married my cousin—it's a small world, especially in Bermuda.) We sat around the conference table as the men talked. We then took pictures, and I was so pleased that they showed my mentor such great respect.

The Chimes of Hope Concert

On June 17, 2003, Rev. Dees shared his love of music with and for the people he loved. When he was the pastor of Bethel A.M.E. Church, Rev. Dees sometimes opened his sermons or closed them with song. About a year before, he called me and asked for my assistance to organize a concert. He knew that I had directed many dramatic performances for the A.M.E. Church and had been proud of my play, *Battle for Freedom*.

Years prior, I had formed a drama group called "Solid Rock Foundation." This group consisted of members from various denominations, not just the A.M.E. Church. This group helped with the plays I wrote and directed over the years. The members of this group could be called upon at any time to assist with not just putting on plays, but holding public speaking workshops as well. Marsha Burrows and Kellyanne Gibbons (Smith) were instrumental in helping me with these

The
Solid Rock Foundation
Presents
The Chimes of Hope Concert
An Evening of Classical and Sacred Music
Featuring
Reverend Lloyd E. Dees, Vocalist
Dr. Anne Yarrow, Violinist
Tuesday, June 17, 2003
8:00 PM
St. Paul Centennial Hall - No 15
Court Street
Hamilton, Bermuda

The Chimes of Hope Concert
June 17, 2003

events. When Rev. Dees told me about his plan to hold a concert, he asked if my group could assist him. I assured him that they would be happy to be involved.

The event was billed as "The Chimes of Hope" and was publicized as, "An evening of classical and sacred music, presented by The Solid Rock Foundation." Rev. Dees had introduced Ann Yarrow to me, and she became a friend of mine. I escorted her, Mr. Randolph Hayward, and Rev. Dees around Bermuda when she visited the island with him. She is a wonderful person with a jovial spirit. Being a renowned violinist it was wonderful to include her in the event.

The preparation for the concert was well worth the effort. My mother, an honorary member of my organization, proved invaluable once again as she almost single-handedly prepared the patron list. She was determined that this event would be a resounding success. She invited her many political allies, all of the Bethel A.M.E. Church congregation, as well as people from the other churches that she knew—and it seemed she knew everyone.

Solid Rock Foundation members, most of whom perhaps were not familiar with Rev. Dees or his singing ability and certainly were not familiar with the violinist or pianist, worked diligently to publicize the event. They prepared the programmes, radio advertisements, and secured St. Paul's Centennial Hall. The event was held at 8:00 p.m. on Tuesday, June 17, 2003.

In the programme, I made introductory comments and the participants were highlighted. Again, for historical benefit, I have included part of the programme in Part II of this book. The programme introduced Dr. Anne Yarrow as a conductor and college professor with degrees in music from Yale University and who specialized in the 19th Century Repertoire. In 1993, she was one of three scholars who were invited to and attended a presentation at Grieg's Sesquicentennial Celebration in Berlin, Norway. At the time of the event, she was a member of

Dr. Anne Yarrow

the music faculty of Molloy College in New York, where she founded and conducted the Molloy College Community Orchestra. Additionally, she recorded and produced CDs in Switzerland and New York. Her music, she said, was designed to bring healing and reconciliation to all people.

The programme also introduced Laura Tompkins, a pianist, organist, and teacher who had graduated from Westminster Choir College in Princeton, New Jersey, where she had received a Bachelor of Music Education, majoring in organ. She had also taught for many years in public schools. She had accompanied many vocalists and instrumentalists and presented plays with the Suffolk Y Chamber group on Long Island, N.Y. She had been a church organist with Rev. Dees when he had served as pastor of the Freeport United Methodist Church on Long Island.

Laura Tompkins

Reading the programme all these years later brings back fond memories.

The programme opened with the invocation given by Rev. Conway Simmons, who at that time, was the pastor of St. Paul A.M.E. Church.

Also in attendance was the P.L.P. Opposition leader, The Honourable Lois Browne-Evans. This is the same person who the President of N.C. A&T had met through Rev. Dees in the early 1970's. The programme noted that Rev. Dees had been an ardent supporter of the Progressive Labour Party since 1979.

Years later, as I reviewed the programme, it seemed a little "high-brow" as the selections rendered classical entries I can't even pronounce: *Sicilienne* by Paradis, *Intrada* by Moffat, *Largo* by Veracini, *Intermezzo* by Schumann, and *Sonatensatz* by Brahams. I imagine that the A.M.E. Church audience members were relieved to hear the included spiritual pieces such as "Balm in Gilead," "Go down Moses," and "Swing Low, Sweet Chariot." Rev. Dees also sang his "Bermuda Song," which he wrote and dedicated to the Honourable Jennifer Smith, JP, MP, Premier of Bermuda, and she gave what was noted as "Premier Expressions."

I believe it was the *Worker's Voice,* the Bermuda Industrial Union's newspaper, that reported the following:

> Since 1979, Reverend Dees has been an ardent supporter of the Progressive Labour Party and has participated in many of its activities. He came in January 1998 for the great victory celebration and presented a poem to Premier Jennifer Smith—which he had written especially for the occasion, titled "Ode for the Premier." Now, Reverend Dees is returning to Bermuda to sing, which is a surprise to many people. This time, he has composed a song titled: "BERMUDA SONG." He will sing and dedicate the song to the Premier, who will be present at the concert on June 17. When asked about his singing, he said, "It is just something that I like to do. I sang in the Sunday School Choir, my high school choir, and my Seminary Glee Club." He gives thanks to the many organists who have nurtured his soul in the many churches in which he has been a pastor.

According to the programme, flowers and other items were given to the participants. The programme pamphlet simply read, "Presentations to All," and the presentations were made by a member of the Solid Rock Foundation group, Ms. Kelly Anne Gibbons.

There were also numerous advertisements printed in the programme from supportive people who sponsored Rev. Dees for this event, including his personal friends, family members, and church affiliates.

Prospect Primary School

When Rev. Dees came to Bermuda for his concert, "Chimes of Hope," I tried to ensure that his trip was a memorable one. Without telling him beforehand, I had taken his recording to a radio station and requested that it be played over the airwaves, though I'm not sure it ever was.

It must have been after the concert that he visited the Prospect Primary School where I served as principal. I do not recall either his violinist or pianist being present, which is why I think the visit occurred after the concert when they had probably left Bermuda. I gave him a tour of the school, and I vividly recall introducing him to the students and staff at the school's morning assembly. To the amazement of the students and to his delight, Rev. Dees had the opportunity to sing a few songs. I remember looking at the faces of the children as he sang iconic *Negro Spirituals* to see their reactions. I also remember thinking that many of them had never heard a

Rev. Dees' Bermuda Song

baritone singer singing *Negro Spirituals*. I can tell you that this was truly a great experience for many, and for Rev. Dees, it was more than simply another performance. He sang with passion, and it was easy to see that he thoroughly enjoyed the experience, singing with the same gusto as if this were a large ticket-buying audience.

After the assembly, I took him to the school's music room, where the students sang for him. I had given the music teacher a recording of his Bermuda Song, the song that he had sent me months before, along with the written sheet music. Ms. Lynell Ponton, a gem of a teacher, had indulged me without hesitation in the past when I requested that she teach the students a song that my music teacher, Ms. Ruth Thomas, had taught me at Francis Patton School. I recalled being so pleased as I walked the hall and heard one young man singing "Ava Maria" at the top of his voice. At that moment, I didn't have the heart to enforce the rule of walking quietly through the halls. When I told Ms. Ponton about Rev. Dees' visit and requested that she teach the students the special song, she did so enthusiastically.

The children were dressed in their school uniforms, shoes polished and hair combed. They had been taught stage etiquette and how to breathe. They stood tall, breathed at the right moments, and sang their hearts out. When Ms. Ponton played the piano while Rev. Dees sat in the seat of honour and listened to the students perform, I was thrilled that he looked so pleased with the students' performance.

Mrs. Dees confirmed years later that this was another highlight that Rev. Dees valued. What strikes me is that when you do for others, you spread joy in the world, and I am thrilled to have been used as a vessel to have given joy to a man who did so much for me.

Two years later, on October 14, 2005, Rev. Dees wrote an article as a commentary from an old friend for the *Worker's Voice*, the Bermuda Industrial Union's Newspaper. In the article, "A Glance Backward and a Look Forward," he wrote:

> Being able to remember is a very precious gift! Being able to hope is the essence of human achievement.
>
> Monday, June 7, 1969, I arrived in Bermuda as a newly appointed pastor of Bethel A.M.E. Church in Shelly Bay. I was received warmly by members of the church and the community. My immediate neighbour was Dr. John Stubbs, M.C.P. After some days, he invited my wife and me to his home for brunch.
>
> I was born and raised on a farm in Alabama U.S.A. But what happened to me after being in Bermuda for about three weeks was a totally new experience: I went into the bathroom and turned on the faucet, but no water came out. I did the same thing in the kitchen and no water came. I made inquiry and was told that "your well is dry." In order to remedy the situation, we would have to wait for rain, or buy a truckload of water. We bought the water! Buying water had never been a part of my experience. So, we learned to use water sparingly.

Some time passed and I was invited to attend a meeting that was held one evening at the Devonshire Recreation Hall. Someone introduced me to an engaging and vivacious young woman named Lois Browne-Evans. I soon learned that this was a meeting sponsored by the Progressive Labour Party, which had its beginning in 1963. My attention was arrested by some of the things that were said that evening, and I gradually became a devotee to the Progressive Labour Party.

On the same day I arrived in Bermuda, the newly appointed pastor of Allen Temple A.M.E. Church in Somerset, the Rev. John E. Brandon, also came. In process of time, we became good friends and shared similar concerns. A major issue at the time was the high cost of living. We, along with many others believed that certain essential items, such as food, clothing, and shelter were too costly. We engaged certain people of interest and held meetings and discussion sessions, which eventuated in forming an organization that we called Bermudians for Reconciliation. The organizational meeting was held in the Parsonage of Bethel A.M.E. Church, and Randolph Hayward was elected president. A great soul!

This organization devoted itself to the matter at hand by monitoring the prices in supermarkets and other stores. Informational and inspirational meetings were held from time to time in different places. There was periodic activity on the grounds of the House of Assembly. During "Holy Week," 1970, Rev. Brandon and I observed a fast—only eating bread and drinking water until Good Friday.

It has been 35 years now, and I cannot remember all the wonderful people who were devoted to this cause: a few names come to mind such as Lonnie Richards, Julia Durham, Rosalie Douglas. The Honourable Walter N. Robinson is remembered for giving his legal expertise and moral support. With his help a petition was drafted on behalf of the Bermudians for Reconciliation which resulted in the establishing of the Bureau of Consumer Affairs by the government of Bermuda. The Bureau stands today!

Because of the prevailing customs in those days, Black organizations did not use the major hotels for meetings and other functions. The Progressive Labour Party had its public functions in the various workmen clubs throughout the island. In early 1971, Bethel A.M.E. Church held a banquet in the Castle Harbour Hotel. In June 1983 the Honorable Louis Brown-Evans invited me to be the guest speaker for the Progressive Labour Party's Father Day Banquet which was held at the Castle Harbour Hotel. That was a distinct honor for me and a fine tribute to Bethel A.M.E. Church.

Now, all of that said and done, I have on a wall in my home, a painting that I shall always cherish. It was done by a young Bermudian girl who, at the time must have been about 12 or 13 years old, and whom I fondly call Shangri-La. It is the painting of the House of Assembly; the top of which looks a bit like the tower of Pisa. It speaks to me of hope!

It has come to me that our Premier the Honourable W. Alexander Scott, has it in his heart to pursue independence for Bermuda. I firmly believe that this is a worthy pursuit! And to the Premier, my heart is open, my hands are extended, and for him my prayers ascend to the One who has the power to change things. So, I urge him to pursue valiantly; and with blended spirits of like-minded Bermudians the triumph shall be glorious!

As I reflect on the words above, I am moved by Rev. Dees passion and will not fall into depression, though realizing that as I write this today, Bermuda is still a British Dependent territory!

Chapter 6

The Speeches

As a man who was recognized for his efforts to serve others, Rev. Dees was asked to speak on many occasions. He was a paladin for justice and every speech he made was delivered to make people think and to educate and influence them. The speeches spoke to his passions, his belief in people, and in correcting wrongs. He exhorted his audiences to *live to make a difference.*

Many people knew Rev. Dees as a stellar "motivational speaker." His speeches, to a wide variety of groups (as well as his sermons in church) provided inspiration and enlightenment and encouraged positive action. He often focused on promoting a positive outlook and resilience in the face of adversity. His words helped listeners believe in their own ability to overcome obstacles and to improve not only their own lives but the lives of others.

As I reviewed the speeches, I was touched by his conscious thoughts and I embraced his words, so powerfully designed to make an impact. His speeches included everyone, even deceased babies and the circumstances surrounding their burial. In one speech, Rev. Dees spoke of a more respectful and better way to say goodbye to babies rather than to just bury them on Harts Island in a place called Potters Field, where the homeless, the unnamed, and the unwanted were laid to rest in unmarked graves.

His words evoked images and emotions in me, as they should in all of us (especially parents) when he spoke about drugs. In every speech, he conveyed his love for people and concern for humanity. His speeches fostered a sense of unity and shared purpose. The first speech is written as an article that Rev. Dees sent to the local newspaper. I am unsure of the exact date, but he felt that he was a part of the Bermuda community and he let his voice be heard. This is what we all need to do: express our beliefs and allow God to speak through us. As I read the speeches listed below for various audiences, I felt his compassion and his sincere love for all people.

Drugs (date unknown)

DO NOT BE OF THIS WORLD! Instead, let's drive the "PUSHERS" and "DOPE PEDDLERS" out of this society. Say NO to anyone and everyone who tries to sell or give you drugs of any kind.

Let's develop a very talkative attitude. Let's tell everything that we know about "PUSHERS" and "DOPE PEDDLERS." If anyone offers you a "fix" remember his face—remember everything about him. Point him out to your friends and warn them to stay away from him. If you have a camera handy, take the "PUSHER'S" picture and present it to the proper authorities.

Parents, if your children tell you about drug sales on their school grounds, do not take it lightly. Make this matter known to the school authorities and demand that they take the matter to the police. It is not enough for us to sympathize with the users; we must ostracize the "PUSHERS" and "SUPPLIERS." These "PUSHERS" and "SUPPLIERS" are leaches in our society, and they eventually bring DEATH. Let's get together and put these leaches out of business.

The Fantastic Mind (date unknown)

Almost like a flash of lightning, it came! This, in full view and completely and immediately recognizable, stood the Brandenburg Gate. It is that magnificent structure of stone and water that stands between East and West Berlin. I was there in 1952. I had not been there before, and I have not been back since. It was an imposing sight! I must have been told of its height, and its width, and its weight, but these I do not remember now.

The Gate was that great divide between East and West—between democracy and communism. It was a Gate! But, in those days, very little traffic passed through, either on foot or on wheels. It was closed on both sides, and guards were posted on both sides: "guards of communism" and "guards of democracy" standing back-to-back. They were in full battle array, and there was no trace of a smile on their faces. I remember taking pictures of these "stone faces." But I don't know where they are now...I wish I could find them.

There was a curious kind of serenity at the gate. People moved slowly, carefully, almost meditatively. It was a feeling akin to that which is present when one is visiting the shrine of a revered saint. People recognize the presence of each other by nodding their heads. There were persons who just stood and stared; some East and some West—some toward communism and some toward democracy. I saw no laughter on their faces, but I saw no tears in their eyes either. It was a longing, penetrating, wondering stare. I surmised that these persons were possessed by both anxiety and desire—two powerful emotions vying within the human soul.

The call came to leave. I left the gate wondering. I boarded my bus, wondering. I rode in silence back to my post in West Berlin...still wondering! I must have been more deeply impressed than I realized: for after 39 years, my mind has awakened these thoughts and memories within me. Why? Who knows! To what end? Who can say? I just thank God for [my] fantastic mind!

A Better Goodbye for the Babies (April 24, 1990)

In the East River, near the Bronx, New York, there is an island called Hart Island. On Hart Island there is a field called the Potter's Field. It gets his name from the Bible (Matthew 27:1-7). It is a graveyard in which strangers are buried. It is the final resting place for the abandoned, the homeless, the unknown, and the not-so-well-known people who die in and about New York City.

Among these are little babies who are brought in little "pine boxes"… sometimes by the truckload. They are laid side-by-side, stacked three deep, in a long hole in the ground. Their pallbearers or grave diggers are prisoners from the city jails on Rikers Island. What a paradox! If these little babies were alive, we would not permit prisoners to come near them. But in death, we gladly commit them to their care. I am not sure as to whether there is to be some redeeming factor for the prisoners, or whether no one else can be found to perform this last act for this pitiful lot of humanity.

If I pastored a church nearby this Potter's Field, I would ask the City Fathers to let these little babies be brought in, and I would give the best eulogy that the Spirit of God and I could compose and express. And, because so many of them have no names, I would name them: "Children of God"…"Niñas de Dios." Then I would go with them to this burial place and give "a baby's Benediction" and a prayer for their fathers and for their mothers.

On the Passing of Time (date unknown)

The years seemed to go by so quickly! Procrastination is the great thief of our age and of our lives. Because of it, much that should have been done is never done. Because of it, much that could have been achieved is never realized. Procrastination makes us believe that there is a better day than today to think noble thoughts and to do noble deeds. It convinces us that the time is not right for either of these.

Procrastination makes us doubt our abilities—always telling us that we are unable now. We are too weak now. We are too poor now. We are made to believe that we don't know enough, always being told that we need more facts in order to act wisely. On and on it goes until 5, 10, 20 years have passed us by. And we wonder why! Then comes the sad reply, "It's too late now."

So let us strive to keep our dreams alive and hope that they will be realized. Time passes so quickly, and sometimes our dreams are carried along with it, and we are buried in the deep grave of forgetfulness—where there is never a resurrection.

This may be a helpful proverb: "Don't put off for tomorrow what you can do today." For those of us who have a farming background—let us "Make hay while the sun is shining."

"Lo These Many Years" (date unknown)

"Lo these many years I have served you…and you never gave me a kid, that I might make merry with my friends." (Luke 15:29)

In the above phrase, we have a preface to a *lament.* A lament is a prolonged expression of disappointment, sorrow, envy, and dissatisfaction. All of these are negative! All of these are erosive and detrimental to human well-being.

In the story of the prodigal son, the older brother lights in on his father and expresses his true feelings…feelings that had been concealed for a long time.

"Lo these many years I have worked hard for you…and you did not give me." He is sorely disappointed, and very angry. His envy and anger affected his fellowship with the other members of the household. He would not go in the house where they were. He deliberately separated himself from them. His deep emotions, as well as his motive were disclosed. He sought the praise of his father for a long time and did not receive it. He surely is an object of our sympathy, even our pity.

The "older brother" is so like us! Or we are so like him. "Lo as many years" we still harbor our resentments, conceal our anger, and cover our disappointments. And all of these erode our sense of well-being. It is very hard for us to keep on going, without being praised, or rewarded. And then, one day, at some critical moment, it happens…we blurt it all out. "Lo these many years I have worked hard, and nobody ever gave me…" From this moment on, however, the cover is broken, and the possibility of healing is present.

My Prayer (date unknown)

God of all Creation, life giver and life sustainer—I thank you for life! Life for me in its fullest, is the constant awareness of your presence and your power. Your presence keeps me from being alone, and lonely. I always have someone toward whom my attention is drawn. Your presence keeps me from being afraid in the midday, at midnight, and at the time of death. "Yea, though I walk through the valley of the shadow of death, I will fear no evil, for thou art with me."

Your presence provides me with a joy that cannot be taken away by all the little negative things which I encounter from day to day. Your presence is like a shining light upon my way, so that I may see how and where to walk, and where to stay. Your presence gives me courage. When I know that I'm not alone, I am able to go places that I otherwise could not go, to say things that I otherwise could not say, and to do things that I otherwise could not do. "In your presence there is fullness of joy, and at your right hand, there are pleasures forevermore."

Thank you, God, for life and your daily presence with me.

I Have Known Wars (date unknown)

There is nothing civilized about war. War is barbaric. There is nothing nice about war. War is ugly and mean. There is nothing wholesome about war; war is crippling and destructive. There is nothing holy about war; war is evil and exceedingly profane.

War is an utter denial of the notion of the evolutionary refinement of the human intellect, and the increasing sensibility of the human mind. War is a morbid expression of men who have come to their wits end. When men become unable to talk to each other, they resort to brute force in a burning attempt to annihilate each other.

In the 1940's we fought a war in Europe and Japan. In the 1950's we fought a war in Korea. In the 1970's we fought a war in Vietnam. In the 1990's we are fighting a war in Iraq. Indestructible havoc wrecked upon the lives of millions of people. Thousands were killed! Thousands have had their bodies broken and dismembered. There are casualties of these wars that most of us have not seen, or known: People with no eyes, no legs, no arms, no healing. There are persons who have been in veteran's hospitals since World War II. Some don't know who they are. There is a great multitude of people who are affiliated with all kinds of body and mind diseases because of these wars. There are widows by the thousands, fathers and mothers mourning the death of their children, and children mourning the death of their parent.

Life is precious! War is destructive! Men started this war and men can stop it. Let us implore our nation, and the other nations involved to "cease-fire" and talk peace, lest we all die a horrible death together.

Chapter Seven

Overview of the Letters

It seems to me only fitting that I document the letters sent to and by Rev. Dees throughout his life, as they highlight the impact he made on those he served. As I write this chapter, I am grateful to God for the opportunity to have known Rev. Dees and thankful, too, for the impact he made on my life and on the lives of others. I, like the Apostle Paul, feel compelled to extend my thanks for all that he did for me. Paul said in Philippians 1:3 "I thank God every time I remember you," and I have thanked God so many times over the years for Rev. Dees.

Philippians 2:3 advises us to, "Do nothing from selfish ambition or conceit, but in humility count others more significant than yourselves." This was the essence of Rev. Dees, and this was evidenced in the many letters he received, kept, and entrusted to me. There were almost fifty letters that I read and reread and organized by date. They revealed, very concretely, how he touched people's lives. They are a testimony to a life well lived. I have recorded who sent each letter and the reason for them. Conclusively, these letters provide legitimacy and further insight into his character while serving as a record of his many accomplishments. Part II includes sample letters in their entirety.

The first letter, dated May 7, 1987, thanked Rev. Dees for awarding a framed citation and scholarship to John E. Carrington, and he asked that Rev. Dees extend gratitude to the Black Clergy Caucus of New York on his behalf. Mr. Carrington was grateful to Rev. Dees for recognizing him for such an award. He described receiving it as a once-in-a-lifetime experience. Rev. Dees took the time to thank others for their contributions.

The Bible tells the story of the ten lepers, and Luke 17:15-16 states that, "When one of them saw that they were healed, he came back. He praised God in a loud voice. He threw himself at Jesus' feet and thanked him." The man was a Samaritan. When Jesus saw the Samaritan, he immediately wondered about the other nine men who had been healed and he asked, "Weren't all ten healed? Where are the other nine?" I smiled when I noted that Rev. Dees took the time to say thanks and honoured Mr. Carrington when he was alive. So often we honour people after they have passed, but the Bible reminds us to lift up our fellow man. Hebrews 13:16 says, "And do not neglect doing good and sharing, for with such sacrifices God is pleased." As I read the letters I am encouraged to do a better job of recognizing others.

The Lawrence Public Schools expressed appreciation to Rev. Dees for his work on their behalf. He had participated on their testing panel and their letter (April 28, 1987) applauded his insightful comments and frank discussion, which made for an effective presentation. Rev. Dees had also assisted them with their Superintendents Advisory Committee meeting which addressed minority concerns. They noted that this had been their first formal attempt at parental education. True to form, Rev. Dees was always ready to educate others.

On February 1, 1988, Mr. Baron and Mr. Ferraro, Jr. wrote to thank Rev. Dees for being an initiator and founding member of the Superintendent's Advisory Committee. He noted that Rev. Dees had been instrumental in establishing communication between the administration, the Board, and the minority community at large. Mr. Baron and Mr. Ferraro, Jr. acknowledged the significant manner that Rev. Dees enriched community life in the district.

Marilyn Sherman, in her letter to Rev. Dees on November 2, 1987, expressed how sorry she was to hear that he could not complete his term as a member of the Continuing Education Advisory Committee, as he had accepted a new appointment. She noted that he was a valuable contributor to this committee. Although sad that he could not fulfill his term, she extended best wishes for his future endeavours and thanked him for his willingness to serve.

Because Rev. Dees assisted where he could, the principal of Freeport High School in New York on March 10, 1988, thanked him for delivering the invocation and benediction at their 95th Annual Commencement Exercises.

Additionally, the letter he received on March 28, 1989, from Principal Harding M. Morgan, of John W. Dodd Junior High School in Freeport, New York must surely have filled both Rev. and Mrs. Dees with joy. This is where their daughter, Janet, attended junior high and the letter congratulated them on her successful S.A.T. examination results. The letter stated that it was rewarding to have a student like her at Dodd as she did not allow any activity to deter her from her academic accomplishments. Like her father, she was focused.

The letter written to Rev. Dees on June 25, 1990, from Principal Morgan again thanked Rev. Dees for delivering the invocation and benediction at their graduation ceremony. When you go out of your way to help others, it is always a good feeling when you are rewarded in return. I have been told by many people that family members are often neglected by those dedicated to community services, but Rev. Dees spoke to me often with pride about how his children were doing.

Dr. Ann Yarrow, a friend of Rev. Dees and one who respected him tremendously, sent a letter on October 16, 1991, to The Dr. Martin Luther King, Jr. Celebration Committee nominating Rev. Dees for the 1992 Nassau County Dr. Martin Luther King, Jr. Recognition award.

It was interesting to discover the letter sent by Joseph W. King, Chief of Police of the Freeport Police Department, on February 10, 1992, inviting Rev. Dees to their Community Relations Breakfast to be held at the Freeport Recreation Center on Saturday, February 29, 1992 at 9:30 a.m. The purpose of the breakfast, he stated, was to open communications between community and business leaders, as the Freeport Police Department played an integral role in the community and they wished all facets of the community to understand their role. Obviously, the presence of Rev. Dees to this event added legitimacy.

As all accounts have shown, Rev. Dees fought for justice and was not afraid to involve himself in causes he found disturbing. This was evident when Rev. Dees tried to help his fellow clergy friend who had been charged with child molestation. He sent a news article to Edward I. Koch on March 10, 1995, of Robinson, Silverman, Pearce, Aronsohn, & Berman, perhaps seeking his intervention in the case dealing with the accusation. Mr. Koch replied, "Dear Lloyd, the case of Rev. [...] which is described in the article which you left with me is certainly a sad one. It is sad that he would be convicted based largely on the boy's testimony when the boy was three years old and there was, apparently, no physical evidence. There was a period in this country when almost anyone charged with sexual molestation of a child was near automatically convicted. I do not have the facts in this case other than the article and that is not really adequate on which to make a judgment. Regrettably, there is nothing that I can do to help you or him."

In 1997, Rev. Dees planned to retire, and his friends planned a celebration for him to which all could not attend. He received a lovely letter from Oswald P. Bronson, Sr., the President of Bethune-Cookman College on June 13, 1997, conveying his regrets. He extended his hearty congratulations for the gala affair celebrating his forty years of marriage and his forty years in ministry. He noted that the celebration "recognizes the significant contributions you have made to the church and to untold individuals." He went on to say that "in these days when there is a moral and spiritual drought pervading the human family, it is reassuring to witness a ministry, such as yours, that brings hope and blessings and abundance." He enclosed a check representing a dollar for each year that Rev. Dees had been in the ministry.

On December 23, 1997, Mr. Ernest S. Lygth, of The United Methodist Church, sent Rev. Dees an acceptance letter acknowledging receipt of his invitation to participate in a service of dedication at 2:00 p.m. on January 19, 1997, at the Westchester County Courthouse Plaza. He had been asked to bring greetings and offer the prayer. He noted that he was looking forward to sharing in the ceremony naming Dr. Martin Luther King, Jr. Boulevard. The letter sent to Rev. Dees on January 30, 1998, from The City of White Plains, Office of Mayor Joseph M. Delfino, stated that the mayor personally wanted to thank him as well as the Ministers' Fellowship Council of White Plains for making the dedication ceremony of Martin Luther King Jr. Boulevard a reality.

On December 14, 1998, Ernest S. Lyght of The United Methodist Church, New York Area, acknowledged the letter Rev. Dees sent to inform him of his desire to retire on July 1, 1999. He thanked Rev. Dees for including him in this important decision and asked that Rev. Dees continue to keep him informed as he "worked through the details."

On March 11, 1999, Rev. Dr. Charles H. Straut, Jr., of Kings Highway United Methodist Church, Brooklyn, NY, sent a letter to Ms. Orr, thanking her for the invitation to attend Rev. Dees Retirement. He noted that although, unfortunately, he could not attend, he requested that his sentiments regarding his respect for such a committed, compassionate, and caring man; one who had served selflessly over the years, receiving insufficient recognition of his efforts be expressed on his behalf.

On April 19, 1999, Rev. Dees received a letter from Mr. Noel N. Chin on behalf of the Butler Memorial United Methodist Church, thanking him for sharing their 87th annual celebration and delivering a timely and challenging message that gave a sense of history. Again, here is a testament to how Rev. Dees infused pertinent information into talks he was asked to deliver. His message was timely and challenging. I wish I could have heard this message, but the fact that he was asked to deliver a message on the occasion for the 87th annual celebration says a great deal and shows how much respect they had for him.

Rev. Dees received a letter on June 4, 1999, from Delores, his sister, and family members, Prince and Pamela Willis, offering their congratulations on his retirement. They also thanked him for being a "beacon of light." Delores noted that the family looked to him with awe and a sense of pride.

On June 23, 1999, Mary Pitt sent Rev. Dees an article about his coming to Trinity United Methodist Church back in 1977. She reminded him that he and his family had been an inspiration to all. She said, "We love you and you will be truly missed." This acknowledges yet another impact he made in the lives of all those he touched.

On November 1, 1999, Bishop Robert C. Morgan, President of the Council of Bishops, received a letter from Rev. Dees. By this time, he had recently retired as a member of the New York Annual Conference, after serving 15 years in the African Methodist Episcopal Church and 27 years in the United Methodist Church. Rev. Dees informed the council that it had been 31 years since the dissolution of the central jurisdiction, where the original goal of "One United Church" had not been realized. True to form, very direct and without apology, and perhaps to the chagrin of some, he highlighted that the goal was far from being reached. He advised that in upcoming meetings of the Council of Bishops the next year, opportunities to re-articulate the goals and aims of this body would be a priority.

On June 22, 2000, Rev. Dees received an apology from Walter H. McKelvey of Gammon Theological Seminary for taking so long to respond to his letter, but as he explained, his wife had passed away. He agreed that Rev. Dees' letter to the Council of Bishops seeking to broaden Interdenominational Theological Center (ITC) involvement was on target. Rev. Dees went to great lengths to send his letter to the Council of Bishops. He informed others so that they too, could share the knowledge and perhaps be inclined to become a part of the solution.

On September 12, 2000, Rev. Dees received a letter from Bishop Woodie W. White, Resident Bishop of the United Methodist Church, Indiana area, informing him that the Council of Bishops had identified racism as one of their priorities for the quadrennium and a comprehensive effort was in the works to be implemented across the church. This must have been very satisfying for Rev. Dees, who had been lobbying for this cause for some time. He had written to those he thought could "speed up the agenda," prodded those who he felt had lagged in their deliberation to ensure success for this initiative, and here he received acknowledgment that his efforts were not in vain. The bishop informed him that he had prepared an Episcopal Pastoral letter on race to be read in every congregation. Additionally, the 18 districts in the Indiana area had held a day-long event on racism and he had prepared a video that was used. Bishop White noted that follow-up efforts were anticipated, and he thanked Rev. Dees for the reminder.

On December 28, 2000, Mayor Lee Brown of the City of Houston wrote to thank Rev. Dees for the letter of encouragement Rev. Dees sent to him. Mayor Brown expressed that he appreciated supporters who understood the values and initiatives of his administration. Again, Rev. Dees supported others, understood their value, and let people know that he would be available to assist whenever he could.

February 27, 2001, Bethune-Cookman College, President Oswald P. Bronson wrote to Rev. Dees, noting that while going through some old papers, a letter from Rev. Dees, dated March 17, 2000, surfaced. He thanked Rev. Dees for the letter expressing appreciation for the College's Chorale Concert. He recalled their friendship while at the Interdenominational Theological Center with profound gratitude and appreciation. He highlighted Rev. Dees' witness as a minister of Jesus Christ and wished him well upon his retirement.

On March 30, 2001, Bishop Ernest S. Lyght of the United Methodist Church, New York Area, wrote to thank Rev. Dees for sending him a copy of the sermon Rev. Dees preached at Asbury Memorial Church in Savannah.

On March 26, 2002, Dr. Allen N. Pinckney, Jr., of the Long Island District, wrote to thank Rev. Dees for his letter concerning the issue of cross-cultural racial appointments. He noted that he had given critical thought to the matter and had articulated the very important concerns to those under his influence.

On May 28, 2002, Rev. Thomas Mills, Jr., wrote to thank Rev. Dees for accepting his invitation to be his guest speaker on June 30, 2002.

On June 25, 2002, Mr. William W. Hutchinson of the United Methodist Church wrote Rev. Dees to thank him for the copy of the letter Rev. Dees sent to Bishop Watson.

On July 12, 2002, Mr. Chester Jones, General Secretary of the United Methodist Church, sent Rev. Dees a letter on behalf of the General Commission on Religion and Race, and also wrote to thank him for the copy of the letter Rev. Dees sent to Bishop Watson.

On July 26, 2002, Mr. James King, Jr. of The Kentucky Annual Conference, wrote to thank Rev. Dees for his letter on July 10. He expressed concern about the church moving forward toward the goal of "one church" noting that they, in Kentucky, were working toward cross-racial appointments. He expressed appreciation for Rev. Dees' availability for "interim" and short-term work and said that he would keep his letter on file if such a need arose.

On October 21, 2002, Mr. Henry Bradford, Jr. of Huntsville, Alabama, wrote to thank Rev. Dees for sending him a copy of the Bermuda song.

On September 4, 2003, Rev. Dees received a letter from Henry Bradford, Jr., thanking him for the Chimes of Hope Concert program.

November 19, 2003, Henry Bradford, Jr. wrote to thank him for keeping in contact.

On July 11, 2005, Bishop Ernest Lyght of the United Methodist Church wrote to thank him for the CD.

On September 9, 2005, Mr. Hubert C. Sapp, Chairman of the Effingham County Board of Commissioners, wrote to inform Rev. Dees that he had been voted to serve on the Coastal Georgia Regional Development Center Aging Services Advisory Council.

On May 10, 2006, Mr. John Barrow from the House of Representatives, Washington, D.C., wrote and thanked Rev. Dees for getting involved in voter participation and for sending him a CD concerning voter registration.

On October 18, 2006, Mr. Vernon D. Martin, AICP, Executive Director of the Coastal Georgia Regional Development Center wrote to congratulate Rev. Dees on being selected Chairman of the Aging Services Advisory Council and thanked him for his attendance at the Capital for Senior Week in February.

On May 10, 2007, Mr. Vernon D. Martin, AICP, Executive Director of the Coastal Georgia Regional Development Center wrote to thank Rev. Dees for honouring the director (him) for his service. He noted that Rev. Dees had done an outstanding job as chairman and that people like him help vanguard services for seniors.

On October 15, 2007, Rev. Dees wrote to Mr. R. Gerald Turner, President of Southern Methodist University, expressing concern for having the Bush Presidential Library located on their campus. One trustee was reported to have been a financial supporter and the same trustee was a

CEO of a major oil company seeking to secure a deal for his company so as to receive an advantage in the supply of Iraqi oil. Rev. Dees stated that the university bearing the name Methodist should not put itself in the position of practicing partisan politics and embracing a trustee seeking to profit from the spoils of an unpopular war. He copied the letter to numerous people.

On October 23, 2007, Rev. Dees received a response to his letter from Mr. R. Gerald Turner, President of SMU, acknowledging receipt and expressing different views. He noted that when he was a graduate student at the University of Texas, the LBJ library was placed on that campus and there were demonstrations against it. Now there would be demonstrations if they sought to remove it. That memory has encouraged the UT trustees to compete with SMU for the current president's library.

On January 17, 2008, Rev. Dees received a letter from Mr. Johnny Isakson of the United States Senate, Washington, D.C., wishing him well in preparation for Senior Week and thanking him for leading the trip to celebrate the event and helping participants learn more about state government.

On September 6, 2010, Nancy, Godmother of Janet, wrote to thank him for his card and expressed that his thoughtfulness was appreciated at a time when it was needed.

On November 4, 2010, Mr. Jack Hill of the State Senate, Atlanta, wrote and thanked Rev. Dees for the framed photo of them that Rev. Dees sent to him and emphasized his thoughtfulness.

On June 24, 2011, Rev. Dees received a letter from Patricia Crowley, County Clerk of the Effingham County Board of Commissioners, informing him of his reappointment to the Area Agency on Aging.

On July 5, 2011, Mr. John Barrow from the Congress of the United States, House of Representatives, Committee on Veterans' Affairs Oversight and Investigation, wrote and thanked Rev. Dees for contacting him to support preserving Medicare and Social Security. Mr. Barrow noted that when Medicare was created in 1965 only half the people over 65 had health insurance, and many of those had only limited coverage.

On August 15, 2011, Bishop Bill Lyght, of Asbury United Methodist Church, Savannah, Georgia, wrote to invite Rev. Dees to attend Gammon Theological Seminary. The intent was to introduce the new president of Gammon Theological Seminary and to tell their story outlining the vision and plans for future growth.

On April 1, 2013, Ms. Deborah Scariano, of the Coastal Regional Commission, wrote to thank Rev. Dees for giving his time and talents to the Advocacy Committee. The Georgia State Alzheimer's Association expressed that the committee was a big "hit." The letter contained the legislative update on the Georgia Alzheimer's Dementia State Plan Task Force, noting that by 2050, up to 16 million Americans will have Alzheimer's disease. The next step for the Advocacy Academy was to address the Coastal Regional Delegation in the November/December time frame in preparation for the 2014 legislative session. Rev. Dees was invited to be a part of this legislative committee.

Also, on April 1, 2013, Ms. Patty Lyons, CO-AGE Chair, Georgia Council on Aging, wrote to congratulate Rev. Dees for being nominated for one of the Martha Eaves Advocating for Positive Change Awards, and asking that he attend the April 25 Coalition of Advocates for Georgia's Elderly (CO-AGE) meeting where he was to be recognized.

All of these letters help explain who Rev. Dees was, what he did to help his fellow man, and, ultimately, what he did for the Kingdom of God. In his quiet, dignified manner he fulfilled his purpose. He was, from all accounts, a good and faithful servant.

Chapter Eight

A Life Well Spent

In this final chapter, the conclusion of a life well spent, I am humbled and appreciative of all that my mentor and friend, Rev. Lloyd E. Dees, did for me, the people of Bermuda, and the communities he served. I hope my life can be lived in service to others, with humility, dignity, and a boldness for Christ.

As I listened to Mr. Robert Holden on a Hay House recording, I understood how his affirmation expressed the life of Rev. Dees. His affirmation included, "I am a pencil in God's hands. I'm here to write love letters from God to everyone in the world…I sit patiently before God and listen to the thoughts of God. I find it easier to write because God does the work. All I do is listen, take notes, and enjoy the process." This brings to mind 1 Samuel 3:10: "Speak, Lord, for your servant is listening."

Bishop Noel Jones once spoke about talents and skills and how important it is to ensure that we use our gifts to glorify God. He spoke of how Satan works against us, but we are in God's presence to do his will. This resonated with me because it has taken me years to write this book, but I had a mission to fulfill. Before he died, I promised Rev. Dees that I would write it. I also did not yet understand who he actually was. He came into my life and impacted me in such a profound way that I desire to serve others as he did. He loved God and he did his best to engage people with humility and love and worked to make a difference.

Memorial

On April 23, 2016, my husband, Stanton Thompson, my mother, Julia Durham, my sister, Shelby Durham-Jackson, and I attended the memorial service for Rev. Dees at Trinity United Methodist Church in Savannah, Georgia to celebrate the life of my mentor and friend. On this occasion, I renewed my vow to write his story in the presence of the congregation. Additionally, I was privileged to read the poem I had written for him and delivered at his retirement banquet in New York. I also had the honour of delivering remarks from two former premiers of Bermuda.

Before we left Bermuda, The Hon. W. Alex Scott, CBE, JP sent the following communication to a Mr. Smith of the press in Bermuda:

> Dear Mr. Smith,
>
> Earlier yesterday I left a voice mail message informing you that I would forward a short Press Release [see attached] outlining the tremendous service rendered to Bermuda, and her citizens by the late Rev. Lloyd Dees. He was both a pastor and community leader who served here in the seventies.
>
> To this day, the contribution he made through his spiritual presence, and interest in making Bermudians more aware of their power as informed consumers, has caused him to be fondly remembered and respected by many.
>
> Hopefully, you will be kind enough to share the news of his passing and memorial service with your readers by publishing the enclosed release.
>
> Thanking you in advance.
>
> Regards,
>
> Hon. W. Alex Scott CBE, JP

Following is the press release the Hon. W. Alex Scott CBE, JP included in his letter:

> REVEREND LLOYD E. DEES—"HE LIVED THE LIFE HE PREACHED"
>
> News has been received in Bermuda concerning the Memorial Service for the much respected Reverend Lloyd Dees, who was the pastor of Bethel African Methodist Episcopal [A.M.E.] Church in the early seventies here in the island; who passed away on February 4, 2016.
>
> In informing the wide circle of friends here on the island, and members of his local Bethel family, of his passing [and memorial service] after a protracted illness, Mrs. Julia Durham, her daughter, Dr. Shangri-La Durham-Thompson, Mr. Randolph Hayward, and the Hon. Alex Scott, former Premier of Bermuda, extend their heartfelt sympathy and condolences to Reverend Lloyd Dees' family, wife Dolores, and two children, daughter Janet, and son Jason [who was born in Bermuda].
>
> This weekend, traveling with a small delegation of Bermudians to Savannah Georgia, was Mrs. Julia Durham, a community activist and original member of the "Bermudians for Reconciliation," a pressure group started and led by Reverend Dees and John Brandon, which paved the way for generations of Bermudians who followed to become active and make their contribution to Bermuda. In this regard, commenting on the very large impact Rev. Dees had upon her life, Mrs. Julia Durham's daughter, Dr. Durham-Thompson declared that: "I was like an adopted daughter to him;" in fact, he had been very instrumental in her attending North Carolina Agricultural & Technical State University, where at the time he was the campus pastor.
>
> While Mr. Hayward recalled the activism of his friend Lloyd Dees when he had been instrumental and responsible for the formation along with Rev. John Brandon of the "Bermudians for

> Reconciliation Group," which through its newsletter and activism had managed to, by reporting regularly on the prices of staple products, like bread, milk and the like, both educate Bermudians to their rights and power as consumers. Mr. Hayward observed that consequently, this had led to the lowering of prices throughout the competing supermarkets and stores all over Bermuda. In fact, he reminisced: that after the two pastors had organized a March to Parliament with Rev. Dees even embarking upon a hunger strike to bring a focus and attention to the high cost of living in Bermuda—the pastor's activism, and that of the group, had eventually caused the creation of the Consumer Affairs Office by the government of the day.
>
> Rev. Dees became a strong spiritual influence for Bermudian leaders and Premiers. He returned to the island on occasions to support Dame Jennifer Smith in the eventful, historic, 1998 General Election, writing a poem to salute the landmark victory.
>
> Former Premier Alex Scott revealed that it had been the recruitment of himself by Rev. Dees, and Rev. John Brandon, into their consumer pressure group that had provided him with his first involvement in the local pressure group—and eventually politics. In expressing sympathy to the Dees family, he wanted them to know that Bermuda and Bermudians have been made a much better place and had received a blessing because Rev. Dees had passed this way.
>
> The Durham family will leave Bermuda this weekend and lead a local delegation to pay respects and celebrate the life and contribution of an exceptional man of God at the memorial service and repass which will be held in Trinity United Methodist Church in Savannah, Georgia, USA.

The memorial service was a heartwarming event. We had the pleasure of reconnecting with the Dees family. It was so wonderful to see Janet and Jason. Jason spent a great deal of time with us at our hotel sharing the music he had created. We took time to visit places of interest in Savannah and spent time with Mrs. Dees at her home. She was still as health-conscious as ever, going to the gym to exercise weekly, and she encouraged me to do the same. At the service we talked with Marcus Brandon, and he promised to keep in touch and to send me the information I would need for this book.

The church was packed and it was the first time I recall attending a United Methodist service. Both Black and white people were in attendance, as you may have expected. They were all very gracious. After the service, we had a repast in the church hall where everyone greeted each other and reminisced about the impact Rev. Dees had made on their lives. Following is the funeral program in full.

[Press Release]:
REVEREND LLOYD DEES - "HE LIVED THE LIFE HE PREACHED"

News has been received in Bermuda concerning the Memorial Service for the much respected Reverend Lloyd Dees, who was the Pastor of Bethel African Methodist Episcopal [AME] Church in the early seventies here in the island; who passed away on February 4th., 2016.

In informing the wide circle of friends here in the island, and members of his local Bethel family, of his passing [and memorial service] after a protracted illness, Mrs. Julia Durham, her daughter, Doctor Shangri-La Durham Thompson, Mr. Randolph Hayward, and the Hon Alex Scott, Former Premier of Bermuda, extended their heart felt sympathy and condolences to Reverend Lloyd Dees family, wife Delores, and two children, daughter Janet, and son Jason [who was born in Bermuda].

This weekend, travelling with a small delegation of Bermudians to Savannah Georgia, was Mrs. Julia Durham a community activist and original member of the "Bermudians for Reconciliation", a pressure group started and lead by Reverend Dees and John Brandon, which paved the way for generations of Bermudians who followed to become active and make their contribution to Bermuda. In this regard, commenting on the very large impact Rev Dees had upon her life, Mrs. Julia Durham's daughter, Dr. Durham Thomson declared that: "I was like an adopted daughter to him"; in fact, he had been very instrumental in her attending A&T University where at the time he was the campus pastor.
Page 1.

Rev. Dees Memorial Announcement, April 2016

Memorial Service
Celebrating the Life of
The Reverend Lloyd E. Dees

April 23, 2016
2:00 p.m. Trinity United Methodist Church
Savannah, Georgia

Preludes	My Shepherd, Handel *The Lord is my Light,* Allitesen
	Psalm 121, H.C. Baker
Special Music	*Largo* - G.F. Handel
	Hubert Baker, organ / Anne Yarrow, violin
Words of Grace	The Reverend Enoch Hendry
Prayer	
The Epistle Lesson	2 Corinthians 4:3-18, Janet Dees
Reading	Dr. Shangri-La Durham-Thompson
Reflections	Jason Dees
Congregational Hymn	*It Is Well With My Soul* #377
The Old Testament lesson	Isaiah 43:1-3
Eulogy	Mr. Hendry
Special Music	*If I Can Help Somebody,* Mr. Baker
The Gospel Lesson	John 11:25-26
Dismissal with Blessing	
Postlude	Holiness Unto the Lord, L.N. Morris

A repast will be held in Trustees Hall following the service for the Dees family.

The Reverend Lloyd E. Dees

Rev. Dees

The Reverend Lloyd E. Dees died on Thursday, February 4. He was 85 years old. First ordained as an A.M.E. pastor, the Reverend Dees served that denomination from 1961 until 1972. That year he joined the Western North Carolina Conference of the United Methodist Church. He served churches in N.C., West Virginia, New York, New Jersey, Bermuda, and Georgia in a long and faithful career! He was a chaplain at North Carolina Agricultural & Technical State University as well as a Human Rights Commissioner in W.V. Upon retiring in 1999, he and his wife moved to Rincon, GA where he continued to serve United Methodist churches in the Savannah area, including the historic Trinity United Methodist Church, Mother Church of Savannah Methodism.

An Alabama native, he graduated high school from the Camden Academy (a Presbyterian mission school) where he worked to supply room and board. He enrolled in college at the age of 27 and followed his undergraduate studies with a Master of Divinity degree (w/honors) from the Interdenominational Theological Centre, in Atlanta. He continued his studies at Union Seminary (New York City) and Princeton Theological Seminary.

He was a tireless advocate, especially for the aging. The Reverend Dees was honored by the Georgia Council on Aging; Receiving the Martha Eaves Advocate for Positive Change Award (twice). He was a founding member of the Board of Directors of Habitat for Humanity in Freeport, N.Y. and the co-founder of Bermudians for Reconciliation during his tenure in that British territory. In retirement he was a volunteer with the Effingham Democratic Committee and the NAACP.

As a singer, Lloyd lent his voice to any number of charities. With violinist Anne Yarrow (performing together at *Chimes of Hope*), he lent his talents for fund raising and in support of churches and non-profit organizations. Lloyd's voice was instantly recognizable. He often sang the inspirational *If I Can Help Somebody,* with a gracious spirit and a kind heart!

In 1957 Lloyd married Dolores Mills. Married nearly 60 years, the Dees' have two children: Son Jason Lloyd (Crystal) of Port Wentworth, GA and daughter Janet of Chicago, Illinois, who survived him. He is also survived by seven brothers and one sister; brothers-in-law, sisters-in-law and several nieces and nephews.

Remembrances to Trinity United Methodist Church or Hospice Savannah.

Remembering Rev. Dees

Janet Dees (Daughter)

Many people knew my father as a minister, activist, and advocate for justice. For me, he was all those things, but also "just" my dad. It is difficult to say just a few words about someone with whom I had such a longstanding and complex relationship, as parent-child relationships inevitably are. He was a daily presence in my life in a way that only a handful of people, my brother and mother among them, may understand. It is also difficult to push past the complicated emotions and grief at his passing that still lie just below the surface of daily life, even after nine years.

Rev. Dees and Janet, 1992

What I miss the most about my father is his laughter and our shared sense of humor, sharing and discussing books and political issues. I would give him serious books and funny cards as presents. One of the memories that stands out is visiting my parents as an adult and spending mornings with my dad watching the call-in TV show "Washington Journal" on C-SPAN. From 7-10 a.m. We would drink coffee and eat our breakfast and talk back to the TV about whatever political issues were being debated that day.

Finally, my father loved to dance, and I have fond memories of dancing with him at special occasions like family reunions.

Jason Dees (Son)

My father always said, "Son, always have a desire/hunger for knowledge."

Rev. Dees and Jason

Mr. Martin Dees (Brother)

Lloyd was one of eleven children, ten boys and one girl. He was the fourth, and I was the seventh. In our early years, we did not have serious communication or association because (1) the difference in our ages, (2) he went off to boarding high school (Camden Academy in Camden, Alabama) away from home, as had all the brothers before me. Our association grew as communication and transportation grew. It was in the latter years that Lloyd and my association grew strong. Lloyd and I called each other more and more frequently, and when he started his new avocation with singing and producing songs, we communicated even more. I helped him obtain copyright protection to several of his songs, including "The Bermuda Song." I went to Bermuda with him when he presented "The Bermuda Song" in Bermuda.

In his latter years, he let me know he was waning. He said to me a number of times that, "I am eighty-five and I have had a good life." At the end of his life's journey, I flew to his home to see him on the last day.

Lloyd was independent, and he believed in civil rights from an early age. For example, if he worked for someone, he expected that he would be paid immediately.

Lloyd was the son of Martin and Maggie Dees from Wilcox County, Belview, Alabama. They had eleven children: Herman H. Dees, Edward, Earnest, Lloyd, Henry (deceased), Franklin, Martin, Otis, Delores, Dan (deceased), and Clarence (deceased).

There was no public high school for blacks in Belview and Lloyd worked on and off campus and was supported by the Presbyterian boarding school.

Dr. Anne Yarrow (Violinist)

He was the first African American pastor of the Freeport Methodist Church in Long Island. He was concerned about people, and I was not surprised when I discovered that he had worked with Habitat for Humanity. He was a very dapper dresser, very stylish. He had a great love of the arts, and we became great friends, in part because of our love for music. I performed in numerous concerts with him. He had a distinguished baritone voice, and he loved to sing Negro Spirituals which he sang with his whole heart and soul. In fact on December 12, 2015, only a few months before he passed, he released a CD of Negro Spirituals called *Soulful Sounds*.

Rev. Dr. John E. Brandon (and wife, Minnie)

Throughout the years of my friendship with Lloyd, there were tough times and great times, and there were thick and thin times. Along the way, there were many projects we shared, and there was laughter and brotherhood in each and every one. I am thankful for the friendship journey that I shared with my friend Lloyd. It was a journey filled with memories, too numerous to count.

Mr. Marcus Brandon (Rev. Brandon's son)

My father indicated that Rev. Dees was an avid social activist throughout all the years he knew him. I am proud to know that he and my father were to each other confidant, friend, and colleague. Rev. Dees was a thoughtful man of strong character who tackled injustices in the Church and in the community in which he lived. I was told that he counselled, mentored, and helped many men and women in ministry.

Mrs. Julia Durham (Parishioner, Bethel A.M.E. Church, Bermuda)

Rev. Dees was my pastor at Bethel A.M.E. Church, a man of great depth whose sermons always carried profound, underlying messages. I deeply admired his unwavering commitment to speaking out and working on behalf of the Bermudian people. Over the years, we developed a close friendship, and he often sought my assistance.

Although my professional responsibilities prevented me from taking a more public stance, as I worked with him and Rev. Brandon, I was actively involved in the Consumer Affairs Bureau initiative at Rev. Dee's encouragement. I appreciated that he took a personal interest in my children, particularly Shangri-La, playing a pivotal role in her journey to study at N.C. A&T State University.

No return to Bermuda was complete without Rev. Dees and sometimes, Rev. Brandon, visiting with me. They were both fearless men of God, steadfast in their convictions and dedicated to their calling.

Mrs. Eloise Furbert (Past Educator, Bermuda)

I first met Rev. Dees when he invited my husband, F.S. Furbert, and me to a service at Bethel A.M.E. Church. My husband, Mr. F.S. Furbert, was the principal of the Berkeley Institute, and he always invited great speakers to the school on Friday mornings to speak to the students. Rev. Dees was invited on a few occasions to inspire the students. He was a very friendly person who did not hesitate to spread friendships beyond the bounds of the A.M.E. Church. He was a gracious individual, and never sought to draw attention to himself. We remained friends until his passing.

Rev. Dr. Larry Dixon (Retired Presiding Elder of the A.M.E. Church)

Rev. Dees was a true Church Leader, a gentleman, and a prophetic voice for the Kingdom. Our conversations often touched on the Church and broader societal issues, always guided by the principle that "while we are in the world, we are not of the world." I recall that Rev. Dees had an impeccable sense of style. I once told him, "When I grow up, I want to be just like you!" Precious memories!

[I note that Rev. Dr. Larry E. Dixon is a retired Presiding Elder in the African Methodist Episcopal Church, who spent 46 years as an active Itinerant Elder. In Bermuda he pastored St. John A.M.E. Church in Bailey's Bay, Bermuda, and St. Philip A.M.E. Church in Harrington Sound while serving as Presiding Elder of the West District. Like Rev. Lloyd Dees, he was deeply engaged in the

Bermuda community and played a significant role in the protest against capital punishment in 1977.]

Rev. Dr. Wendell Christopher (Current Pastor, St. Philip A.M.E. Church, Bermuda)

As the former Director of Social and Political Action for the Second Episcopal District—covering Maryland, Virginia, North Carolina, and Washington, D.C.—for over 16 years, I can say without hesitation that Rev. Dees and Rev. Brandon helped shape my life more than almost anyone outside of my immediate family.

Bermuda's Opposition Leader, Dame Lois Browne-Evans, was my cousin, and the Hon. Frederick Wade was my uncle. However, I recall the writings of Rev. Dees and Rev. Brandon and believe they influenced my involvement in social activism. Growing up in "the back of town," they taught me to recognize my worth—that I was just as important as anyone else.

I remember how boldly they spoke out against injustice, advocating for a Bermuda where all people were treated equally. Their voices, I believe, had a profound impact on many, including Rev. Dr. Larry Lowe, an A.M.E. minister, now deceased who became a member of Parliament.

During Rev. Dees's tenure in Bermuda, the oligarchs ruled, and many lived in fear of speaking out. Those with mortgages feared they would be revoked, while those without one feared jeopardizing their chances of ever getting one. In that climate of intimidation, Rev. Dees and Rev. Brandon stood firm. They spoke truth to power, and they inspired me.

I particularly remember Rev. Dees as incredibly approachable—a genuinely kind, down-to-earth man. His presence, like his words, made a lasting impact.

Betty Monroe (Congregant)

Rev. Lloyd Dees was a blessing to the Freeport United Methodist Church. He truly understood and taught the doctrines of God, and his dedication to the Lord's work touched many hearts and souls daily. We are forever grateful for his guidance, wisdom, and unwavering faith. Rev. Dees' warmth, generosity, and biblical qualities made him not only a powerful pastor but a true and loyal friend.

Linda Hendrickson (Current President, Board of Trustees, Freeport United Methodist Church)

I recall walking into the church one day and seeing Rev. Dees mopping the floors. When questioned about it, he said he was doing the Lord's work. I told him that this was not the pastor's job, but he replied that Jesus did many menial tasks, and he wanted to be like Jesus.

Julien Leotaud (LAY leader, Freeport United Methodist Church)

When I look back at the association with my friend Rev. Lloyd E. Dees, I cannot help but think that being in his company was one of my better life experiences.

He was not only a genuine human being, but was my Spiritual Advisor and Mentor. He changed the course of my life and helped me develop confidence in my Christian beliefs. When I gave thought to what I should say and what would best describe my friend, the words that came to mind are on a passage from the book of Micah 6:8 that reads, "Do what is just, show love, and live in humble fellowship with our God."

During my lifetime, I have known many men who are Holy in Heart and Life, but one equal to my friend Lloyd E. Dees I have yet to meet. May his memory be everlasting in life.

Hope Springs Eternal

It has been over fifty years since Rev. Lloyd Dees left Bermuda, but his efforts and those of Rev. Brandon and others to address the rising cost of living continue to be a challenge for Bermuda today. Although rising costs of living are not limited to Bermuda, in 2024, Bermuda was ranked number one for the high cost of living plus rent index by NUMBEO. The Bermuda Industrial Union, under the leadership of President Chris Furbert, and the Progressive Labour Party, under the leadership of Premier David Burt, continue to try and address this complex issue.

I could not end this book without acknowledging an article in *The Royal Gazette* by Gareth Finighan, dated December 14, 2024, and published under the headline, "Premier Predicts Slate of Tax Breaks in Next Financial Year."

In this article, Premier David Burt outlined a comprehensive package for tax breaks and strategic investments, not only to help alleviate financial pressure on the Bermuda population, but to lay the groundwork for future prosperity. The government's plan includes over 45 million in tax relief for the 2025 to 2026 financial year.

Beyond seeking to ease the cost of living, the Premier calls for strategic investments to strengthen Bermuda's social fabric, with $50 million dedicated to the launch of a universal healthcare system. Premier David Burt described 2025 as a transformative year for Bermuda. His vision honors the spirit of Reverend Lloyd E. Dees, whose unwavering dedication to justice and community was a hallmark of his life.

As Bermuda steps into a new chapter, we find hope and trust because the Premier says, "These measures are designed with fairness at their core. They reflect our understanding of the real challenges faced by our people and our determination to provide meaningful relief to taxpayers. This is a plan that will ensure a fairer Bermuda for all."

The complete article can be found at: https://www.royalgazette.com/politics/news/article/20241214/premier-predicts-slate-of-tax-breaks-in-next-financial-year/

Finally, although this work shows how and why Rev. Lloyd E. Dees worked tirelessly to make a difference wherever he lived in the world, I hope this book serves as inspiration to help others especially those with inadequate resources, the downtrodden, and those treated unjustly. Someone once said, "Bad things happen when good people look the other way."

The quote "Do what you can, with what you have, where you are" is widely attributed to Theodore Roosevelt. It encourages making the most of your current situation and available resources, rather than waiting for ideal conditions.

"Do what you can:" this part emphasizes action and taking initiative, even if it's a small step. "With what you have:" encourages using the resources and opportunities you have available to you, rather than waiting for more. "Where you are:" this acknowledges that we are all in unique circumstances and that our environment may not be perfect. However, we should still make the most of it.

This quote is often seen as a reminder to:

- Stop procrastinating and start taking action.
- Don't wait for perfect conditions.
- Embrace the challenges and opportunities in your current situation.
- Be resourceful and make the most of what you have.

As a tribute to Rev. Dees and other "Onward Christian Soldiers," let us, too, stand for justice and strive harder to make a difference.

Part II

Anthology of Reference Material

Chapter 9

The Protest Magazines

November 1969 . . . . p. 179

January – March 1970 . . . . p. 189

October – December 1970 . . . . p. 203

March 1971 . . . . p. 217

September 1971 . . . . p. 233

November 1969

THE PROTEST MAGAZINE

The Protest Magazine is an earnest endeavour on the part of the editors to speak to some of the significant and controversial issues in the A.M.E. Church and in the Society. It endeavours to constructively criticize many of the outmoded and antiquated procedures of the A.M.E. Church which actively hinder the church in performing its duties as Christ would have it in the world today.

Also, this magazine does not attempt to make a false dichotomy between the spiritual on the one hand and the social on the other but tries to state very realistically that man is a whole and the spiritual cannot be stressed successfully over that of social, psychological, or political.

CONTENTS

The Magazine 3
About the Editors 4
Pastoral Appointments in the A.M.E. Church 6
Speaking About the Church 10
Is the A.M.E. Church Really Serious? 11

About the Editors

Lloyd E. Dees was born in Camden, Alabama; but he has spent most of his adult life in New York City. He served for two years in the United States Army, spending almost a year in Berlin, Germany. Mr. Dees received his B.A. degree from Shelton College with a major in Philosophy. He received his B.D. degree from Interdenominational Theological Center in Atlanta, Georgia. While at I.T.C. he became a member of the International Society of Theta Phi, for excellence in scholarship. He was also the recipient of the Sammye F. Coan Memorial Award for high academic achievement during his seminary career, and the Henry McNeil Turner Memorial Preaching Award for outstanding achievement in homiletics. He has also fulfilled half of the requirements for the Master of Theology degree in Christian Ethics at Princeton Theological Seminary. At the present time, Reverend Dees is the pastor of Bethel A.M.E. Church in Shelly Bay, Bermuda. Reverend Dees is married to the former Miss Dolores Mills of New York City. He is an avid ping-pong player and a lover of the New York Mets.

Rev. John E. Brandon is the pastor of Allen Temple A.M.E. Church in Somerset, Bermuda. He is a native of Louisiana where he received his early education. Rev. Brandon received his (A.A.) Associate of Arts Degree in Education from Campbell College, Jackson, Miss.; (B.A.) Bachelor of Arts Degree from Morris Brown College in Psychology and Sociology, Atlanta, Georgia; and the (Th.M.) Master of Theology Degree in Ecumenics, Missions and World Religions from Boston University School of Theology, Boston, Mass.

Rev. Brandon has served on the Executive Board of the United Christian Youth Movement in Georgia (Georgia Council of Churches); he has worked for two summers (1965-1966) with the Pennsylvania Council of Churches in the Migrant Ministry; served as Co-Chairman of the

Consultation on the Black Church; a member of the National Committee of Black Churchman; and is a member of a number of honour organizations and societies.

PASTORAL APPOINTMENTS IN THE A.M.E. CHURCH

By

Rev. Lloyd E. Dees

Many questions may be asked concerning pastoral appointments in the A.M.E. Church. And undoubtedly many answers can be given. Perhaps this is so because of the role that the pastor has been given and the total operation of the church. But I do not propose to ask all the questions; and I am sure that I could not give all of the answers. Basically, I am concerned with whether the present system of appointing pastors serves to enhance the mission of the church. Coupled with this basic concern is the question as to whether democracy should be more evident as a guiding principle in making pastoral appointments.

Some persons will perhaps say that we do not have a democracy. However, these persons should be reminded that bishops are elected by the people and that this is indeed characteristic of a democracy. But, when I speak of democracy in this context, I have in mind a greater degree of fairness, a greater awareness of justice, a greater inclination towards encouraging self-expression, and a more sympathetic consideration for the wishes of other people. I also have in mind the question as to whether favoritism is replacing justice when it comes to the appointing of pastors. Further, one wonders whether the spirit of democracy would permit arbitrary decisions to be made that might affect the lives of hundreds of people. The latter statement, of course, is a judgment; due in part to the writer's observation of certain patterns that are too prevalent in the appointing pastors.

As we proceed, therefore, it should be kept in mind that it is my intention to raise certain questions about the operation of the A.M.E. Church, and certain relationships within the church, as these relate to pastoral appointments. The questions are being raised in order to see if something may be done to enhance the operation of the church, and the relationships within the church. All of us together must scrutinize the subject and underline every possibility. We must strive to see things as they are, and we must not try to cover those issues that should always be in the open. We must think seriously about our church as it is now existing throughout the nation, and in parts of certain foreign countries. And when we observe certain inequities, we must be willing to admit that these exist.

Let us now take a closer look at the pastor and his appointment. Ideally—according to the law and tradition of our church—a pastor is appointed to his charge annually at the time of the Annual Conference. In support of this assertion, I shall quote two historical statements which have reference to pastoral appointments. The first one is taken from the *History of the A.M.E. Church,* by Bishop Daniel Alexander Payne (p. 281). "The bench of Bishops (General Conference of 1852), decided that the preacher having the charge of a circuit or station is the pastor of that charge until his appointment to another is announced in the Annual Conference to which he belongs..." The particular circumstances which gave rise to this decision are not quite clear. But it is quoted because it indicates that the time and place of pastoral appointments (ideally speaking) should be the Annual Conference. (When we use the word "ideally" we are allowing for emergencies, such as sickness and death, etc.,). Significance should also be given this statement because it is a ruling of the Bench of Bishops which undoubtedly had the welfare of the church at heart.

The second statement was made almost a hundred years later than the first. To the General Conference of 1948, the Committee on the Revision of the Discipline made the following recommendation: "The following requirements shall be observed by the bishop when fixing the pastoral appointments; he shall appoint preachers to pastoral charges annually after consultation with the presiding elder. The presiding elder in turn shall inform the minister of said appointment at least twenty-four hours before appointments are publicly announced... Whenever the appointment of a minister is changed, he shall be upgraded, or assigned to an appointment commensurate with the one from which he has been moved (provided his work in the charge from which he is being moved has been satisfactory per presiding elder's report and the local church from which he is being moved). All laws in conflict with the above are hereby repealed." (*Encyclopedia of Africa Methodism 1948*, page 659, by R.R. Right Jr.).

The decision of the "Bench" in the General Conference of 1852 stated that the preacher is the pastor of a charge until his appointment to another is announced in the Annual Conference to which he belongs. The recommendation of the General Conference of 1948 states that "the bishop shall appoint preachers to pastoral charges annually." One may raise the question as to whether the terms "annually", and "Annual Conference" mean the same thing. The writer is inclined to think that they do not. The term "Annual Conference" has referenced to a certain geographical area in which are situated a certain number of churches. It also has reference to an organized body of people who meet once a year to administer the affairs of these several churches within its boundary. Further, it has reference to a fixed time and place determined beforehand by its members, and delegates. This writer interprets the "decision of the Bench" in the General Conference of 1852 to mean that it is at this fixed time and place that the pastor's appointment is announced. The term "annually" also has reference to something occurring once a year. But the time and place of this occurrence does not have to be fixed, nor determined beforehand by an organized body. The recommendation of the General Conference of 1948, therefore, can be interpreted to mean that the bishop may appoint pastors at any time during the year. One may say that those who wrote this recommendation had the Annual Conference in mind, but we cannot escape the fact that it tends towards ambiguity. This tendency notwithstanding, it is the writer's opinion—ideally speaking—that at the Annual Conference session is the time and place for pastoral appointments.

Another point which this recommendation makes is that the bishop and the presiding elder should have consultation, and that the presiding elder should inform the pastor of his appointment at least twenty-four hours before his appointment is announced in public. Many pastors may doubt whether such a consultation actually takes place, but they know whether the presiding elder informed them of their appointments twenty-four hours in advance. Ask many pastors, and they will tell you that they were utterly surprised—and in some cases utterly shocked—when their appointments were read on the Sunday afternoon of the Annual Conference. But suppose the presiding elder actually fulfilled his function in this connection, can we be satisfied with this twenty-four-hour time factor? It is the writer's candid opinion that pastors deserve much more than this. Beyond this, it seems to me that democracy would demand that a consultation be held with the bishop and the pastor. After all, it is he who is to receive the appointment. And it is possible that he may be able to shed more light on his capabilities than anyone else. We must admit, however, that there are some pastors who are consulted prior to the announcing of their appointments. But, on the whole, these are those who are commonly referred to in our church as "big pastors", who are assigned to "big churches." In general, there seems to be no felt, or apparent need to confer with "little pastors" who are assigned to "little churches."

There was something else in this recommendation to the General Conference of 1948 that should be considered. This recommendation states that "whenever the appointment of a minister is changed, he shall be upgraded or assigned to an appointment commensurate with the one from which he has been moved (provided his work in that charge from which he has been moved is satisfactory as per presiding elder's report and the local church from which he is being moved). Perhaps to many persons especially pastors—this sounds like a wonderful idea. And perhaps some pastors see in this idea a kind of safeguard for themselves. A closer look, however, should reveal much more than this. In the first place, this recommendation puts a tremendous burden on the bishops of our church. Anyone who has a fair knowledge of the A.M.E. Church should know that there are more small congregations than there are large ones. And anyone who knows anything about the "mind" of the A.M.E. Church should know that upgrading means moving from a small congregation to a larger one. Following this kind of logic, and given the present conditions in our church, some pastors will never be "upgraded." And finding a charge commensurate with the one from which a pastor is moved is not as easy as it sounds.

But beyond this is the kind of mentality that may be detected in this recommendation, with respect to the changing of pastor's appointment. It is the writer's candid belief that the presupposition upon which such a statement is predicated is that the pastor in the A.M.E. Church must begin his pastorate at the low rung of the ladder, and through a long and tedious process, work his way upward. And even the casual observer knows that this practice is widespread in the A.M.E. Church. But the principle of democracy would demand that a pastor be given a charge on the basis of his qualifications, and not on the basis of an outmoded mentality.

From my point of view, the above practice is having a tremendous ill effect upon the whole church. I believe that it has set in motion a diabolical, and perpetual struggle among the ministers of the church. And I further believe that this practice has created an element of distrust that is destroying the morale and spiritual fiber of the A.M.E. Church. And after the destruction of the morale and the spiritual fiber, death comes. Let us, therefore, take heed to the following words:

> "And to the Angel of the church in Sardis write: the words of him who has the seven spirits of God and the seven stars. I know your works; You have the name of being alive, and you are dead. Awake, and strengthen what remains and is on the point of death, for I have not found your works perfect in the sight of my God. Remember then what you received and heard; Keep that, and repent. If you will not awake, I will come like a thief, and you will not know at what hour I will come upon you. Yet you have still a few names in Sardis, people who have not soiled their garments…" Revelation 3:1-4.

SPEAKING ABOUT THE CHURCH

(Charley and Pete)

Yesterday (Monday) I decided to stay in bed and relax. Sunday had been a very busy day for me. I had taught a Sunday school class at 9:30 a.m., preached at 11:00 a.m., 4:00 p.m., made a hospital call at 6:00 p.m., preached at 7:00 p.m. and lost pounds in the process. It was about 8:30 a.m., when my doorbell rang. I tried to ignore it, but the caller was persistent. I staggered to the door, and there was my friend Peter, the pastor of Vine Street A.M.E. Church. I forced myself to invite him in, and he came in gladly. I forced myself to offer him a seat, and he sat down gladly. I dropped myself into a chair and focused my sleepy gaze at him. Peter said to me, "Charley I couldn't sleep last night." In my sleep laden voice I said, "my name is Charles." "Did you call the doctor?" "I wasn't sick, I was thinking." "You were thinking all night, Peter?" "Yes," he said. I raised myself up in my chair in utter amazement—(Peter thinking all night). "I was thinking about the church." "You were thinking about the church?" I asked. "The A.M.E. Church." "You might have been better off if you were sleeping," I said. "Charley, sometimes I don't understand you." "Don't call me Charley! My name is Charles." "All right don't get excited. I just wanted to talk with you about the church." "All right Peter, go ahead and talk." "Well first I was thinking about the meeting that is going to be held next week; I think it's good because it will give us a chance to get together." "Have you received a program?" I asked. "No, I haven't," he said. "So, what are we going to talk about when we get together?" I asked. "Well, I'm sure there will be some kind of program Charley." "Don't call me Charley." "All right Charles!" "Well even if there is no special program, it will be good to get together just to talk." "What do you think that we should talk about?" I asked. "We should talk about what happened at the last General Conference." "You mean about all of that noise and confusion, all of that destruction of property, and the archaic manner in which bishops were elected?" "Why are you so critical Charles?" "Thanks for remembering my name." "I should have known better than to try to talk with you," he said. "Well, I was only trying to suggest some topics for discussion. Maybe you would rather talk about the rumour that we will not be welcomed in the city of "brotherly love" again, or the rumor that one of our bishops threatened to resign at the last Bishops' Council." "I see that I'm not getting anywhere with you Charley, I think I had better leave. We will have to talk again, when you are in a better frame of mind." "When you come back to talk about the church, please don't come on a Monday at 8:30 in the morning, Pete." "Don't call me Pete! My name is Peter."

IS THE A.M.E. CHURCH REALLY SERIOUS?

By John E. Brandon

What reason can the A.M.E. Church give for its participation in the Consultation on Church Union? Are we observers pretending to be full participants? Are we going along for the ride? Can we state unequivocally our position? Can we say that since A.M.E.'s do believe that: there is one Lord and one salvation; therefore one church—but of necessity, a black church and a white church; that when A.M.E.'s say, "Our Father", white denominations refer to the same "Father" when they say, "Our Father;" that the whole church is answerable for the ecumenical effort; that it is a movement of, and by God and is ours by the Holy Spirit which embraces all divisions; and that "all have sinned and come short of the glory of God." Now if we can assume the proceeding, then ecumenism poses the same challenge to the A.M.E.'s as it does to any white denomination. Some might say that we participate in COCU., "because we are Christians, and we must seek unity continuously with all of God's people." While these statements may be true enough, they should not blind us to the kind of honest and just unity God would have us seek unity without power is dangerous.

At this point in history, the A.M.E. Church must thoroughly assess and reexamine its position in COCU. The A.M.E. Church indeed must examine its position in the whole ecumenical movement. The result of such examination is that we cannot avoid taking an attitude towards COCU., and that if that attitude is not a positive one, and yet a critical one, then we shall have to put forward an exact declaration and justification of such a position. If we are really serious, we must begin to ask ourselves some questions: Why hasn't any special effort been made to inform the local congregations of what COCU. is all about? COCU. or any other similar kind of ecumenical organization cannot function without the support of the various local congregations. Are bishop's willing to give up their positions of power for the possibilities of COCU.? How will we handle the question of property, congregations, bishops, general officers, and many other considerations involved in COCU.?

In light of the seriousness of the preceding questions, the A.M.E. Church must answer soon. In answering, we must of necessity keep in mind the historical situation of black and white relationships in the church and the present condition of those relationships today. As expressed by Bishop F.D. Jordan at the last COCU. meeting in Atlanta, Georgia, "We remember that white

Christians don't really believe in the black religious experience, but feel it is some pre-civilization expression."

If events of the seventeen hundreds with regard to the A.M.E. Church and other black denominations as they relate to white denominations were any indication of the future, as surely, they were, what can we expect to be different today in COCU.? The question of our seriousness becomes even more pressing when we look at these historical situations. Ever since the white man made his way to Africa to take slaves back with him, there has been conflict. From this confrontation and the intervening stormy centuries of white mastery and black resentment, we now have the most explosive situation in the world today.

If some of the issues of race are not resolved in COCU. now, we cannot even talk straight about union. If A.M.E.'s are willing to accept a kind of union that is not one of justice, sharing of power, and full participation, we will end up with no support from black people. This sharing of power must of necessity be a pre-union action. Already are black participants in COCU. looked upon with suspicion by young black clergy, seminarians, and others of the black community.

In the present ecumenical thrust, A.M.E.'s must reassess relationship at all levels if we are really serious about this business of ecumenism. How can we trust the white denominations of COCU. to deal justly with us when they don't deal justly with their own members who are black like we are? The white Christian Church is faced with a tremendous problem of reconciling its professed principles of equality and justice with the practices of segregation and discrimination. We must begin to say in no uncertain terms what ecumenism means to us.

My suggestion, first of all, is that black denominations must make that "big" effort to unite so that when we do come to talk seriously with white denominations, we will talk from a stronger base of power. If this does not take place soon, we will only continue to haggle in splintered groups of A.M.E.'s, C.M.E.'s and A.M.E.Z's trying hopelessly to do the impossible. We should not begin with COCU. if we are really serious about ecumenism, but with unity with our black sisters and brothers who have been divided from us for too long. We should not let haggles overpower keep us apart. Basically, we have the same doctrine and liturgy. If we are really serious, we will begin to take notice of the fact that we as a black people can never meet the power of the white church as divided as we are. They (white denominations) can unite any time they feel like it, as has been shown with the merging of the Methodist Church and the E.U.B. church.

There is no doubt that the historical relationship between the black man and the white man effects the present state of affairs in ecumenical organizations. There does exist a problem of racism. In many white churches as has been down through history, white people raised the question of the propriety of blacks preaching to whites. There is also today in many places, great opposition to whites and blacks worshipping together in God's house. Dr. Harry V. Richardson states in his book, *Dark Glory,* that,

> "... Many of these difficulties, (white and blacks worshipping together) were said to be solved in the separate church or mission presided over by white pastors; Who were generally regarded as a missionary to the blacks. It avoided social mixing: It permitted special preaching to slaves; and it provided the one element about which there was so much uneasiness—white supervision of black gatherings."

Therefore, we cannot overlook our history as a black people in assessing our position.

The trend of events in recent years on the national and international scenes in racial confrontations have brought to the attention of churchmen and all people the situation which lay dormant in the black community for many years. In order for A.M.E.'s and other black denominations to really deal with problems facing the black community, we must unite. It seems to me that black denominations uniting is also the only way of dealing with the hard core of racism in the white church. This might be called a step toward black solidarity. I do not believe that the unity of the church is any more threatened by blacks uniting than it is already. It can only strengthen our relationship to the entire church.

The kind of ecumenism sought by white Christians has to be countered when white Christians' motives say that "in the dark all things are dark": That is, there is indeed no other way to include blacks, except in justice and a recognition of differences—differences in ways of worship, preaching, and an entirely different experience. There is no real gain in ecumenism unless there is recognition of unity and diversity, justice, and in shared power. If we as A.M.E.'s are serious, we cannot tolerate false beginnings or relationship with white denominations. We must agree upon the principal features of ecumenism, now! Ecumenism must express a whole view of the world. However, it does not disregard the reality of the past nor of the present or of future "possibilities." But, brethren, are we really serious?

January – March 1970

THE PROTEST

Editors: JOHN E. BRANDON AND LLOYD E. DEES©

Published Quarterly, to stimulate thinking, and affect change within the Church and Society.

Subscription rates: in Bermuda, $2 per year: outside Bermuda, $2.50 per year, single copy .65c.

Make check or money order payable to

LLOYD E. DEES

Shelly Bay, Bermuda

©John E. Brandon is Pastor of Allen Temple A.M.E. Church, Somerset, Bermuda.

Lloyd E. Dees is Pastor of Bethel A.M.E. Church, Shelly Bay, Bermuda.

CONTENTS

No Vision, No People 3
Speaking about the Church (Charley and Pete) 6
An Urgent Call for Action 8
Expressions 12
A New Thing (A Sermon) 13

NO VISION, NO PEOPLE

by

John E. Brandon

Is it possible for any people—nation, or institution to survive without vision? In developing a response to this question, one must have a knowledge of the concept "vision." Vision is not an isolated happening, rather, it takes into consideration the present, the past and the future possibilities. It is more than something seen in a dream, a trance, or some supernatural appearance that conveys a revelation or an object of the imagination. We can speak here of two kinds of vision—physical and spiritual. The consequences of poor vision or lack of vision, whether physical or spiritual, can result in tragedy. For purposes of illustration, we can cite the instances of where two ships in a fog collided because the physical vision was impaired by the fog, and where the Israelites who were not content in the wilderness suffered the consequences of poor spiritual vision or no vision at all because they could not "see" the Promised Land.

The writer of Proverbs captures the idea of "vision" that I am speaking of when he states in Proverbs 29:18: "Where there is no vision, the people perish…" For vision in this sense is foresight; it is to conceive and visualize, to form, to bring forth, it is to develop ideas, plans and designs necessary for a people—a nation or an institution to survive in God's ever-changing world. We might say that vision is one of the purest forms of reporting upon an immediate awareness of the will of God. Without this kind of vision, it is possible to perish! To perish is to be ineffective when we ought to be effective; to be impotent when we ought to be potent; to worry about trivialities when immensities face us—problems of racism, injustice, and undemocratic processes. If the African Methodist Episcopal Church would be a potent factor in the lives of its people, it must commit itself seriously to God's fight for justice which ought to spring up in all its activities and programs to the point of saturating and permeating the very fiber of the institution itself.

The A.M.E. Church must do more than pass resolutions and print smooth sounding words and phrases in the discipline. It must constantly plan on a national and international basis from a central point of operation. I am not talking about each district with its own "planned – pre-planned" planning council, but rather, I am speaking of a massive examination and thorough-going look at the present structure of the A.M.E. Church. It is at the moment, quite evident that such a program is needed if we will not perish from lack of vision. Certain changes in structure need desperately to be scrutinized and developed in the area of placement of ministers, ecumenical intentions, and recruitment of young men for the ministry. This kind of examination and planning must become a reality because we are now faced with the fact that "tomorrow is today." We are confronted in the A.M.E. Church with the fierce urgency of now. We cannot afford procrastination. Life often leaves us standing bare, naked and dejected with a lost opportunity.

We can look at many areas of the A.M.E. Church where there is a seeming lack of vision. First, let us look at the situation of our schools and colleges. At the moment, the A.M.E. Church is trying to maintain ten schools and colleges in the United States and Africa without a great deal of success. Why don't we use the money being spent on some of the smaller schools (which are barely surviving) for purposes of strengthening two or three of our better equipped and potentially productive schools? Some of the money now spent on certain schools could be used for scholarship aid to students who otherwise might not be able to attend college. These scholarships would not only be available to students in the States, but wherever there are A.M.E. Churches.

Secondly, the A.M.E. Church must seriously seek union with her sister churches—the African Methodist Episcopal Zion Church and the Christian Methodist Episcopal Church. Can we envision the day when Episcopal power does not stand in the way of the union of our sisters and brothers who are divided from us, denominationally? Basically, we have the same liturgy and doctrines.

Thirdly, what vision or lack of it keeps us in the stalemate we seem to be in when it comes to expanding at the Interdenominational Theological Center in Atlanta, Georgia, particularly, in a time when there is a great need for trained ministers? It is indeed sad that when church officials speak of expansion, they are usually speaking of a few more smaller churches, made up mostly of two or three members.

Fourthly, is it vision or lack of it to divide small conferences into such small districts throughout the A.M.E. Church for the sake of only creating jobs—what else? My concern at this point is for the people who have to suffer the consequences of "episcopal vision." Sometimes "episcopal vision" is what Shakespeare called in *Measure for Measure*; "Proud man dressed in a little brief authority…plays such fantastic tricks before high heaven…the angels weep." The statement, "together we stand, divided we fall" should be considered very carefully. Such an open manifestation of district divisions opens the way for psychological aloofness in many districts of the A.M.E. Church, which is incongruent with the church's concern for the spiritual development and cohesiveness of its people. The A.M.E. Church must have a vision for the future—a future of what lies beyond history—of that toward which history is pointing. However, I do not make any claims to deny or simplify the enormous complexity of existing structures and general conditions. But all forms, traditions, and procedures that become inadequate must be repeatedly revised and changed. We cannot in the name of Him who is able to keep us from perishing, allow ourselves to be content. Our bishops must not lose themselves in the past, but find and put into action that revolutionary spirit of our forefathers. However, the past should not be romanticized to the point of prohibiting future progress. The church needs more than the few progressive bishops it now has. They must be joined by others, because time marches on and waits on no one.

Black people should have remained and perished in more ways than one in the all-white Methodist Church, but Richard Allen had a vision for his people worshipping without being harassed and pulled off their knees because they were black. The A.M.E. Church was born in protest because someone had a vision of a better day. Could it be that today the black church has lost its zeal for freedom in the midst of the alluring white power structure? As James H. Cone has said in his book *Black Theology and Black Power*:

> The black minister remained the spokesman for the black people, but, faced by insurmountable obstacles, he succumbed to the bribery, the cajolery of the white power structure and became its foil. The passion for freedom was replaced with innocuous homilies against drinking, dancing and smoking; and injustices of the present were minimized in favour of a Kingdom beyond this world.

It is evident that today, our "vision" in the church must extend beyond mere symptoms.

We might say that to have vision is to see beyond the skyline. That is, to see not just today, but tomorrow. People perish when the range of vision is confined to any one place, whether it is a church, in a sick room or on a highway—depending on whether it is spiritual vision or visual physical vision. If a person who is sick cannot see his or her way out of the sick room, it is possible to remain in the sick room. But the person who sees beyond, can mount up strength never before realized. Noble souls and institutions have always seen beyond the skyline. They have found the secret of life which has eliminated most of the worries and enlarges the scope of vision. The people or persons who looks farther than the narrow circle of his visible world is challenged by the bigness of the universe. That person or institution who has the vision of tomorrow finds something beyond his reach that allures and inspires to higher and better living. A church that is able to see future possibilities is also challenged. We are required in the A.M.E. Church to see ourselves in the midst of a revolution asking our attention. We cannot afford to divide ourselves at any level. We must continually build upon what we have. Our vision of tomorrow has to be well thought out and methodically carried out.

As we seek the vision of Christ for our local churches and the entire A.M.E. Church, let it not be one of illusion. The New Testament gives us a touchstone by which we may judge all such spiritual insights, and know whether they come from God. The genuine work of the Holy Spirit is to exalt Christ as Lord, not give some new revelation, but to guide us into all truth by taking the things of Christ and showing them to us in His Divine Light. There need not be "no vision," there need not be "no people"—an ineffective church—because we *have* the capacity of foresight—of vision, and necessary action; we have the resources and the manpower to deal with our present condition and the needs of our times.

* * * *

Speaking about the Church

(Charley and Pete)

Pete: Charley, my friend, I'm glad that this day has brought us together.

Charley: You seem to be in a very rare mood today. Am I in for some kind of surprise?

Pete: Surprise Charley? I always thought that you were beyond surprises. I've known you for a long time, but I've never known you to be concerned about surprises. Could it be that you are beginning to have feelings?

Charley: I have known you for a long time also. And in all of that time I cannot truthfully say that I've ever been surprised by you. On the contrary, almost every time that we have met, I have had to listen to some of your faulty ideas about the A.M.E. Church. I don't know what I've done to cause you to have this kind of attitude, but I warn you to be careful.

Pete: That's you Charley! That's always you; the innocent one. You go about sticking people with your pen and always try to keep a straight face.

Charley: Am I to conclude that you have been struck with my pen?

Pete: I called you my friend a while ago, but I hope you understand that I was just being sarcastic. I read that article you wrote the other day. And when I had finished, I wanted to get my hands about your throat. Who do you think you are, some kind of prophet?

Charley: That's who I am indeed: some kind of prophet.

Pete: You are a pompous neophyte—a philosophical babbler; that's what you are. You speak as if you were the epitome of wisdom. What do you know about the moral and spiritual fiber of the Church?

Charley: When one moves about with his ears, and eyes open he sees and hears and he is able to draw certain conclusions.

Pete: You see and hear all right, but what you see is hidden from everybody else.

Charley: Perhaps that makes me some kind of prophet.

Pete: You are an arrogant brat! I've been in this church for years, and it has treated me well. You don't know half of the story.

Charley: I pity you! Your spiritual perception has grown dim. What you are seeing most these days is yourself. That is a sign of death. And that is what our church is doing to so many pastors—killing them.

Pete: Wow, what kind of church do you want?

Charley: You are asking the wrong questions Pete. You must remember that it was Jesus who said: "Upon this rock I will build my church."

Pete: You are very good at quoting scripture.

Charley: You shall know the truth and the truth shall set you free.

Pete: All right! Can't you say something else?

Charley: Something smooth, and pleasing?

Pete: Say what you want to say!

Charley: What I want to say may break your heart.

Pete: If it is the truth, say it. Who can withstand the truth?

Charley: Listen to this parable: A certain man made a visit to a zoo. And as he passed through, he observed the manner in which a keeper was feeding some birds. There were about one hundred birds in all. The keeper was passing the food through a small opening in the cage, so that about four or five birds received all of the food—except for a few crumbs that were scattered as they ate. The feeding lasted for several minutes and when the keeper went away, the ninety-five hungry birds turned on the five full birds and viciously trampled them to death.

AN URGENT CALL FOR ACTION

by Lloyd E. Dees

The Office of Urban Ministries and Ecumenical Relations has been in existence since the General Conference of 1968. But there is a good possibility that many members of the A.M.E. Church have not heard about this new department. One reason for this lack of knowledge is that their 1968 discipline was just recently published, and many members do not as yet possess one. However, it seems to me that, there should have been another channel through which this information could have been given. The possibility is that an informed church will become a better church. In this regard, it might prove beneficial to give some consideration to this new department. We should at least give some thought to what the department is, the reason for its existence, and what it intends to accomplish.

What is it?

> "This office is to constitute the Connectional Agency of the African Methodist Episcopal Church in the area of Social Action and Ecumenical concern." (1968 Discipline, p.p. 648-49).

According to the above definition, the Office of Urban Ministries, and Ecumenical Relations is one of status, and importance. It is connectional in its standing, and is set up to deal with pressing social problems and reconciliation among the churches. Therefore, this Agency has been given a tremendous responsibility.

Why it came into being?

There have been some unwritten remarks, and statements to the effect that this Office came into being by the General Conference to serve as a means to curb the power of one of the bishops of the Church who was perhaps a bit too progressive in his thinking, and in his acting. The degree of credence given to such a statement is of course a matter to be determined by the individual. However, there are times when men will say things "in the dark" that they don't dare say "in the light."

But one should rather think that it was the adverse social conditions which are so prevalent among our people, and the strained relationships that are so widespread among the different religious denominations that gave rise to the idea, and the inception of this important office. One might say that the times in which we live demanded the creation of such an office within the

A.M.E. Church. Or, one might say that the Church has begun to show a greater concern for the world, and the total life of the individual. Perhaps somewhere among these concepts the truth will be found.

What does it intend to accomplish?

The statement of the function, and the aim of the Office of the Urban Ministries and Ecumenical Relations may be found on page 649 of the 1968 Discipline, and it is quoted below:

"Separately, and in cooperation with other agencies it shall promote and conduct Seminars and Institutes for both ministers and laymen. It shall develop curricula, prepare and distribute study material and other information.

The Director shall:

> Promote, in every Urban area the coordinated mobilization of our efforts to attack the characteristic problems of urban society—poverty, unemployment, poor housing, inadequate, ill-conceived education, and social disorganization. He shall seek to use the results of scientific and technological developments; and to cooperate with other agencies, ecclesiastical, governmental and social, which share the objectives of this office, to the end of making more effective the total witness of the Christian Church in meeting the problems of our society.
>
> He shall encourage the churches, individually as well as collectively, to undertake no community service alone, which could be made a joint project with one or more other churches. In this way the Office will seek to implement the will of the African Methodist Episcopal Church to make its contribution to the ecumenical movement of our day, in church union and cooperation."

When one reads the above statement he should be able to see that the Office of Urban Ministries and Ecumenical Relations was designed to have the essential function within the church, and in our society. Its aim is also lofty, and praiseworthy. Poverty and poor housing are two of the evils that are having a devastating effect upon the lives of thousands of people in our society; and anyone who devises a plan to work for the elimination of these deserves words of commendation.

Inadequate education, and unemployment are two other ills that are plaguing the lives of so many people—especially black people. And it is quite appropriate for the church to devise means to deal with these ills. But, for this we cannot praise the church; we can only say amen, because it is realizing its responsibility. When the church addresses itself to these elements in our society which tend towards its disorganization and dissolution, it is fulfilling its reconciling role in the world. Such an undertaking on the part of the church deserves the interest and cooperation of all its members.

The Episcopal salutation of the 1968 Discipline seems to carry the same tone, or embody the same idea as the statement concerning the Office of Urban Ministries and Ecumenical Relations. The following is a quote from that salutation:

> "We address you at a time of unusual political, social, economic, moral, religious and spiritual strain; At a time when the entire world structure seems to be breaking at the seams; and when once more we face the 'hour of Babel', (the confusion of tongues); And the Armageddon of Nations (the catastrophic battle of warring humanity). From this final calamity we must be saved. It is the privilege, duty and challenge of the Church of Jesus Christ to now renew its early vows and engage itself in this higher calling of salvation for our generation."
>
> (1968 A.M.E. Discipline, p.1).

One can hardly deny that this is a worthwhile, and pertinent statement. And the fact that it is an expression of the Bishops of the Church should give it more relevancy, and urgency. When the Bishops of the Church agree and express their agreement in such a statement as the one we have before us, it should be taken with all seriousness, and every effort should be exerted to put their ideas into practice. The Bishops themselves should exert the full power and influence of their office to see to it that their words, and ideas, and the words and ideas of others so similar in meaning to theirs, do not remain enclosed between the covers of the Discipline. The statement of the Bishops, and that of the Office of Urban Ministries and Ecumenical Relations speak of "salvation for our generation." They speak of an essential function, and a purpose worthy to be accomplished.

The Great Tragedy

But the great tragedy is, that during the past eighteen months little or nothing has been done to put these noble ideas into practice. And, whereas we do not accuse the church for a lack of meaningful expression, it has brought judgment upon itself because of its inaction. The ideas contained in the above statements were not meant to rest within the archives and libraries of our Nation, but they were meant to be active in the streets of the cities of our Nation. The beauty of the words contained in the above statements was not meant to be realized by gazing upon them as they lay dormant on the printed page, but it was meant to be seen in the transformation and reconciliation of the lives of men. The beauty of these statements was meant to be seen by the church being so actively engaged in society that it will cause ignorance to give way to knowledge, poor housing to give way to better homes, unemployment to give way to adequate employment, slavery to give way to freedom, injustice to give way to justice, despair to give way to hope, and hate to give way to love. That will indeed be beautiful! And that will truly be "salvation for our generation."

The church has set forth a plan. There is now an urgent call for action. The call is being made by the thousands of drug addicts who roam the streets of our cities; The millions of people who are trapped hopelessly in the rat-infested houses of our nation. The call was coming forth from the ill-educated children in our nation, the oppressed people of our land. The call is urgently coming forth from the pastors and laymen of the A.M.E. Church who are sensitive to the social ills of our nation and our world, who know that the Church has a directive from its Lord to be in the world "where the action is."

The A.M.E. Church needs to be reminded that it has a commission from its Lord to "go into all the world and preach the gospel…" The Church needs to be reminded that the Lord of the church is urgently calling for Labourers. "The harvest indeed is great, but the laborers are few." What shall we do? Shall we continue to procrastinate? Shall we continue to say that we do not have sufficient manpower? Shall we continue to say that we do not have sufficient funds? No! We must not continue our procrastinating; we must begin to act. We have manpower and we have money. What we need is a more judicious appropriation of both of these. And if the understanding of our mission is not as keen as it should be, and if the timidity in our midst is more than is should be, perhaps the following words may be a tremendous help to us:

> "The spirit of the Lord is upon me, because he has anointed me to preach good news to the poor. He has sent me to proclaim release to the captives and recovering of sight to the blind, to set at liberty those who are oppressed, to proclaim the acceptable year of the Lord." (Luke 4:18-19).

The call to the A.M.E. Church is for action. NOW!

EXPRESSIONS

We go to Church, and we go to Church
And we learned the golden rule
But when it comes to politics,
We need to go to school.

Your brothers are calling you,
don't you hear them?
Stop shouting sister! and listen.
Listen to those drug addicts
Down on Fourth Avenue.
Listen to those big shots uptown,
They need you too.

Give me that old time religion;
I just want to wither away
for the Lord.

I went to prayer meeting
the other night,
And I thought God was dead—
Everybody was mourning.

"This is the day of distress, of rebuke,
and of disgrace; children have come to
the birth, and there is, no strength
to bring them forth."
(The prophet, Isaiah)

Before they let a "little child lead them,"
They will put him to death,
And commit suicide themselves.
"The people who walk in darkness,"
are still looking for the
"Great Light."

A NEW THING

(A Sermon) Lloyd E. Dees

Let us be quiet, and listen to what the Bible has to say concerning the New Thing that God is doing in the history of mankind.

> Thus says the Lord who made a way through the
> sea, a path through the mighty waters.
> Remember not the former things, neither consider
> the things of old. Behold, I am doing a New Thing,
> even now it is springing to light. Do you not
> perceive it? A way will I make in the wilderness
> and rivers in the desert! Isaiah 43:16, 18-19

There are two outstanding things that God is asking us to do in this passage: (1) forget, or put behind us the things that should be a part of our past. "Remember not (forget) the former things, neither consider the things of old." (2) God wants us to look, and see, "Behold, (look) I am doing a New Thing, even now it is springing into light. Do you not perceive it?"

The church has tremendous difficulty in putting behind the things of yesterday (the things of old) and seeing the things that are springing forth today (the New Things).

> Let us listen further.
> Thus says the Lord God: I ignore the troubles of
> the past. I shut my eyes to them. For, behold
> I create new heavens and a new earth. The past
> shall be forgotten and never come to mind.
> Men shall rejoice forever in what I now create.
> Isaiah 65:16-17

The call is to break away—do not be enslaved by the past. But there still remain those among us who believe as did the Preacher of so many years ago.

> Vanity of Vanities, says the Preacher,
> Vanity of Vanities: all is Vanity.
> What has been is what shall be;
> What has gone on is what shall go on;
> And there is nothing new under the sun.
> Is there a thing of which it can be said:
> Lo, this is New? It was already in existence
> in the ages which were before us.
>
> Ecclesiastes 1:2, 9-10

The apostle gives this answer:

> Therefore, if anyone is in Christ, he
> is a New Creation. The old has passed away;
> behold, all things have become new.
>
> 11 Corinthians 5:17

Let us now listen to what a prophet of the New Testament has to say:

> Then I saw a new heaven and a new earth; For the
> First heaven and the first earth had passed away.
> And I saw the holy city, the New Jerusalem…
> and I heard a great voice from the throne saying:
> Behold, the dwelling place of God is with men…
> he will wipe away every tear from their eyes and
> death shall be no more, for the former things
> have passed away…Behold, I make all things new.
>
> Revelations 21:1-5

The prophet saw what God wants the Church to see—the NEW.

Finally, let us hear what Jesus says:

> ... No one puts a piece of cloth on an old
> garment, for the patch tears away from the garment,
> and a worse tear is made. Neither is new wine
> put into old wineskins; If it is, the skins
> burst and the wine is spilled, and the skins
> are destroyed; But new wine is put into new wine skins
> and so both are preserved.
>
> Matthew 9:16-17

"Behold, I am doing a new thing—I create new heavens and a new earth. If anyone is in Christ he is a new creation, I saw a new heaven and a new earth...the former things have passed away. New wine is put in new wineskins."

The mighty hammer is striking. And with each stroke the intensity is increasing. It is shattering the OLD; And the echo is; NEW! NEW! NEW!

IN BERMUDA

Consultation on the Black Church and Social Issues to be held at Allen Temple African Methodist Episcopal Church—Somerset, Bermuda—March 1-7, 1970.

Topics will include:

1. The Black Church in the Midst of Political, Economic and Social Change in Bermuda.
2. The A.M.E. Church and the Black Press.
3. The Black Church and Politics.
4. The Black Church and Black Power.
5. Black Youth and Revolution.
6. The Implications of the Cancellation for Further Action.

Outstanding persons from Bermuda and the United States will be participating in the consultation. The opening service will be on Sunday, March 1, 1970, at 4:00 p.m. at the Allen Temple Community Centre. REGISTRATION FREE $3.00 REFRESHMENTS WILL BE SERVED.

THE PROTEST

Please enter my subscription as checked below:

( ) 1 Year $2.00 ( ) 1 Year $2.50 (Foreign)

Name____

Street____

City________ State ____________ Zip Code__________

October – December 1970
THE PROTEST

Editors: Lloyd E. Dees and John Brandon©

Published Quarterly, to stimulate thinking and effect change within the Church and Society.

Subscription rates: In Bermuda, $2.00 per year: Outside Bermuda, $2.50 per year, single copy .65c.

Make check or money order payable to

LLOYD E. DEES

Shelly Bay, Bermuda

John E. Brandon, A.A., B.A., Th.M., Pastor, Vernon Temple A.M.E. Church, Southampton East, Bermuda.

h.p. - Bermuda

CONTENTS

A Contemporary Look at Bermuda and Africa Methodism 3
Pressure Point 6
Expressions 7
Lest We Forget 8

A CONTEMPORARY LOOK AT BERMUDA AND AFRICAN METHODISM

by

JOHN E. BRANDON

Bermuda is a small island not more than twenty-five miles long in the middle of the Atlantic Ocean with a population of over 50,000—65% of which are black. Any visitor to this island would immediately exclaim how beautiful it is only after a short stay.

Bermuda lies in close proximity to the United States and is affected by the U.S. more than Bermudians would care to admit. It possesses the same problems as many other places throughout the U.S. and the world. However, many seem to feel that in Bermuda there is much more of a chance to deal with its problems—mainly because of its size and the fact that many problems pertaining to drugs are not on proportion with many other places, although it is a serious problem. Yet Bermuda is not without its racial crisis equal to any place.

Bermuda is an island that flaunts the idea of being different—different from the West Indies; different from the United States—and this "difference" tends to perpetuate the island syndrome which is detrimental to Bermuda's progress. This is one area in which the African Methodist Episcopal Church plays an important part, because of the church's far-reaching connections in Africa, Canada, the U.S., Caribbean, etc. When we take serious note of the rapid pace of the world day travel and the technological advance, Bermuda must admit with its words and actions that there is simply no more room for "islands" in this world. Although physically separated, Bermuda is economically and politically a "part of the main", and that includes the West Indies, Jamaica, and Africa.

At the time of this writing, government officials are busily preparing for the visit of His Royal Highness, The Prince of Wales. All indications at the moment concerning the royal visit of Prince Charles is that the black reaction is going to be significantly different. Many blacks are raising important questions about the image being perpetuated by such a visit—an image of white dominance. Black consciousness, black awareness and self-identity are no doubt contributors to this change in attitude since the last royal visit. This kind of attitude is not viewed as being negative but is seen by many to be positive in its ramifications.

In the statement issued by the Opposition Progressive Labour Party (P.L.P.) an idea of the attitude of many blacks is expressed. The statement in part reads:

> The P.L.P. wishes to make it clear that its decision (not to attend any of the functions at which His Royal Highness, the Prince of Wales will be present) is not taken out of any personal disrespect for His Royal Highness, the Prince of Wales, who undoubtedly is a very charming and sporting young man, but who, in our view is the supreme embodiment of British Colonialism and Imperialism. (October 15, 1970)

The African Methodist Episcopal Church might disagree on political statements, but it must deal with the atmosphere and mood which undoubtedly made such a statement possible—mainly, the concern of a segment of the community about important issues. The A.M.E. Church is the largest institution in Bermuda that is owned, operated, and supported by black people. Yet it finds itself caught up in red-tape procedure and to a great extent in the cajolery of the white power structure. Of course, it is naive to assume that it would not be in some measure a protector of the system. It is no wonder that young blacks are attacking and opposing so-called Christian beliefs. Many "Christians" tremble with fright in the face of anyone calling into question their understanding of what Christianity is all about. "Many years of indoctrination and the misuse of the Christian Religion has resulted in a gross misconception of that Religion on the part of many black people." (Lloyd E. Dees, *The Protest* Magazine, April-June Issue, 1970)

The A.M.E. Church can play a more important role in the life of the community in Bermuda and indeed the world, but, at the moment, the church is not as effective as it ought to be. This is not true only because of the traditional ideas of committees and meetings, but because some have failed to see that God is constantly making all things new. God can even work with committees, although committees in the A.M.E. Church, most of the time seem to be unduly monotonous and a waste of energy. We at times need committees and the A.M.E. Church is not exempt from these necessities. However, the actual form and habits of these committees need constant scrutiny in light of the essential purpose of the Church, lest by curious self-perpetuating habit of all human organizations, committees become our masters—or even prisons—rather than operative, functioning, and viable forces.

There does exist a social action committee in the Bermuda Annual Conference, which is set up to function throughout the year, but it is bound by bureaucratic procedure, causing it to be ineffective at crucial times. What are we up against in the Church? Are we intellectually, spiritually and morally bankrupt? It would seem so. The vitality of the A.M.E. Church must not be sapped by continuous alienation of young radicals and questioning minds who frequently look to the A.M.E. Church Bermuda for creative thinking.

We cannot continue to live on the progress and creative thinking of our forefathers—Bermuda and indeed the world seek our leadership. The inability to act when it really counts is an intentional reflection of a problem that permeates the whole of African Methodism.

Could it be that we in Bermuda experience a situation somewhat different from that of African Methodists Stateside? We might explore this situation for a moment. Would we be more effective in Bermuda if our Bishop resided here? How would this enhance the stature of African Methodism in Bermuda? Would the Bishop over a short period of time lose his effectiveness by being in the forefront of issues in the community? These are questions we cannot adequately answer at present, but we can conjecture that since we have no resident Bishop, more frequent and longer visits might be in order.

Yet again, this line of thinking raises more questions. Why should the Bishop have to live in Bermuda when he has presiding elders who are official representatives of the church and who should be capable of speaking out on issues affecting the community?

That we are in the midst of social change there is no doubt. And it must be understood that the church is a responding community, a people whose task it is to discern the action of God in the world and to join in his work. This action of God occurs throughout what theologians had sometimes called "historical events" but might better be termed "social change." This means that the Church must respond constantly to social change (Harvey Cox, *The Secular City*, 1965). And in order to respond effectively, the African Methodist Episcopal Church in Bermuda or the Church anywhere must be free from the power structure.

As we look at the future of the A.M.E. Church Bermuda, we might take a moment to examine what we are able to know about the future of the church.

Many people romanticise and indulged themselves in unrealistic dreams of the new heaven and the new earth where justice and equality will reign, but we must be the instruments to bring about that justice and equality on earth with God working through us. It has been established by many before me that if one can give a knowledge of the great historical events, he has a means to clues to the farseeing intellect.

The first business of consideration is the demand of the Gospel and then its application to circumstances of our own lives and to the needs of the times. The future of the African Methodist Episcopal Church in Bermuda greatly depends upon the ability of its membership to see themselves less confined to the service of the altar and to look upon the ministrations of worship, for which we all have responsibility as a service of faith, not as mere service to a "religion." Religion is a separate order of activities; faith transforms every activity and calls nothing profane except that sin profanes by removing it from the offerings of all things to God. (Yves Congar, *Ecumenism and the Future of the Church*, 1967). The future of the A.M.E. Church in Bermuda as in other parts of the world will greatly depend upon its ability to assume the shape of its servant Lord. Therefore, African Methodism like Bermuda cannot separate itself from the fact that it must be involved—as God so loved the world that he gave...

* * * *

PRESSURE POINT

The minister's wife: Person or position?

Is the minister's wife given the opportunity to be herself (a person) or just assume a position designed by the minister and/or the congregation?

Presiding Elders

For your next quarterly conference, why not put all of your reports, along with the elders assessment, into an envelope—mail them to him and save him a trip!

THINK ABOUT IT!
EXPRESSIONS

by Lloyd E. Dees

MOMENTUM

Strive! Black folk Strive!
Who knows what lies beyond this dark night?
Keep awake Black folk, and you'll survive.
Freedom is coming, but after the fight.
Strive! Black folks Strive!
We have come too far to give up now.
We must not faint we must stay alive.
If we want to see what we are fighting for.
Strive! Black folks Strive!
This is not the end of the day.
We have a goal to realize
And no one must take it away.

Searching

When you speak to me
I hear turbulence in your voice,
your threat screeches with contempt.
When I look into your eyes I see hate
hot hate striving to leap out like
a hungry flame to devour my BLACK FACE.

A Saying

There is a saying:
They don't know what they want,
and have no idea where they are going.
NEGATIVE—I SAY.

For My People

I stay awake at night thinking—
        thinking for my people.
All through the day and night
I am hoping and longing—for my people.
When I am overwhelmed
        and my tears begin to flow,
        they are tears for my people.
        When my tears cease and smiles appear,
        they are smiles for my people.
I do not always smile
        sometimes I get angry—
        but that too is for my people
My prayers, sermons and my songs are for my people

I go without food, frequent the legislative halls,
I protest the high cost of living, and I am
MISUNDERSTOOD—for my people.
I get very lonely sometimes—for my people.
It is for my people that I live
And someday I will die—for my people.

LEST WE FORGET

by Lloyd E. Dees

The black man's struggle for freedom and fulfillment in America has been a long and difficult one. And the intensity of that struggle has fluctuated from "hot to cold", from "strong to weak", and vice versa. When we consider the years from 1954 to the present, we are able to observe certain events and personalities that were stimulants in this difficult struggle. The Supreme Court decision of 1954 concerning segregation in the public schools was undoubtedly the most outstanding stimulant of that year. The rendering of that decision may be likened unto a shining light for a lost man groping in the darkness of midnight. But the glow of the light soon faded. The deliberate speed with which the Court's decision was to be executed proved to be too "deliberate." The hands that were light as they clapped for joy became heavy and sagged from sorrow. The faith that was revived with the ability of the nation to do right gave way to doubt and skepticism—even frustration and despair. It had to be frustration to a people who had been mistreated, and punished by an unjust law when they discovered that the ruling of the highest court in the land was being ignored—and that without punishment.

Although the Supreme Court's decision of 1954 encountered difficulty in its execution, it nevertheless gave a great degree of stability to the civil rights movement. "Separate but equal" would no longer be a part of the Constitution of the United States. This indeed was the crossing of a tremendously high hurdle. And it served as a basis for forward movement. But the slow execution of the Supreme Court's decision caused the civil rights movement to lose much of its momentum. "Usually, the Supreme Court's decision in Brown v. Board of Education is thought of in connection with the beginning of the current Civil Rights Movement. But the decision itself did not hurtle Negroes into the dramatic action to secure equal education, nor was it a command to Southern school officials to end segregation immediately." (Joanne Grant, *BLACK PROTEST*, p. 252) Immediate action was what the Negroes wanted, but the Court's ruling indicated that they might get action by and by. The Court's decision was an impetus in the beginning, but later it proved to be an impediment.

In 1955 in Montgomery, Alabama a Negro woman had grown very tired "after spending a full day working on clothes that white people wear." She boarded a bus that white people owned and placed her tired body in the first empty seat that she could find. As it happened, the seat in which she sat was too close to the white section of the bus. When a white person entered the bus, this black woman was told by the bus driver to get up and give the white person her seat. This was nothing new for Mrs. Rosa Parks. She had heard the rough voices of white bus drivers many times ordering Black people to "move back" so white people could take their seats. She was used to giving white people her seat—even white men. But on this particular day Mrs. Rosa Parks was tired. The tiredness of so many years of "working all day on the clothes that white people wear," and of so many years of standing on the buses that white people owned had overwhelmed her. She was physically tired. She was mentally tired. She was spiritually tired. She was too tired to obey the white man any longer. She kept her seat.

The refusal of Mrs. Parks to give a white person her seat, and her consequent arrest served as a rallying cry for thousands of Negroes in Montgomery. It might not be stretching the point to say that Mrs. Parks epitomized the tiredness of all the Black people in the South. She was a decisive impetus in the civil rights movement. What happened in Montgomery was known throughout the world, and literally millions of people—black and white—became sympathetic to the Black man's struggle for freedom and fulfillment. And some people would say that out of the Rosa Parks and Montgomery situation emerged the greatest exponent of civil rights and human freedom that the nation had ever known—Martin Luther King, Jr. It is significant to note that the Black people in Montgomery were too tired to stand on the buses, but they mustered enough strength to walk until they could sit on the buses and rest. Montgomery, and all that happened there notwithstanding, was summed up by Martin Luther King, Jr. as only "A stride Toward Freedom." But it was a good stride.

In 1957 in Little Rock, Arkansas a little Black girl wanted to get a better education. She tried to enter all-white Central High School. This was about three years after the Supreme Court's decision of 1954. "She walked alone" between an angry crowd of screaming whites, and a contingent of national guardsmen—with fixed bayonets. She was courageous. But she went away in fear and dejection. She was deeply hurt because she was so young—and she believed. She believed in her nation. But her nation failed her. She was small. But her nation was not big enough to fully support her. She had hopes. But her hopes were crushed in and by her nation. Poor little Black girl! Black people saw and read about what happened in Little Rock. The courage and dejection of Elizabeth Eckford gave new courage and determination to Black people throughout the nation. They saw the need to keep striving. They saw the need to strive harder and harder. They saw the need of striving together. There were many Black people who were shaken by Little Rock, but at the same time were steadied by the courage and the indomitable spirit of Elizabeth Eckford.

In 1960 in North Carolina three young black girls sat at a lunch counter in a Woolworth store. They vowed not to move. Black people had spent a lot of money in that store. They had spent a lot of money STANDING in that store. They had watched White people sit in that store and eat, and talk, and relax. These young Black girls had stood in that store and bought sodas and sandwiches which they had to take out into the streets to eat and drink. But they had seen young White girls buy sodas and sandwiches which they could drink and eat sitting at the lunch counter. There was a tremendous difference in standing and eating and sitting and eating—a tremendous difference. Young Black people throughout the South were keenly aware of that difference. They had been aware of that difference for a long time—even though they were young. When one had to live from birth to college age before he is able to sit at a lunch counter to drink a soda and eat a sandwich—that is a long time.

What made those young people sit at their counter? Were they tired? Were they hungry? Were they seeking attention? Perhaps all of these and more. But there is no doubt that they wanted a better society in which to live. They wanted freedom. Freedom to sit or freedom to stand. Freedom to say yes and freedom to say no. Freedom to go where they wanted to go. And underlying all of this, there seemed to be a sincere desire to bring about "righteousness in the land." These young people were very convincing in their effort. And whereas Black people had been very fond of saying "we will stand by you", they could now say—with a deep sense of meaning: "we will sit by you."

The sit-ins of 1960 gave birth to the Student Nonviolent Coordinating Committee which was for several years of formidable force in the civil rights movement. The following is the statement of purpose of that newly formed organization:

> "We affirm the philosophical or religious ideal of nonviolence as the foundation of our purpose, the presupposition of our faith, the manner of our action. Nonviolence as it grows from Judaic-Christian traditions seeks a social order of justice permeated by law. Integration of human endeavor represents the crucial step towards such a society.
>
> Through nonviolence, courage displaces fear; love transforms hate. Acceptance dissipates prejudice: hope ends despair. Peace dominates war: faith reconciles doubt. Mutual regard cancels

> enmity. Justice for all overflows injustice. The redemptive community supersedes systems of gross social immorality.
>
> Love is the central motif of nonviolence. Love is the force by which God binds men to himself and man to man. Such love goes to the extreme; It remains loving and forgiving even in the midst of hostility. It matches the capacity of evil to inflict suffering with an even more endearing capacity to absorb evil, all the while persisting in love.
>
> By appealing to conscience and standing on the moral nature of human existence, nonviolence nurtures the atmosphere in which reconciliation and justice become actual possibilities."

It is quite obvious that this statement is permeated with the doctrine of Martin Luther King, Jr. Therefore, the Student Nonviolent Coordinating Committee and the Southern Christian Leadership Conference began to walk the road to freedom together. This enlarged the movement and provided a more active role for the young people. All of which gave a tremendous impetus to the civil rights movement at that particular time.

In 1963 "they marched on Washington." They came by the thousands. They came—Black and white—from all over the nation. Those who could not come watched "them" go. They came by train, car, bus and plane. Old stalwarts were there; Neophytes were there. Seventy-five year old Asa Philip Randolph—who some twenty odd years before had proposed a "March on Washington"—was in the forefront of the march. By the means of television, the whole nation watched them as they went hand in hand marching for jobs, and things; And FREEDOM. Old people, young people, and little children heard them sing in one BIG voice;—"we shall overcome," "we shall all be free." They heard John Lewis of the Student Nonviolence Coordinating Committee say: "The revolution is at hand, and we must free ourselves of the chains of political and economical slavery." But most of all they heard the Reverend Martin Luther King, Jr. thunder forth his most famous speech: "I have a dream." His voice was loud and clear. His emotion was deep and profound. Everyone who heard him could tell that he was serious. Many weeks and even months after that notable day in August "Washington" was very evident in the lives of many Americans—especially Black Americans. They were indeed sharers of the same dream. One could walk the streets of large cities and hear young Black people singing, "we shall overcome." One could pass the playgrounds of the small towns and the yards of the rural South and hear little Black girls and boys of the nation saying, "I got a dream." One could visit a Black Church in any part of the nation and hear young and old singing together; "we shall overcome—deep in my heart I do believe—we shall overcome some day." The March was tremendous. It was moving! It gave Black people new hope. The spirit of the March was catching; It revived the dreams of Black people throughout the nation. But:

> What happens to a dream deferred?
> Does it dry up like a raisin in the sun?
> Or fester like a sore—
> And then run?
> Does it stink like rotten meat
> Or crust and sugar over—
> Like a syrupy sweet?
> Maybe it sags like a heavy load.
> Or does it explode? (Langston Hughes)

In 1966, a young Black man, more than a thousand miles away from home got an idea. He would walk from Memphis, Tennessee to Jackson, Mississippi. James Meredith, who entered the University of Mississippi by force of federal troops was now a law student at Columbia University. Meredith said that his undertaking would dramatize that all pervasive and overriding fear that dominates the day-by-day life of the Negro in the United States, especially in the South and particularly in Mississippi. It was now almost four years since Meredith had his confrontation at the University of Mississippi. But he was still bound by the chains of fear. Mississippi was his home, and Meredith had been afraid all his life. He said that one purpose of his march was to "get rid of this fear."

It was a beautiful Sunday afternoon in June when Meredith and a few of his friends left Memphis. Jackson was about two hundred hot miles away. It happened on highway 51. It happened in Mississippi. It was a Monday—the very next day. Meredith was BLASTED with a shotgun by a white man who crawled out of the bushes. The whole nation was told that Meredith was dead—but he was not. The dream of which King spoke, and of which Black people sang in 1963 was frustrated in less than three years. The emotion that gripped the hearts of Black people was one of anger—deep anger exuding in spurts.

Black people—and some whites—converged on Memphis from throughout the nation. Martin Luther King, Jr. came. Whitney Young, Roy Wilkins, and Floyd McKissick came. And there was Stokely Carmichael—fuming. These and others organized the Meredith March and walked into Jackson. That which began as a one man's march was now a mass demonstration of angry Black people. It was there in Jackson—in the Deep South—that the cry of Black Power was raised. Perhaps it was there in Jackson that the "dream deferred" EXPLODED—at least for a number of Black people. To many people, Black Power was startling and frightening. And criticisms were raised immediately by Black and White. Bayard Rustin stated that "black power" not only lacks any real value for the civil rights movement, but its propagation is positively harmful. It diverts the movement from a meaningful debate over strategy and ethics, it isolates the Negro community and it encourages the growth of anti-Negro forces. Senator Edward Brooke stated: "That slogan Black Power has struck fear in the heart of Black America as well as in the heart of white America… The Negro has to gain allies—not adversaries." Vice President Humphrey stated: "There is no room in America for calls for racism, whether they come from a throat that is white or one that is black." Martin Luther King, Jr. said: "It is absolutely necessary for the Negro to gain power, but the term Black Power is unfortunate because it tends to give the impression of Black nationalism." President Lyndon Johnson stated: "We are not interested in black and we are not interested in white power, but we are interested in American democratic power with a small d." The language of Roy Wilkins was very strong. In his denunciation he used such words as "separatism", "wicked fanaticism", and "black death."

But there were authors who were more kindly disposed toward Black Power. James Farmer was in accord with the emphasis that was given to Negro "dignity" and "self-esteem", but he wished "the term Black Power had not been devised." Representative Adam Powell hailed Black Power with enthusiasm. But he was not in accord with such ends as black supremacy, and black nationalism. He denounced the manner in which Black Power was expressed by Stokely Carmichael. But he went on to claim Black Power as a working philosophy for a new breed of cats—tough, proud young Negroes who categorically refused to compromise or negotiate any longer for their rights, who reject the old-line established white financed, white controlled, whitewashed Negro leadership. Powell also said that the phrase Black Power meant only a "dynamic process of continuous change toward a society of true equals." For him Black Power has positive connotations. It indicates a radical shift of emphasis from being helped to helping one's self.

It may be said that Black power is an affirmation of positive potentials, and a yearning desire "to be" and fulfill that "being." It is a cry for "blackness" to exude and give coloration to the encompassing and suppressing "whiteness" of American society. It is a cry to be "me" according to a formula that is derived from the hearts and souls of Black people and not according to a formulae that is prescriptive by White people. It is a recognition that so many white formulae have led to non-fulfillment. With Black Power as a working philosophy, the emphasis is more on "I." The philosophy of coalition in the civil rights struggle emphasized the "we"; we shall overcome—black and white together. When the term "we" is used by Black Power advocates, it has reference to Black people getting together. Blacks have been a dependent people for a long time—far too long a time. They have been degraded and indoctrinated with lies about themselves, and with lies about white people. They have had to remain silent and suppress their emotions—contrary to what many whites may believe. They have been given their "place" but they are never quite sure of its exact boundary. They are told that if they are to succeed in this nation, they must work and educate themselves. But jobs are withheld from them and education is second rate—it's a vicious circle. They are required to adhere to rigid standards which they had no part in setting. White people are driving Black people in this country to "black rage." And they have the audacity to ask: why?

I think that Black Power has added a healthy dimension to the civil rights struggle. Black people are now becoming able to embrace their blackness in a positive and proud manner. Young people are beginning to put the emphasis on what "I" can do rather than on what others can do for "me." Black Power is causing Black people to be "born again." It is my contention that the philosophy of coalition did not possess this kind of "regenerative" spirit. There is something mystical about Black Power which Black people call SOUL. This mystical element enables Black Power to transcend American society and touch Black people throughout the world. It is drawing all black people into a universal struggle for freedom and fulfillment. This SOUL is like "fire shut up in the bones" of young Black men and women. It will move them onward, and a LONGER STRIDE TOWARD FREEDOM will be achieved.

March 1971

THE PROTEST

Editors: John E. Brandon and Lloyd E. Dees©

Published Quarterly, to stimulate thinking and affect change within the Church and Society.

Subscription Rates: in Bermuda, $2.00 per year; Outside Bermuda, $2.50 per year; single copy, .65c

Make Check or Money Order

Payable to:

LLOYD E. DEES
A&T State University
Greensboro, North Carolina

©John E. Brandon A.A., B.A., Th.M., Vernon Temple African Methodist Episcopal Church, Southampton East, Bermuda.

Lloyd E. Dees, B.A, B.D., Director, United Christian Ministry, A&T State University, Greensboro, North Carolina.

CONTENTS

1. Editorial Comments 1
2. A History of Bermuda 3
3. An Artist Look at Bermuda 7
4. Interesting Bits of History 10

(a) An Account of an Interesting Meeting

(b) An Interesting Letter

(c) A Former A.M.E. Church

5. An Interview 13

THE PROTEST

EDITORIAL COMMENTS

THE LATE BISHOP GEORGE WILBUR BABER—1898-1970

This magazine extends warmest sympathy and understanding to the family of the Late Bishop George Wilbur Baber, consecrated a Bishop in the African Methodist Episcopal Church in the year of our Lord, 1956-64. Bishop Baber has served the church well. May his soul rest in peace. He headed the first Episcopal district from 1956-64 which includes BERMUSA. The Second District, Bermuda, and the entire church will miss him.

BERMUDA ASSIGNMENTS

The situation of pastoral assignments to the Bermuda Annual Conference in the African Methodist Episcopal Church is one that needs immediate attention.

In light of stigmas attached to pastors who serve or have served in Bermuda and the sometimes unfortunate occurrences which take place between the American pastor and the congregation, it is time that the present procedure of assignments be examined and rectified. Now, it is understood that any problems which take place between the Bermuda congregation and the "foreign" A.M.E. pastor can possibly occur in the United States also. However, Bermuda, being a colony with British connections and isolated from any mainland territory, carries its own set of problems for the American pastor and his family, particularly, if one is not prepared to make certain sacrifices.

A pastor should not be assigned to Bermuda simply because there is an opening or because Bermuda is for "upstarts" only. Maybe this is not the case, but this whole matter should be carefully studied. Past experiences have demanded better reasons for assignments than the foregoing. Prospective pastors for the Bermuda Conference and the expectant congregation in Bermuda ought to have the opportunity to know before the official assignments are made what each other's expectations and needs are.

This is a matter which any of our bishops (who serve districts which extend outside the U.S.A. but are connected officially with the mainland) must eventually deal with more seriously. Everyone concerned will be much "happier" for it.

BERMUDA ANNUAL CONFERENCE—TWO DISTRICTS

Many A.M.E.'s in the Bermuda Annual Conference are becoming increasingly concerned about having two districts in such a small area the size of Bermuda. The cry is that there is "too much needless conflict in the programs among our churches." "Things are not as 'together' as they use to be," some say. "When we had one district, we all supported each other," the talk goes on.

The concern for one district is sure to come up in the next Annual Conference in April. If one district comes about this year, many A.M.E.'s in Bermuda will be forced to discover whether or not their ideas of "togetherness" and "supporting each other" are only sentimental reminiscences (which cannot be recovered as they are remembered) or whether two districts really hinder maximum participation on the part of the A.M.E.

It will come to light if two districts present THE PROBLEMS or if failure to support each other penetrates much deeper.

A HISTORY OF BERMUDA?

By

John E. Brandon

Who is writing Bermuda's history? Over a year ago while the writer of this article was pastoring in Somerset, Bermuda, his Woman's Day speaker from the United States reminded all who listened of Bermuda's lack of a written history, especially of the black man. She stated that upon receiving an invitation to come to Bermuda, she immediately began to search for Bermuda's history. She wanted to know who were Bermudians, the history of its people—she wanted to get an historical perspective. She wanted to know where she was going. She was also sadly disappointed.

Most of what is written about Bermudians is contained in brochures, books, and pamphlets for tourists which portray Bermuda as a luxurious vacation island having a white population majority. There are few if any meaningful writings of the black man's struggle in a British colony.

Just as the Woman's Day speaker wanted to know where she was going, a history of Bermuda, in a larger context is necessary for the people of Bermuda, especially black people, to properly begin to chart a course for the future. Many persons in Bermuda would and do discourage in words and action any endeavor of blacks to recover a true history of themselves. Some fail to realize the importance of a historical perspective. If you don't know from whence you have come, you will certainly have difficulty in going in the right direction.

The most recent history of the black man and his achievements in Bermuda are recorded in a book by Miss Eva N. Hodgson entitled: *Second Class Citizens, First Class Men*. This writing only covers a period of 10 years 1953-1963. However, it should serve to inspire a more comprehensive study. Miss Hodgson, I believe, has voiced the general attitude of Bermudians when it comes to setting history in its proper perspective. She says in the Foreword: "Colored…friends…cautioned me…although, in their opinion, all that I had written was accurate, they pointed out that John the Baptist spoke the truth and lost his head." They were concerned for my "welfare." This kind of fear of deadly reprisals still holds captive Bermuda's progress in many areas—real or imagined, it exists. In this writing, the writer is mainly concerned about black history, because the white man's history has already been written. Black history will put it more clearly.

One can take bits and pieces of history of Bermuda which is in no way adequate. Take for example, what does Cup Match mean from the black man's point of view: *Second Class Citizens, First Class Men*, the author gives us a hint:

> Cup match is a day when the Negro protested against their bondage by throwing off all care for two days. The Cup Match was the only truly spontaneous holiday for the people of Bermuda. It was then, as now, the one and only true symbol and celebration of the black man's Emancipation. Those two days of cricket, held on Emancipation Day, and springing originally from the picnics of the Friendly Societies remain, today, an event…in the lives of the Bermudian Negroes.

However, the author goes on to express concern that Bermudians would even lose that small bit of history, in practice, on the Cup Match. The author states:

> Perhaps soon he will lose even that. In the first flush of his moment of success which seems to have met this new thrust forward, after a decade of collective, if sporadic, protests, he may come to believe that his past, unlike the past of others, is irrelevant to either its present or his future. And that continuation of Cup Match is, in some strange way, a form of unnecessary protest. Now that he is

> being permitted, slowly with hesitation, and with no little reluctance and compromise, to share in other local events he may well be persuaded that Cup Match, which was his from inception and which he created, is no longer of significance. Now he can participate in the Floral Pageant. Now Negroes are no longer marshalled along the sides of the street like children sat in a row to watch a meaningless pageantry. Now, perhaps, he will care for only those bits and pieces of Bermuda which, for so long, have been denied him. And if that should be so, then the Colored man in Bermuda will be doomed, in the future, to an even greater curse than in the past. He will not only have lost what the centuries of slavery have snatched from him, but deliberately, and shamelessly, he will have turned his back also on those dark silent days of torment which have molded both him and his present (pp. 38-39).

Will the black church's history in Bermuda be lost too? The African Methodist Episcopal Church has played an important role in the life of black Bermudians as Miss Hudson recounts in her book:

> The African Methodist Episcopal Church in Bermuda, a branch of the American church begun by a Negro who was turned away from the white American church, has been as much a symbol of protest in Bermuda as it has been in America. It was for many years, the only place, other than the Friendly Societies, where a Bermudian Negro was, even if only temporarily shielded from the insults and insinuations of the white segregationists...It is small wonder that John William Cann felt that the advent of African Methodist Episcopal Church brought with it "light and liberty" which gave to the ranks of the masses a spirit of independence... The very existence of the A.M.E. Church in Bermuda has belied the white man's illusion that, until the middle of the 20th century, Negroes in Bermuda were content, and there was peace. There was stillness, but there has been no peace at the heart of the Negro.

It is feared that the black church, especially the A.M.E. Church has lost some of that vigor of its founding fathers. This fear is expressed by the Black Beret Cadre (a group of young black people organized to educate blacks) who said in their position paper:

> The black Church of today has set itself apart from the many problems that afflict the Black Community. At this time, it is of very crucial importance that the church moved to correct this situation: a time when the masses of black people are demanding change—revolutionary change. Slave Christianity concerned itself with the individual and deliberately emphasized the "other world" so that black people would not be concerned about the everyday problems of this world. Black Christians must be made to realize that Jesus did not build a church but a movement…

Many people recall, (as one can often hear) with delight the name Dr. Edgar Fitzgerald Gordon. His story along with many others is a part of Bermuda's rich history. There is a sense of accomplishment and pride when his name is spoken. In a newspaper article (*The Daily Star,* Toronto, March 16, 1946) it stated that:

> Dr. Edgar Fitzgerald Gordon, 50-year old son of a colored Trinidad land proprietor and livery stable owner and a Portuguese woman, who came to Bermuda in 1924 to practice medicine, took his newly won seat in the 300-year-old House of Assembly on March 8, amid a cold silence. Twice before, in the 1933 and 1943 general elections, he had been balked in reaching his goal; On the first occasion by a court action and next by a friend's fickleness. For almost a year, as president of the Bermuda Workers Association, Dr. Gordon has lashed the House of Labor meetings throughout the island. With white Bermudians secretly suspicious of his West Indian origin, Dr. Gordon gradually grew more and more workers on his side in a country where trade unionism is illegal.
>
> Dr. Gordon put forth the following five point plan: 1. an extension of the franchise to the extent of making it universal, 2. introduction of an income tax to relieve the burden put upon poor

> people by customs duties, 3. removal of intimidation "which at present makes representation here a pointless mess" 4. opening of the civil service to qualified colored people who now can aspire to an office no higher than that of postman, and 5. trade unionism and a better relationship between employee and employer.
>
> If he fails to get his way in the House, he said, as soon as the membership of the Workers Association reaches the 7,000 mark, he will bring a petition from the association to England requesting the appointment of a royal commission to investigate conditions in Bermuda and the Bahamas.

No nation of people ever began and never will begin from a kind of tabularasa or empty life empty state. All of the events which have gone before should serve to guide the future. These events will have to be put down in some uniform manner. One can speculate that no adequate Black Studies program in Bermuda can be what it ought to be without a more complete history of its people. With just a sample, it does not take a tremendous stretch of the mind to gather that Bermuda's blacks have a rich historical background. It is not enough for Bermuda to always refer to the United States and Europe, although in order to have a complete historical background, all must be considered. Bermuda must find its own true identity in the midst of the trappings of a tourist economy. It is by coincidence that at the writing of this article, concern is at the same time expressed in a search for local art forms. Art can play a very important role in preserving Bermuda's history once the time is taken to develop it and make it more expressive of the Bermuda scene. Black artists on the island will have to organize themselves to assure that a true picture of the black man in Bermuda his portrayed.

The Bermuda Recorder (January 9, 1971) states in the editorial that:

> For many years entertainers and educators alike have been stressing the unhappy fact that there is no real art form which could be claimed as peculiarly Bermudian. Evidence of this can be seen in the search each year by the Pageant Committee for an outfit that could typify Bermuda at the Miss Universe competition during the segment requiring the girls to wear native attire. The best we have been able to offer is the military aspect.

It is too easy to become lost in the crowd. A nation, a colony, an individual must seek and find its own unique identity if each is to survive very long as such and make a positive contribution. It is all right to say "let us live together and love one another." But each individual, nation, or colony, whatever the case may be, is unique. It seems that the thing to do is to find ways to make differences complement each other and allow for the uniqueness.

Bermuda's history is rich, the African Methodist Episcopal Church's history in Bermuda is also rich. So, there is a history within history, yet there is only one history. May this history not be lost in practice or in written word so that generations to come will be able to chart their course well. May the artists do their part and the historians do theirs.

AN ARTIST LOOKS AT BERMUDA

Charles Lloyd Tucker is a native Bermudian, and he knows his homeland well. There are few people in Bermuda whom he does not know, or who do not know him. Much of his knowledge about Bermuda and its people has been passed on to him by his mother, who is now 91 years old.

Mr. Tucker has his own studio (Morrox) in Shelly Bay and he also teaches art at the Berkeley Institute. He is quite popular with the students at his school. He admits that the African Methodist Episcopal Church has had a tremendous influence on his life. Since his childhood he has been a member of Bethel A.M.E. Church in Shelly Bay.

Here, Mr. Tucker discusses some of his paintings with his pastor, Rev. Lloyd E. Dees. This picture was taken at an exhibition of his work at the Hamilton City Hall. The colorful scenes are quite prominent. The physical beauty of Bermuda is difficult to surpass. But what lies beneath this beauty?

Mr. Tucker admires one of his latest paintings, *I Have a Dream*. He says that: "It symbolizes the black youth of Bermuda who are longing to be "somebody" but somehow are being frustrated in the process. It is also the artist's dream of fulfillment for all the youth of Bermuda.

Here, Mr. Tucker discusses one of his latest paintings with Rev. Dees. This one is entitled: *"Let my People Go."* It is the artist's cry of freedom for his people: *A Moses for Bermuda*.

A footnote to the above:

Charles Lloyd Tucker died suddenly of a heart attack on Monday, January 11, 1971, after the above material had been prepared. It was decided to print the material as it was prepared. The editors are indebted to Mr. Tucker for the design on the cover of *The Protest*.

A FORMER A.M.E. CHURCH

The building shown is a former African Methodist Episcopal Church in Tucker's Town, Bermuda. The story behind the sale of this building and property is a long one, but yet a familiar one. Tucker's Town in Bermuda is what might be termed a white and wealthy part of the island. Many black people used to live in that area as evidenced by the presence of the A.M.E. Church. However, when the government of Bermuda decided that Tuckers Town should be set aside as an exclusively white domain, the A.M.E. Church there was "bought" by the government and is now used as a dormitory to house the "servants" of the wealthy persons who bought the property from the government.

This Church has been relocated at Harrington's Sound, Smith's Parish, Bermuda. It is the St. Phillip African Methodist Episcopal Church.

INTERESTING BITS OF HISTORY

An account of an interesting meeting

(The Berkeley Educational Society)

(Twelfth Annual Meeting)

The Twelfth General Meeting of the Berkeley Educational Society was held in the Town Hall, Hamilton, on the evening of the 25th, July. The chairman, Mr. S.D. Robinson, presided. The meeting was opened with a prayer by the Rev. Mark James. In the routine of business, the Secretary read the Report which is as follows:

In placing before the public the twelfth report of the above named Society, the Committee feel grateful to Almighty God for the continued progress that has attended the affairs of the Society. Although the results of their efforts on the whole have been comparatively small (considering the great importance of the object in view) nevertheless the Committee are encouraged to persevere in the good work. The total amount standing to the credit of the Society is 367 pounds. 0.3. Of this sum 351 pounds 12.5. are invested in mortgages on real estate and bearing interest after the rate of 7 percent per annum. The balance in hand will be invested as soon as a favorable opportunity offers.

The object of the Society which is to invest money for the purpose of establishing a school or schools for the higher education of the people, (a much felt need in these islands) is generally known. If many who now stand aloof would become members of the Society, the object would be soon attained. The Committee do not hesitate to say that if the same spirit which actuated the people at the outset had been continued, today the Society would be doing effective work; facts and figures bear them out in the assertion.

It is earnestly to be hoped, however, that the people will be aroused from their seeming lethargic state and exhibit of more liberal and patriotic spirit. As the people require an education in keeping with other things in Bermuda which unmistakably denote progress the Committee feel not to be discouraged or to relax their exertions toward the accomplishments of the scheme in hand, and trust that the Divine blessing will rest upon their future endeavors.

The subjoined resolutions were submitted, and duly adopted:

1. That the Report be read as adopted.
2. That as we are living in an age remarkable for its intellectual advancement—it behooves the people to be better educated, that they may credibly discharge the duties that will devolve upon them.
3. That since there does not exist in this Colony a high school—accessible to the people, the public would manifest their deep interest in the country's welfare by aiding, with their money and sympathy, to establish such an institution.
4. That the meeting pledges itself to put forth a more united and determined effort to establish a school under the auspices of the Berkeley Educational Society, so as to meet the present and growing demands of the people—and thus merit their cooperation.

The following were elected officers of the Society for the ensuing year:

Chairman, Mr. S.D. Robinson
Vice Chairman, Mr. John Barrett
Treasurer, Mr. H.T. Dyer
Secretary, Mr. S. Parker, Jr.

Hamilton, July, 1892
Closed with the Benediction
Samuel Parker, Jr.
Secretary, B.E. Society

Taken from: *The Bermuda Colonist Newspaper*, 1892

AN INTERESTING LETTER

To the editor, Bermuda Colonist:

Sir: "In your last issue you refer to the proposed Collegiate Institute for which the Rev. J.A. Johnson left Bermuda to raise funds. Will you allow me space to express my hearty concurrence with its object, and at the same time suggest a change in the Constitution of the governing body in the proposed scheme. Two days before sailing, Mr. Johnson, with Mr. J.H.R. Jackson M.C.P., called on me and gave an outline of the proposal. As in many ways it gave me hope of the realization of the object that my father had in view during his stay in Bermuda, forty years ago. I felt able to commend it to the consideration of the Trustees of the Berkeley College fund; And no one will rejoice more sincerely than I at its success.

But there is a clause in its Constitution which will, I fear, hamper its usefulness and restrict the support given to it, especially in reference to the old fund; I mean that which places it under the auspices of the Bermuda Annual Conference of the A.M.E. Church. I hope no one will waste his energies trying to convert me from bigotry; nor suppose I wish the church of England to be substituted. Not so. It is to be a secular school; and I am not afraid of that word.

But in that case why place it under the control of an exclusive religious body, presumably devoted to Methodism, and distinctively to the African section of their body? The only test for admission is to be of good character and ability, neither creed nor color being taken into account. Why then limit the governing body to one sect and color? Acting on Byron's words: 'Who would be free themselves must strike the blow', the first step has rightly been taken mainly by those whose children would be excluded from the existing Grammar School by race prejudice. But I venture to suggest that this prejudice will only be perpetuated by the clause (1) of the Collegiate Institute's Constitution. Let the Executive Committee work in their secular character, and seek to form a strong governing body by including more English officials as ex-officio members. A Board of Trustees holding office for one year, at the will of the Conference, will not ensure the requisite stability of such an Institution; and a change such as I have indicated will, I am sure, call forth the 'hearty support' of many others beside."

Your Obedient Servant,
W. Berkeley Dowling
April 9, 1891

AN INTERVIEW

(A Student Interviews a Pastor)

Question: We hear all the time that the Bible is relevant; that it speaks to the needs of the poor, the outcast (so-called) our society, yet many so-called Christians would seem to deny this "relevancy" in their words and actions. Would you comment on this? Can you justify these Biblical claims?

Answer: There are many things that happen in this world which can be justified by referring to Biblical Teachings. Slavery, for instance, has been justified by the use of Scripture. Therefore, I will not attempt to merely justify by Scripture what I have to say, but let the facts speak for themselves as they relate to the teachings of Christ.

It is a fact which no one can deny that Jesus cast his lot with the poor, those treated unjustly, the outcasts; And He would have us do no less. Examine St. Mark 10:21; St. Luke 1:5; 6:24-25; St. Matthew 21:31.

The Christian today is commanded by no other than Jesus himself to "deny" himself, take up his cross and follow Him. Deny ourselves the comfort of modern day living, if need be, in order to follow Him. This is a tremendous command which most Christians fail to heed.

Question: How do you account for the fact that Bermuda, a so-called Christian colony, can raise over $80,000 for an overseas cause and yet find it difficult to adequately care for its own less fortunate?

Answer: First, I want to say that everything and everybody termed Christian, ain't Christian! But I suppose the impact of this disaster had a lot to do with the kind of response received. It is always good to help in this manner, but yet there seems to be something hypocritical about the kind of aid when situations like Pakistan exist much closer to us and failed to receive an equal response.

Also the publicity of the Pakistan disaster would appeal to a place like Bermuda—that is, being a place that lives or dies according to the image it portrays abroad.

Question: Didn't the ferry that turned over in the islands to the South of us get publicity?

Answer: Yes it did. But Bermuda is striving to disassociate itself from that area, this is one difference. Although a word of sympathy was expressed, further consideration by Bermuda's power structure was not taken; even though many Bermudians have relatives in that area—or those islands. The Pakistan disaster was more of a world-wide concern makes another difference to Bermuda. Large nations were involved.

Question: Are you saying that this is good?

Answer: Only that it is good to be concerned about others, but the issue goes further. Some people will now have a chance to become known as "great philanthropists," and maybe receive honors from the Queen. Again, it is much easier to deny immediate problems than it is to deal with them. Bermuda has pretended for a long time that it did not have any problems. Therefore, to concentrate on distant disasters allows Bermuda to think less and less about its immediate situation—at least for a short period of time. This kind of attitude further substantiates the lie. If you can, for instance, convince yourself that you are a wealthy person, you would find it difficult to admit by word or action that you are in need, or a member of your family is in need—to do so would damage your reputation as previously established. Therefore you suffer because of your pride, and others suffer with you. Many people say there are problems in Bermuda, yet there is a seeming attitude that a problem is not a problem. You know what I mean; that Bermuda's problems are different. Bermuda is much like the man who convinced himself that he is wealthy and needs nothing, except what he is already getting.

Question: Would you say that this kind of attitude is repressive?

Answer: I can answer yes, if you mean by repressive, that natural or normal activity or expression is prevented, whether openly or secretly, knowingly or unknowingly; I can answer yes if you mean to put down by force; subdue; to check; contain by or as if by pressure; to curb. Many unfortunate conditions are subdued, and therefore do not get proper attention.

Question: In your opinion, what are some of the results of repression?

Answer: As I have said, oftentimes real problems do not get proper attention because they are prevented from expressing themselves. In any society or community that represses free expression, it becomes a breeding ground for potential revolutionaries. Subtle and yet open repression in a so-called democratic and free society could have devastating results. In other words, repression of any kind and courageous reaction against it. The last disturbances in Bermuda are evidence.

Question: What changes or efforts to change the course of events do you note in Bermuda since the last disturbances?

Answer: I can see as reported in an editorial in the local newspaper that very little if anything has changed. We hear the same rhetoric coming from the power structure. Many black and white people still feel that the government will not do anything about the price spiral, although, we have heard the situation mentioned in government circles. Many black people, especially the young are still frustrated over the fact of no place to turn for redress of grievances. If there is such a place, it is obvious that it needs a new image.

Question: Changing our line of thoughts lightly, does the church have anything to say for revolution?

Answer: Many have been wondering what the church says about revolution. The church talks about revolution, but does not recognize how potentially revolutionary it is. For instance, there is constant reference to how Jesus defied the Roman Empire and how he would have us follow after him. There is a tremendous problem here of relating knowledge and experience when it really counts. Most Christians find it difficult to act upon their beliefs or they don't really believe in the first place.

Question: What is revolution to you?

Answer: From this point, I agree with Dr. James Cone in his book, *Black Theology and Black Power,* that "revolution" is not merely "a change of heart" but a radical encounter with the structure of white racism, "with the full intention of destroying its menacing power..."

Now it is most important not to confuse revolution with protest or rebellion. "Revolution is more than protest. Protest merely calls attention to injustice. It is the refusal to be silent in the presence of wrong to which others are accommodated." Dr. C. Eric Lincoln explains this in the *Union Seminary Quarterly* under the title, *Cultural Perspective* (Vol. XX111 No. 3, Spring, 1968). Dr. Lincoln states that "revolution sees every particular wrong as one more instance in a pattern which is itself beyond rectification.

Revolution aims at the substitution of a new system for one adjudged to be corrupt..." For instance, black preachers were convinced that the evil of slavery was bad and they urged slaves to revolt against it. Mr. Harold Cruse in his book entitled, *Rebellion or Revolution*, explains, "A rebellion is not a revolutionary movement unless it changes the structure arrangements of the society or else is able to project problematic ideas toward that end." He further states that, "Rebellion is by nature, limited in scope. It is no more than an incoherent pronouncement. Revolution, on the contrary, originates in the realm of ideas." Specifically, it is the injection of ideas into historical experience.

Question: Is the Christian free to carry out such a revolution?

Answer: Allow me to put my answer in the form of another quote from Dr. James Cone:

> The Christian man is obligated by a freedom grounded in the Creator to break all laws which contradict human dignity. When man denies his freedom and the freedom of others, he denies God. When black people affirm their freedom in God, they know that they cannot obey laws of oppression. By disobeying they not only say Yes to God but also to their own humanity and the humanity of the white oppressor.

I believe God is angry! I now recall these dreadful words of the book of Genesis (6:5-8):

I will destroy man whom I have created on the earth...

Who will find grace in the eyes of the Lord?

September 1971

THE PROTEST

8th edition

THE PROTEST

Editors: John E. Brandon and Lloyd E. Dees©

Published Quarterly (March, June, September, December), to stimulate thinking and effect change within the Church and Society

Subscription rates: $2.50 per year, single copy, $.75

Make Check or Money Order payable to:

IN THE UNITED STATES	IN BERMUDA
Lloyd E. Dees	John E. Brandon
A&T State University	P.O. Box 146
Greensboro, North Carolina 27411	Southampton East

©John E. Brandon, A.A., B.A., Th.M., Pastor, Vernon Temple African Methodist Episcopal Church, Southampton East, Bermuda: Bright Temple, Warwick.

Lloyd E. Dees, B.A., B.D., Director, United Christian Ministry, A&T State University, Greensboro, North Carolina.

CONTENTS

1. PROLOGUE: THE VOICE OF BLACK CHURCHMEN 1
2. CONSULTATION ON CHURCH UNION 2
'That They May Be One'
3. THE KINGDOM, AND THE POWER, AND THE INFAMY 7
4. EXPRESSIONS 11

THE PROTEST

Magazine

PROLOGUE: THE VOICE OF BLACK CHURCHMEN*

We are morally obligated to confront ourselves and our white brothers with the requirements of our Judeo-Christian faith. We cannot and will not be equivocal with the ethical and moral principles involved.

—United Church of Christ Ministries

"...White Protestant denominations (could) stop worrying about organic union among themselves and reproachment with Roman Catholicism and begin to enter, on an unprecedented scale, into ecumenical relations in the life and work with the five great all-black denominations and about twenty-four smaller churches that comprise more than 90 percent of all black Protestants in the U.S.A.

—Gayraud S.Wilmore, Jr.

What is at stake here is not the question of two churches, one black and one white, but rather the heresy of a "henotheistic" Christ; i.e., one whose headship of the church abhors racism officially but worships it at its shrine unofficially.

—Grant S. Shockley

Of God: God does not command impossible things. But he commands, he asks us to do what we can—and also to ask what we cannot.

Of others: Whether they like it or not, they are our brothers. They will only cease to be our brothers—when they cease to say, "Our Father."

—St. Augustine

Black men are organizing for the power to determine their own future in the church. Once the masses of blacks know they count, then we can move to reconciliation.

—A. Cecil Williams

*Subject taken from the thesis by John E. Brandon, Boston University, 1969, entitled "BLACK CHURCHMEN—A NEW CHALLENGE TO TRUE ECUMENISM."

CONSULTATION ON CHURCH UNION

'That They May Be One'

By John. E. Brandon

The Consultation on Church Union which was organized in April, 1962 as a direct response to the sermon, "A Proposal Toward the Reunion of Christ's Church, preached by Dr. Eugene Carson Blake (December 4, 1960) now composes nine denominations as follows:

The African Methodist Episcopal Church
The African Methodist Episcopal Zion Church
The Christian Church (Disciples of Christ)
The Christian Methodist Episcopal Church
The Episcopal Church
The Presbyterian Church in the U.S.
The United Church of Christ
The United Methodist Church
The United Presbyterian Church in the U.S.A.

COCU, as it is commonly known, has as its specific purpose "the formulation through union of a dynamic united and uniting church." "A Plan of Union" has been presented to the represented denominations for study and action. COCU states that "the specific purpose of this union is not the merger of denominations," but an effort to "begin anew." After having read the Plan of Union one cannot but be impressed by the amount of work and careful effort made to deal with some of the very touchy and important issues involved in such a proposed union. And no doubt, as the Plan of Union recognized, that, "efforts to unite in a common obedience...will release divisive forces. Nonetheless, we must obey God, who is calling us to accept the costliness of union."

COCU presents a challenge to the entire Church of Jesus Christ as we know it in its present form and shape. COCU presents a challenge because it proposes dramatic changes in the present structure of a part of Christ's Church, Dr. Preston N. Williams of Harvard Divinity School states that:

> "If some changes do not occur, it will mean the death of both black and white churches. Both churches as they are presently constituted fail to take seriously God's demand for justice and righteousness. This failure has meant an increase in atheism and

> secularism among blacks and whites. It may mean in the near future a COCU without any blacks, a community without any Christian Church."

Let us take a further look at the Plan of Union for the Church of Christ Uniting (COCU, Princeton, New Jersey, 1970). Although the plan covers a large area of concern there is one issue that is unfortunately omitted. The race issue cannot be so blatantly overlooked. It is an important matter which COCU must deal with. It would not take the white denominations of COCU very long to form a "united and uniting church" void of any blacks, simply because many white people feel there is no race problem if there are no blacks to "contend with." This is like a country or a smaller community being "free of racial problems" because "only whites" are allowed to live as residents. This is a false view, because the race issue goes further than visual contact, but points to the sick condition of the heart which is not cured by distance.

However, the Plan of Union recognizes that such a plan "cannot cover everything," but the race problem has to be confronted honestly in such a Plan. One statement in the Plan indicates that, "…the church will provide compensatory treatment of those who have been excluded in the past." This statement is not enough! More than that will have to be said. That is, what is compensatory treatment? Who have been excluded and by whom? It is not even enough to say that, "…the church (the united and uniting church) will embrace the unity of all persons, regardless of race, age, sex, wealth, or culture…" If the Church of Jesus Christ cannot speak to the issue of race, who will? The Plan of Union will have to be more explicitly spelled out on the matter of race.

Mr. E.U. Essien-Udom states in his book, *BLACK NATIONALISM*, (Dell publishing Company, 1962) that:

> "There are few major world problems which are not somehow colored by the race question. It is evident, though not often openly admitted, that race and color play some part in contemporary thinking and global political strategy of the major powers. That race and colour will continue to be of importance in the world community in the second half of the 20th century, no one can deny."

The words of Dr. Gayraud S. Wilmore ("The Case for a New Black Church Style," Church in Metropolis, No. 18, 1968) still holds true, that:

> "...One thing is certainly clear as one studies the COCU reports, unless the Consultation is more willing to dialogue on the thorny issue of race...there is even less hope that black churchmen will do more than go along for the ride until the white brethren get the message..."

Unless there is the necessary in depth vision and penetration, the result of black and white union can only be confusion.

Many will probably ask, "Why all these questions and statements on race when we are about to unite. Our Lord wants us to be one." One what? We must ask ourselves. Let us deal for a moment with the words of our Lord which are so often used as a basis in efforts of unity and union "that they may be one." Careful consideration must be given to the kind of oneness indicated. Mr. Ian Henderson in his book (*Power Without Glory—A Study in Ecumenical Politics*, Hutchinson of London, 1967), raises this question concerning oneness when he says:

> "That they may be one." These words are an injunction of our Lord. There is therefore the more need to ask soberly what kind of oneness they enjoin. For there are at least three kinds of oneness.

These three kinds of oneness may be illustrated as follows:

1. Two souls with but one single thought. Two hearts that beat as one.
2. Oxford and Cambridge are virtually the one way into the Foreign Service.
3. One Volk, one Reich, one Fuhrer.

As we look at these types of oneness, we can easily see that each is different. "In the first of these statements, oneness is an expression of love. It is true that we do not love properly unless we respect the otherness of the person whom we love." As the author further states:

> "In the second of these statements, oneness expresses a claim to exclusiveness. Here, oneness does not join (as it does when it is a synonym for love) but severs. Certain entities (in this case entry to the Foreign Service) which no other entities of the same kind possesses (characterize the second statement). In the third of these statements, oneness expresses a will to power. If a will to power is so

> strong that it can tolerate no rival then it will naturally express itself in a demand for oneness."

The author does not "think that the prayer of the Johannine Christ 'that they may be one' lays as any obligation on us to seek a oneness which gives expression to a claim of exclusiveness or a will to power." Therefore, it would behoove COCU to take a serious look at whether or not it is bent toward the same kind of situation where a fight for power becomes the focus of attention and result of all the efforts at union, or, that the Church of Christ Uniting becomes exclusive. That is to say, there is a danger of the Church of Christ Uniting becoming the only way to union for other churches.

Let us consider other statements of the Plan of Union. The following ones are very interesting:

1. "There can be no ecumenism worthy of the name without a change of heart."

and

2. Christian diversity is abused by the separateness of the denominations, the competition between congregations, and the hostility within local fellowships. Such diversity is generally expressed only by bringing all our differences into one household.

The first statement says that there can be no ecumenism if the heart is not right. In other words, to mention or change of heart presupposes that the heart is in a loveless state. The second statement seems to assume that "by bringing all our differences into one household" they can be "genuinely expressed." The word that stands out here is "genuinely." Does it mean that love will then exist after we have come together in one household? This raises a question which many have sought to answer. What comes first, love or union?

Without being overly hostile, we must listen to the critics of ecumenical efforts. Mr. Ian Henderson in his book, *Power Without Glory* states:

> Putting all Christians within one denomination will not cure the sin of lovelessness for the obvious reason that the worst examples of lovelessness do not occur between but within denominations.

> Every parish squabble and every...vendetta is an equal offence against love which no amount of ecumenical ecclesiastical merging can cure.

The change of heart that is needed before we can have ecumenism, still seems to be a long way off. If we say it is not a long way off, what do we base such a statement upon? The question of what comes first, "love or union" can very well answer itself, because there cannot be any unity of lasting value without love being woven in it and through it. Douglas Jones in his book (*Instruments of Peace: Biblical Principles of Christian Unity*, Hodder & Stoughton, London, 1965) states:

> Man left to himself, his aggressiveness untamed, will never cease to cause new conflicts as soon as one set of divisions is healed. Without an answer to man's personal problem, the hope of unity... is a romantic dream.

The previous quote is not to say that efforts at unity must cease because there will be new conflicts. The concern here as stated by many black churchmen in union efforts goes beyond the question of who possesses the authentic, true faith, but to a problem of basic human relationships. Many white people are spending a lot of time on doctrines, liturgies, etc., which are important, but does not touch the main source of the conflict. The argument of the authentic faith gets bogged down in religious questions and answers and never gets down to man's personal problem of lovelessness and proclivity toward obsession for power and other sins.

"None of the uniting churches will lose the continuity and richness of its own life, but each will find its life marvelously renewed by union with the other uniting churches." This statement is taken from the Plan of Union. It also raises questions. How will each be renewed? If "the specific purpose of this union is not the merger of denominations," and yet each church that will unite "will not lose the continuity and richness of its own life," how do A.M.E.'s, for instance, preserve their identity?

We need only to look at a few pages of history in order to note the kind of unfortunate situation that forced black people out of white churches. The following letter is in the form of a petition written in 1867 and presented to the white members of the Fairfield Baptist Church by 38 black members of the congregation. This letter is taken from Dr. Harry V. Richardson's book, DARK GLORY, Nashville, 1947:

To Elder William Kirk and the members of the Fairfield Baptist Church:

Beloved brothers: Grace be unto you and peace from God, the Father of our Lord Jesus Christ. From an earnest desire to act in all things with an eye single to the glory of God and for the unity of that common faith which constitute us in Christ Jesus, we have thought it advisable to counsel on the subject of our future Church relationship. So that whatever may be done we may at least preserve that peace and harmony which ought to characterize those of the same faith and order and promote the prosperity of the cause which, through your instrumentality, had been the means of calling us into the light and knowledge of the glorious gospel of the Son of God. Without alluding to the Providence that so mysteriously changed our social and political relation, we conceive that under the new order of things we are not only advanced in our religious privilege, but that solemn and weighty responsibilities impose upon us a new class of duties in which we should be wanting in fidelity if we did not seek to place ourselves in that position in which we could best promote our mutual good, both in reference to ourselves and our posterity. In this new relation the subject of a separate church organization presses itself upon us as the best possible way in which we can best promote those indispensable interests, such as the ordained ministry, a separate congregation with all the privileges of a church organization, stated church meetings, regular religious service, Sabbath schools, etc. But just in this point the question arises: Can we not do this and preserve the unity of the faith and continue in church fellowship with our white brethren; and thereby perpetuate our church identity, so that in all the general interest of the church we may be mutually interested and to some extent collaborators? To effect this may require the concurrent action of all the members of the congregation concerned; and the object of this communication is to ask your attention to this subject with the hope that such an arrangement can be made as to induce a general church meeting at some convenient time and place for this purpose,

> that our identity may be preserved or perpetuated if possible; and if not, that we may receive your parting benediction and blessing, as well as your endonation (endorsement) of our Christian character and standing. All of which is most respectfully submitted for your prayerful consideration and action. Hoping that unerring wisdom may guide us in the way of all truth, we remain, dear brethren in the bonds of Christ.
>
> Yours Fraternity,
> Samuel Conway, Secretary
> Herman Kenner, Chairman

This petition was unanimously granted. Two white members donated small plots of land on which a temporary place of worship was erected for the new congregation. This letter speaks for itself. The situation of white church structures are still the same.

The Plan of Union states (in the Service of Inauguration) that: "The acts of unification... bring to an end the long period during which the uniting churches existed in separation from one another. They are acts of repentance..." Now, the question is, who is repenting? The acts of repentance—do they mean that the 38 black members in the above church, because of white racism and Richard Allen of the African Methodist Episcopal Church have to repent because they stood up as men made in the image of God? And without distinguishing who needs repentance, do we all simply engage in an act of repentance? Now, this does not mean that blacks are exempt from repenting for sins, but the question raised here is whether in the case of separation by denomination, blacks are the ones who need to repent. By gathering everybody together in an act of repentance, both black and white does not hide the fact that whites are the ones who need to repent in this case. Without any change of heart on the part of whites, do "the 38 in the Fairfield Baptist Church and Richard Allen of the A.M.E. Church" walk right back into the same situation they left over 100 and 180 years ago respectively?

The consultation on church union will have to consider more urgently and seriously the petition of blacks within its ranks. More work is needed on the form and shape that certain action toward blacks and minorities will take to alleviate the question of race. "That they may be one." What kind of "one" shall we be?

THE KINGDOM, AND THE POWER, AND THE INFAMY

By Lloyd E. Dees

I begin this article with a Biblical admonition and I shall end it with one:

> "…Not by my might, nor by power, but by my Spirit says the Lord of hosts." (Zechariah 6:6)

In November 1946, after about 150 years of its existence, the African Methodist Episcopal Church held its first extra session of the General Conference. The main reason for the extra session had to do with an action taken by the Bishop's Council which directly affected two bishops of the Church. In June of 1946 the Bishops Council made a determination concerning the New York Annual Conference. It was the decision of Council that the affairs of that conference were not being properly administered by the Bishop who had been assigned to the First Episcopal District of the General Conference of 1944. The Bishop's Council took an action which it thought would remedy the situation. The ruling was to relieve the Bishop assigned by the General Conference of his duties in the New York Conference, and to assign an "associate bishop" to administer the affairs of the conference. The records indicate that although the Council was in agreement on this action, an injunction was obtained in the New York Supreme Court by the General Conference assigned bishop to prevent the "associate" bishop from exercising authority in the New York Conference. This set in motion a chain of "messy" events which eventuated in the first extra session of the General Conference.

At this point in its life the church began to travel unchartered paths. Such paths almost always arouse fear, apprehension and uncertainty. What to do, how to do it, when to do it, and who had the responsibility to do it were major problems to be faced at that time. The church had the Discipline, but it was fraught with ambiguities. Confusion reigned. Bitter disputes were common. A number of meetings that were called were literally broken up. Bishops were divided into two camps and pastors followed suit. But the extra session of the General Conference was called and held in Little Rock, Arkansas. The major action taken by that conference was the suspension and expulsion of a number of bishops. The Bishop of the First Episcopal District was expelled by a "standing vote of 999 to 35." The Bishop's Council later assigned one bishop to preside over the Philadelphia, Delaware and Maritime Conferences of the First Episcopal District, and the "associate" bishop to preside over the other Conferences in that District.

The action taken by the extra session of the General Conference did not put an end to the long controversy. A suit was filed by the bishop who was expelled, charging that his expulsion was illegal. The ruling on the case was made in Philadelphia, Pennsylvania in July, 1947. The decision was that the action taken by the extra session of the General Conference in expelling the bishop was legal. So from a legal point of view the matter ended. But the hostility and bitterness continued. Some of the pastors who supported the bishop who was expelled felt the "heavy hand" of some of the presiding bishops when appointment time came around.

I should like to consider three statements made by the judge in rendering his decision in 1947.

(1) "We are concerned here with the controversies over the call of an extra session of the General Conference and the propriety of its procedure. But before analyzing the issues, it is important to recognize that the differences between the factions of the bishops' group and their followers had affected the affairs of the church in certain sections and precluded the church authority, the Bishops' Council especially, from effectively performing their normal functions. Bitterness had arisen. The majority deemed the minority a rebellious group and the minority believed that the majority sought autocratic power..."

Although the legal aspect of this matter was the main concern of the judge, he felt the necessity of pointing out something which he saw as being more fundamental. Factions had come into existence which would not permit the church to function properly. The matter had come down to whose side one was on, and not so much the right or wrong. It had become a vicious struggle for survival. And perhaps pastors were those who were affected most. The struggle to survive is still with us. This kind of struggle tends to narrow ones concern, and stunt his growth. It tends to influence his choices, and frustrate his plans. This kind of struggle tends to sap the essence of a man's soul and replace it with a substance that is counterfeit. In a struggle of this kind someone eventually dies. The judge made a keen and profound observation; he said "bitterness had arisen" within the church. It was intense bitterness which almost always leads to destruction. And in one way or another many persons were destroyed by this whole episode.

At another point the judge stated that:

(2) "We have tried to set out the legal principles that have been laid down by our courts in a controversy of this kind. We have refrained from going beyond the applicable legal principles involved. By refraining from doing so we are not unmindful for some very important questions

that may perhaps require a reference to if not commented upon by us. Nor are we unmindful of the fact that the legal principles upon which we rely have left untouched in this opinion the question of the security of the tenure of office of the bishops of the African Methodist Episcopal Church under the Discipline. We could not help but be impressed by the almost absolute control of the bishops with respect to the special conferences held in their jurisdictions. (Special sessions of the Annual Conferences must be held in order to vote for the approval of an extra session of the General Conference). This was evidenced by the almost unanimous votes in many of these conferences; the speed with which some of these so-called trials were conducted cannot help but raise a question in the mind of the chancellor."

At this point the judge spoke of something that was already known but rarely, if ever, mentioned in public—the almost absolute power of the bishops. It is no exaggeration to state that whoever becomes a bishop in the African Methodist Episcopal Church comes into an office that is supersaturated with power. Many men have used this power for the good of the church, but others have used it to the detriment of the same. The power of the office of bishops is manifested in many ways. But it perhaps has its most telling effect in the matter of pastoral appointments. The Bishop has the sole power of appointment. And throughout the connection this power hangs heavy over the heads of thousands of pastors. Some bishops try to temper this power by adding the phrase, "in my Godly judgment." But the chances are that this phrase impresses very few people. From the day of his ordination to the day of his death, the pastor is never permitted to forget "who feeds him." "Bishop" is equivalent to power. And in one way or another the pastor is constantly reminded of this. There is a story of a pastor who had gotten out of favor with a particular bishop. It was at Annual Conference. The pastor got up to ask for forgiveness. He was ordered by the bishop to do so from a kneeling position. The bishop said: "Get down on your knees, my brother. Get down on your knees." That was perhaps the day of death for that pastor. But the truth is that in one way or another the pastor is always "down on his knees." Sometimes, in a joking manner, some bishops refer to the ministers in their districts as "my pastors." But that really is no joke.

At this point a fundamental question must be raised. I do not know the answer, and I do not know anyone else who does. But it must be asked and we must give serious consideration to it. The question is: what is the characteristic of the women and men who constantly put so much power in the hands of one man? This fundamental question raises a number of other questions. Are these women and men basically persons of deep faith who have the same kind of faith in their leaders? Is this a combined expression of dedicated Christian men and woman? Is this an expression of women and men who are not willing to share the responsibility for their own destiny? Perhaps there is no one answer to any one of these questions, but I deemed them worthy of consideration.

In another place in his decision of 1947 the judge said:

(3) "No moral stigma has attached to anyone, and it is a church dispute in which personal rivalries, ambitions and rival purposes have blended to a warfare that if persisted in can only destroy the organization of the Church and its great spiritual influences on millions throughout the world."

It seems to me that a fundamental principle is being raised here. It is the principle of the "unity of the body of Christ." Paul says in First Corinthians 12:26: "If one member of the body suffers, all suffer together; if one member is honored, all rejoice together." The judge spoke of a "warfare" that would result in the destruction of the organization of the Church if it was permitted to continue. The writer is of the opinion that the "warfare" has in large measure continued on to this day, in one way or another. How much destruction has been inflicted or influence has been lost is difficult to assess. But one thing seems to be quite evident, and that is that the A.M.E. Church has been falling and rising (?) ever since that first extra session of the General Conference of 1946.

Ten years later the General Conference was held in Miami, Florida. A "major" storm arose there. Again, it had to do with a bishop, or some bishops. Miami is still fresh in the minds of many people. This storm which began in Miami in 1956 increased in intensity and caused a major disruption at the General Conference of 1960 in Los Angeles, California. Another bishop was put out of the church, and he stayed out until the General Conference of 1968. The money that was spent for court costs and other reasons as a result of this action is difficult to count and to account for. The ill will that was created is difficult to measure. Even today, in some parts of the church, bitterness still prevails. My mind harbors the thought that bishops are "killing the church." But if this is true, it is the people who give them the power to do so. What troubles me is that the people, because of the many "beatings" which they have taken, may be existing in a state of apathy. This would indeed be a great tragedy.

Now, after all these years, after all these turmoils, after all these broken hearts, after all these thousands of dollars that have been wasted, we are on the verge of another extra session of the General Conference. There is much confusion, strife, frustration, and in the hearts of some people there is despair. What will happen at this extra session is anybody's guess. But of this one may be sure, if people get mad enough to call an extra session they do not gather to hold each other's hand.

So, there is a good possibility that some more bishops will be expelled. If this happens, bitterness will continue to pervade the church. If any semblance of unity prevails after this extra session, it will be only because God is exceedingly gracious toward us. I think, therefore, that the following biblical admonition is very pertinent to the present state of affairs:

> "… If you bite and devour one another, take heed lest you are consumed by one another." (Galatians 5:15)

EXPRESSIONS

By Lloyd E. Dees

SYMPATHY

Poor little bird who cannot fly,
who cannot live, who cannot die;
with wings that flutter up and down,
and whose little mouth make muffled sounds.

Big strong BIRDS dive from high in the sky,
they look at you and pass on by
Poor little bird, sweet little bird,
how I wish that you could fly!

ADVICE

don't kick him now!
have pity on my friend.
your foot may not be tired,
but his buttock is.

this is not yesterday,
when your heavy foot had full sway.
this today—A NEW DAY,
when brutal feet are chopped away.

A KING

Who is a king?
A king is a man
who gives more than he receives,
who shares, and not hoards!
who sees what is and has visions of what can be.

Who is a king?
A king is a man, who loves
and does not HATE:
who lifts burdens, and not add weights,
who is not crooked, but straight.

Who is the king?
A king is a man,
who does not run, but stands;
who lives not in a palace,
but in the lands.

Who is the king?
A king is a man—who dreams,
and shares his dreams with his brothers,
who lives not for himself;
he lives for others.

Who is a king?
A king is a man—who loves,
and is not forgotten.
I once knew a king;
His name was MARTIN

Chapter Ten

Letters

The following chapter includes many of the letters sent to and from Rev. Dees. I arranged them by date and retyped them as they were aged, faded, and difficult to read. At the end of the chapter, several original letters are shown in their entirety.

Kings Highway United Methodist Church
1387 East Street
BROOKLYN, NY 11210-5433

THE REV. DR. CHARLES H. STRAUT JR. Pastor
Cell Phone: (917) 750-7739
E-mail: chstraut@juno.com

Telephone
Office: (718) 338-6619
Study: (718) 377-7130
Fax: (718) 377-7130

March 11, 1999

Grace L. Orr, General Chairperson
Pastor Dees Retirement Dinner
6 Washington Avenue
White Plains, NY 10606

Dear Ms. Orr:

Thank you so very much for inviting me to take part in the program for the Retirement Dinner of my friend and colleague, the Rev. Lloyd E. Dees. I deeply regret that I shall be out of town for a professional obligation that evening.

Were I able to be there, I would tell the assembled how much regard and respect I have for this compassionate, committed and caring man. He has served selflessly across the years of his career in ways that have not often been of sufficiently high visibility to earn him the recognition that he certainly deserves. However, he is most like his Master in this way, because he does what he does because it is just and right, not because it will earn him a reward, either personal, professional or even pecuniary.

I have counted it a privilege to have been a brother of this ordained ministry, as well as having an opportunity to appreciate his pastoral skills while his District Superintendent, but I have admired him most for his involvement with social justice issues—to an extent which often led those who know him to be filled with both amazement and admiration.

It has been a privilege to have served alongside him, and I wish him Godspeed as he opens this new chapter in service to our God.

For justice and liberation,
The Rev. Charles H. Straut, D. Min.

CHS/me

Butler Memorial United Methodist Church
329 Paulding Avenue
(Rev. W.P. Johnson Place)
BRONX, NEW YORK 10466-4702

REV. NOEL N. CHIN, Pastor

April 19, 1999

Rev. Lloyd Dees
Trinity United Methodist Church
130 South Lexington Avenue
White Plains, NY 10606-2510

Dear Rev. Dees:

On behalf of Butler Memorial United Methodist Church I would like to thank you for sharing our 87th Annual Celebration yesterday.

Your message was timely and challenging. There was also a great appreciation for the sense of history that you brought to the day's celebration.

As God continues to use your many gifts in His service, may He bless you and your family always.

Sincerely,

Noel N. Chin

June 4, 1999

Greetings to Reverend Lloyd E. Dees:

Our sincere congratulations on your retirement after forty-two years in Christian ministry. We regret that we cannot be with you physically to celebrate this momentous occasion, due to the fact that on this same day, I am receiving an honour at my job. Nevertheless, we are pleased that other members of the (family) have come to share with you and mark this event.

I can still remember when the family first learned of your calling to the ministry and the joy we all shared. We all have looked to you with pride, and at the same time, in awe of how you have been so faithful to your work at the various places and in the many ways that you have served. You have served as a beacon light for us. And, we thank God for you and the way in which you have tried to keep us all on the right path.

We wish for you and Dolores many more wonderful years as you find new ways to serve. May God's richest blessings continue to be upon the both of you as you make the transition not only to a new work but also to a new location.

Your sister and family,

Delores, Prince, and Pamela Willis

June 23, 1999

62 Sutton Place
Bloomfield, CT 06002

Dear Pastor and Mrs. Dees,

Enclosed is the article of your coming to Trinity United Methodist Church in 1977. Pastor, you and your family have been a great inspiration to all. We love you and may God continue to bless all of you.

You will truly be missed.

With love,

Mary R. Pitt

P.O. Box 668
Rincon, GA 31326

November 1, 1999

Bishop Robert C. Morgan, President
Council of Bishops
The United Methodist Church
2000 Warrington Way
Louisville, Kentucky 40222

Dear Bishop Morgan,

"Grace be to you and peace from God our Father and from the Lord Jesus Christ."

I am a recently retired member of the New York Annual Conference—having served 15 years in the African Methodist Episcopal Church and 27 years in the United Methodist Church.

My wife and I are now living in Rincon, Georgia—not far from Savannah. My new status and the summer season provided us with the opportunity to visit and worship in several United Methodist Churches in and around Savannah. While worshipping one Sunday morning in one of our "historic" churches in downtown Savannah, I was forcefully awakened to what I knew deep inside and I am sure that all Bishops of our church know as well. Many of our local churches are practicing segregation on Sunday mornings. So, we worshipped in churches where we were the only Blacks in attendance and churches where there were no whites in attendance.

It has been 31 years since the dissolution of the Central Jurisdiction, but, our goal of "One United Church" is far from being reached. I believe it is a noble goal still, and that it should be pursued with vigor and commitment.

It seems to me that the upcoming meetings of the Council of Bishops and the General Conference early next year will provide excellent opportunities for our Bishops to re-articulate our goals and aims, and to encourage the church to re-vitalize its efforts to walk the road that leads toward "one-ness." This—I believe—would be a powerful witness of our Church for the 21st century.

Your faithful servant,

Lloyd E. Dees
cc: The United Methodist Bishops in the United States

June 22, 2000

GAMMON THEOLOGICAL SEMINARY
P.O. Box 92416
653 Beckwith Street S.W.
Atlanta, Georgia 30314

Office of the President-Dean E-Mail: wmckelvey@itc.edu (404) 581-0300

Reverend Lloyd E. Dees
P.O. Box 668
Rincon, Georgia 31326

Dear Lloyd,

My apologies for taking so long to respond to your December 19, 1999, letter. These past few months have been challenging, concluding with the death of my wife on June 9, 2000.

In planning for our December Lecture Series, I will pursue your suggestion with regard to broadening ITC involvement. In the past, the Center has seen this emphasis as isolated offerings and have encouraged participation on a volunteer basis.

Your letter to the Council of Bishops is on target. We will consider your suggestion among others as we plan for the December 2000 Founders' Day/Thirkield Jones Lecture Series.

Continued good wishes.

Sincerely yours,

Walter H. McKelvey
WHMcK/MMcD

THE UNITED METHODIST CHURCH
INDIANA AREA
1100 WEST 42ND STREET • SUITE 210 • INDIANAPOLIS, INDIANA 46208
317-924-1321 • 317-924-4859 FAX

NORTH INDIANA ANNUAL CONFERENCE
SOUTH INDIANA ANNUAL CONFERENCE

WOODIE W. WHITE, Resident Bishop
Hjulian@inareume.org
FAX 317-924-1380

DR. JAMES D. JONES, Executive Assistant
jjones@inareaume.org
FAX 327-924-1380

September 12, 2000

Reverend Lloyd E. Dees
P.O. Box 668
Rincon, Georgia 31326

Dear Lloyd,

Thanks for your continuing commitment to the eradication of Racism.

You will be pleased to know that the Council of Bishops has identified the issue of Racism as one of our priorities for the quadrennium. A rather comprehensive effort is in the works and will be implemented across the church.

Here in Indiana, I prepared an Episcopal Pastoral Letter on Race, which was to have been read in every congregation. Additionally the 18 districts of the Indiana Area will have or already have a day long District Event on Racism. I prepared a video that was used, and follow-up efforts are anticipated after each District Event.

We are definitely still addressing the issue forthrightly, even if you don't see anything in the church press.

Thanks for your reminder!

Sincerely,
Woodie W. White
WWW/kj

CITY OF HOUSTON
Lee P. Brown, MAYOR

P.O. Box 1562
Houston, Texas 77251-1562
901 Bagby 3rd Floor
Houston, Texas 77002
T.713-247-2545
F.713-247-1067
www.ci.houston.tx.us

December 28, 2000

Reverend Lloyd E. Dees
P.O. Box 668
Rincon, GA 31326-0668

Dear Reverend Dees:

Thank you for your recent letter of encouragement. I appreciate it very much when I hear from supporters who understand the values and initiatives of my administration in Houston.

Please accept my very best wishes for the holiday season and a Happy New Year.

Sincerely,

Lee P. Brown
Mayor

LPB:mab

Council Members: Bruce Tatro • Carol M. Galloway • Mark Gildberg • Jew Don Boney Jr. • Rob Todd
Mark A. Ellis • Bert Keller • Gabriel Vasquez • John E. Castillo • Annise D. Parker • Gordon Quan
Orlando Sanchez • Chris Bell • Carroll G. Robinson • Controller: Sylvia R. Garcia

FEBRUARY 27, 2001

BETHUNE-COOKMAN COLLEGE
MARY McLEOD BETHUNE FOUNDER
OSWALD P. BRONSON, SR. PRESIDENT

OFFICE OF THE PRESIDENT

FEBRUARY 27, 2001

Reverend Lloyd E. Dees
P.O. Box 668
Rincon, Georgia 31326

My Dear Friend,

While going through some papers and correspondence, your letter of March 17, 2000, surfaced among filing material. Thank you for expressing appreciation for the Bethune-Cookman College's Concert Chorale. I am delighted to know that their performance was "exhilarating" and spiritually rousing!

I recall our friendship as colleagues at the Interdenominational Theological Center with profound appreciation and gratitude. Therefore, your statement about your retirement led to moments of meditation and celebration, not only for our friendship but also for your witness as a minister of Jesus Christ. It is my hope that we will have the opportunity to visit in the near future.

Thank you, again, for your letter.

Sincerely,

Oswald P. Bronson, Sr.
President
OPB/rh
Dees, Lloyd

640 DR. MARY McLEOD BETHUNE BOULEVARD • DAYTONA BEACH, FLORIDA 32114-3099
(904) 255-1401, Exts. 200/201/374 • (Direct) 252-8667 • (Fax) 257-7027
(E-Mail) bronsonp@cookman.edu • (http):/www.berhunecookman.edu

MARCH 30, 2001

THE UNITED METHODIST CHURCH
NEW YORK AREA
TEL: 914-684-6922 / FAX: 914-997-162
252 BRYANT AVENUE
E-Mail: bishopnyac@aol.com
ERNEST S. LYGHT
WHITE PLAINS, NEW YORK 10605
RESIDENT BISHOP

Rev. Lloyd E. Dees
P.O. Box 668
Rincon, GA 31326-0668

Dear Lloyd:

Grace and Peace be unto you in the name of our Lord and savior, Jesus Christ.

Thank you for sending me a copy of the sermon that you preached at Asbury—Savannah. It was good to hear from you.

Best wishes and may your Lenten journey abound in God's grace.

Faithfully,

Earnest S. Lyght
ESL:erb

MARCH 26, 2002

LONG ISLAND EAST DISTRICT
Rev. Dr. Allen N. Pinckney Jr.
District Superintendent
357 MacArthur Boulevard
Hauppauge, N.Y. 11788-3002
Telephone: 631-366-2396
Fax: 631-366-4842
E-mail: lienyac@aol.com

March 26, 2002

Rev. Lloyd Dees
P.O. Box 668
Rincon, Georgia 31326

Dear Rev. Dees,

Thank you for your letter and your concern regarding the issue of cross cultural/racial appointments. You have clearly given critical thought to the matter and have articulated some very important concerns. As one who has served in cross cultural/cross racial appointments, I am deeply aware of the need for the cabinet and our conference to provide strategic leadership in addressing this critical area in the life of our church.

It is not easy as you have pointed out, and does require tremendous courage to withstand the forces of opposition that prefer to maintain the status quo. I would ask that you keep the cabinet and Bishop in prayer. Please understand that in addition to this very significant issue, the appointment making progress presents very complicated factors and dynamics that the cabinet constantly struggles with.

I ask that you pray that the Holy Spirit will grant us the discerning power to appropriately and creatively match ordained clergy with the very diverse churches that comprise our conference.

Yours in Christ,

Rev. Dr. Allen N. Pinckney Jr.
District Superintendent Long Island East
ANP/bma

"Where All Are Accepted With Warmth And Love"
St. Mary's Road United Methodist Church
3993 St. Mary's Road
Columbus, Georgia 31907-6237
(706)689-8707 / Fax (706)689-1164
Rev. Thomas H. Mills Jr., Senior Pastor
Rev. Stephen D. Jones, Associate Pastor
Minister Peggy Myles
Email Address: StMarysRd@TheRoadUMC.org / Website Address: www.TheRoadUMC.org

May 28, 2002

The Rev. Lloyd E. Dees
P.O. Box 668
Rincon, GA 31326

Dear Rev. Dees,

Thank you so much for accepting my invitation to come and be our Guest Speaker on Sunday, June 30th at 10:00 a.m. You will receive an honorarium of $300. We will also cover your lodging and meals.

We anxiously look forward to you being with the St. Mary's Road Family. If there are any special needs you may have, please give my administrative assistant, Mrs. Jackie McCall or me a call at (706)689-8707.

With Warmest Regards,

Rev. Thomas H. Mills, Jr.

THE UNITED METHODIST CHURCH
LOUISIANA AREA
527 NORTH BOULEVARD
BATON ROUGE, LOUISIANA 70802-5700
(225) 346-1646
FAX (225) 387-3662

WILLIAM W. HUTCHINSON
BISHOP

June 25, 2002

The Rev. Lloyd E. Dees
P.O. Box 668
Rincon, GA 31326

Dear Rev. Dees,

Thank you for sending me a copy of your letter to Bishop Watson. I certainly appreciate the spirit with which your letter is written and the history that is behind it.

We in Louisiana are working hard to make possible some pastoral exchanges between churches of different cultures. We will be instituting those exchanges next summer, 2003, and are excited about the opportunities they hold. If in that process we find a time in which we could use your expertise and advice, we will certainly be in contact with you.

May God's blessings be with you as you continue in service to God and God's church.

In Christ's Love,

William W. Hutchinson
WWH/km

GENERAL COMMISSION ON RELIGION AND RACE
THE UNITED METHODIST CHURCH
100 Maryland Avenue, N.E., Suite 400
(United Methodist Building)
Washington, D.C. 20002-5620
202-5447-2271 • 202-547-4828
(Self Determination Fund) • 202-547-0358 (Fax)
E-mail: gcorr@erols.com / Website: www.umc.org/gcrr

Chester R. Jones, Associate General Secretaries
General Secretary
Kenneth Deere
Yolanda Hawkins
Mable Pone
James E. Taylor
Office Manager
Kathleen A. Thomas-Sano

July 12, 2002

Rev. Lloyd E. Dees
P.O. Box 668
Rincon, GA 31326

Dear Rev. Dees:

Thanks for sending me a copy of your letter to Bishop Watson. As you know racism is still the unfinished agenda of the church. I really appreciate your letter showing a deep interest in the subject of race relations. I will be with Bishop Blythe next week and we'll share this information with him.

Again, thanks for your letter of support.

In Christ,
Chester R. Jones
General Secretary
CRJ:msp

Dictated by Chester R. Jones, signed in his absence to avoid delay
President, Bishop Ellis G. Galvin • 2112 3rd Avenue Suite 301 • Seattle, WA 98121
Vice President and Chairperson, Funding Committee, • Bishop Charlene P. Kammerer • P.O. Box 18750 • Charlotte, NC 28218

Secretary, Rev. Vicky Woods • 211 W. Broadway • Bangor, ME 04401
KENTUCKY ANNUAL CONFERENCE
THE UNITED METHODIST CHURCH
LOUISVILLE AREA

7400 FLOYDBURG ROAD
CRESTWOOD, KENTUCKY 40014
JAMES R. KING, JR.
505-425-4240
RHODA A. PETERS
PRESIDING BISHOP
PROVOST

July 26, 2002

Rev. Lloyd E. Dees
P.O. Box 668
Rincon, Georgia 31326

Dear Rev. Dees:

Thank you for your letter of July 10. I appreciate your concern for our moving ahead in the United Methodist Church toward our goal of "one united church."

We are working toward cross-racial appointments in Kentucky and, in fact, have made some over the past few years. I appreciate knowing that you are available for "interim" and short-term work and will keep your letter on file, should such a need arrive.

Blessings on you in your ministry on behalf of the whole church.

Sincerely,

James R. King, Jr.
JRK/rp

126 Chase Road, N.E.
Huntsville, Alabama 35811

October 21, 2002

Dear Brother Dees,

Thank you for giving me the opportunity to render a service to help another servant of the Lord, meaning Lloyd E. Dees. Your Bermuda Song was very interesting, sentimental, and indeed a lovely original piece of music. If there is no "national anthem" for Bermuda, it just may be that someone will get the idea that your song just could fulfill that need. Who knows?

In association with the national-anthem possibility, here is another matter you might wish to consider. To avoid the indiscriminate use of your music by someone else, to use it as their own piece to submit as a "national" song, you may wish to explore the possibility of having your Bermuda Song copyrighted. That can be done by launching an inquiry at the U.S. Post Office where you can become acquainted with the proper procedure for having the copywriting done. I would not hesitate too long about that aspect of the matter if I were in your place. At least, the matter is worth investigating because both of us know how immoral and unethical some folks can be.

I hope you are pleased with what I have attempted to do in the effort to write the chords (harmony) for your music, which is based entirely on the songs you made on the tape that Henry sent to me. Please also notice that I have placed a HOLD sign on the words, BERMUDA—BERMUDA which was slightly expressed during your singing, and the use of that liberty is excellent because it seems to give dignity to the song. Also, please know the pleasure has been mine. If I can help further, please let me know. Believing that you would not mind, I have sent Henry a copy of the Bermuda Song so that he could see it.

May you continue to enjoy your retirement, which surely is a great blessing from the Lord. The truth is, retirement is somewhat impossible to accurately describe.

Yours and His Cause,

Henry Bradford Jr.

126 Chase Road, N.E.
Huntsville, Alabama 35811

September 4, 2003

The Rev. Lloyd Dees
60 Seneca Street
Dobbs Ferry, New York 10522

Dear Brother Lloyd:

Let me begin by asking your forgiveness for my not having remembered where my correspondence from you about the concert had been hidden. It was hidden so securely that my memory would not accommodate me. Then when I finally remembered, I became the victim of sorrowful procrastination and the time of your performance had come and gone. A second gesture of neglect urges me to seek a little more forgiveness because the lack of my desired financial acknowledgement surely was not intended. My guilt is so disturbing that I would be grateful if you would please send me a mailing address where I might send a "post" concert donation to Bermuda, or to you. I shall be looking to hear.

Thank you for the copy of the lovely Chimes of Hope program. Y'all had some music of high quality on that program; yet, it was not beyond "people appeal" and sure spiritual inspiration. I wish I could have been there. When you get the chance, please let me know how the Premier of Bermuda responded to the tune and text of your song, "Bermuda."

I'm tremendously grateful for your biographical sketch that was included in the program copy. My brother, you are an "electric" Methodist who is at home with the African Methodists as well as the United Methodists. Indeed, that's an interesting combination; And it's almost like the English Anglicans and the American Episcopalians. However, it is clear that you have one thing in mind and that it was to serve God and his human creations.

Henry never told me about your position as campus minister at North Carolina A&T University. Were you serving the university exclusively, and were you serving as a city pastor simultaneously? God permitted me to serve as University Chaplain at Alabama A&M University for forty-two years. Thirty-five of those years included combining that duty with being Music Department chairman there. Thirty-seven of those years, included a third responsibility as pastor of the Church St. Cumberland Presbyterian Church here in Huntsville. The way this combination worked was totally due to the grace of Almighty God. I had good assistance, a caring and understanding wife, a cooperative denomination, and presidents at Alabama A&M who were blessed with… [*Note:* This is an unfinished letter from Henry Bradford, Jr.]

126 Chase Road, N.E.
Huntsville, Alabama 35811

November 19, 2003

Dear Brother Lloyd,

Thank you indeed for all of your correspondence. All of it was absolutely delightful to read. I am still basking in the beauty of the music for strings. You are very fortunate to be in the company of such an experienced performer and a "soulful" interpreter. I still wish I could have been in Bermuda to have heard the harmonious song from the human voice as well as from the violin. Wow!

Although my donation is a bit delayed, the sincerity that prompted it is not reduced in the least; and the truth is, it is even more humbly given. It will be greatly appreciated if you would place the necessary information on the check to indicate whatever use you choose.

I trust that you and your family will enjoy a joyous and exciting Thanksgiving Day. So much is going on in the world; But those of us who are true believers must hear the words that are given in Psalm Ninety-One. Verses nine through eleven are most strengthening as they assure us in the same manner as the scribe speaks to assure his listeners saying, "Because you have made the Lord, who is my refuge, Even the Most High, your dwelling place, No evil shall befall you, nor shall any plague come near your dwelling; For He shall give His angels charge over you, to keep you in all your ways." (NKJV) For that overwhelming confidence, I am grateful in a manner that is indeed matchless and I pass it to you with the hope that both of us are in agreement.

Oh yes, Connie has alerted me about the physical condition of your youngest brother in the Dees clan. I will surely speak to the Lord regularly on his behalf.

Well, we'll talk again soon.
Yours mutually in his cause,

Brad
[Henry Bradford, Jr.]

JULY 11, 2005

THE UNITED METHODIST CHURCH
WEST VIRGINIA AREA
900 WASHINGTON STREET, EAST
CHARLESTON, WEST VIRGINIA 25301
PHONE (304)344-8330
FAX (304)344-8330

LISA M. SHAFER
ADMINISTRATIVE ASSISTANT
ERNEST S. LYGHT
BISHOP

Reverend Lloyd E. Dees
P. O. Box 668
Rincon, Georgia 31326

Dear Lloyd,

Grace and Peace be unto you.

Thanks for being in touch with and letting me know that you are doing well after your June 15 "retirement." Thank you for sending me your CD. I am looking forward to listening to it.

I was not aware of the fact that you previously served at Simpson United Methodist Church, Wheeling. I was at Christ Church, Wheeling on Sunday July 10 for the welcome/celebration of the new Northern district superintendent.

Please give my regards to Dolores. May God's love, joy, and peace be with you.

Faithfully,

Ernest S. Lyght
Bishop

ESL: lms

Effingham County Board of Commissioners

September 9, 2005

Reverend Lloyd E. Dees
P. O. Box 668
Rincon, Georgia 31326

Dear Rev. Dees,

The Board of Commissioners had their regular scheduled meeting on September 6, 2005, and voted to appoint you to serve on the Coastal Georgia Regional Development Center Aging Services Advisory Council. The director of the Council will be sending you information on meeting dates and times.

On behalf of the Board of Commissioners, I wish to thank you for your willingness to serve on the Board. We know that you are well qualified and are willing to devote the time and effort necessary to do an excellent job in this capacity.

Thank you for your continued interest in Effingham County.

Sincerely,

Hubert C. Sapp, Chairman
Effingham County Board of Commissioners

601 North Laurel St. • Springfield, Georgia 31329
(912) 754-2123 • Fax (912) 754-4157

HOUSE OF REPRESENTATIVES
WASHINGTON, D.C. 20515
JOHN BARROW
12TH DISTRICT OF GEORGIA

MAY 10, 2006

Reverend Lloyd E. Dees
P.O. Box 668
Rincon, GA 31326

Dear Reverend Dees,

Many thanks for the audio CD concerning voter participation. You are exactly right—voter turnout is a critical part of an effective representative democracy. I'm hopeful that your work and the work of others will contribute to greater civic involvement and higher voter participation.

Thanks again for caring enough to get involved, and please don't hesitate to contact me again in the future.

Sincerely,

John Barrow

COASTAL GEORGIA
REGIONAL DEVELOPMENT CENTER

October 18, 2006

Reverend Lloyd E. Dees
P.O. Box 668
Rincon, GA 31326

Dear Reverend Dees,

Congratulations! I am pleased to learn that the Aging Services Advisory Council unanimously voted to elect you as Chairman of the Aging Services Advisory Council. Since your appointment to the Advisory Council in June 2005 you have demonstrated exemplary standards by your attendance and advocacy efforts. According to our records you have perfect attendance for all meetings held in 2006. You were also instrumental in advocating for senior citizens by your attendance at Senior Week at the Capitol in February of this year.

I appreciate your efforts on behalf of the seniors in our coastal region, especially those in Effingham County. Again congratulations on your election. If there is ever anything that I can do to assist you, please give me a call at (912) 264-7363, ext. 206.

Sincerely,

Vernon D. Martin, AICP
Executive Director
VDM/ rg

cc: Sharon Dickol, Aging Services Director

Myra Lewis, Effingham County CGRDC Board member
Mayor Michael Gavin, Effingham County CGRDC Board member

Serving the cities and counties of Coastal Georgia
Post Office Box 1917 • Brunswick, Georgia 31521 • (912)264-7363 • FAX: (912)262-2313

COASTAL GEORGIA
REGIONAL DEVELOPMENT CENTER

May 10, 2007

Reverend Lloyd E. Dees
P.O. Box 668
Rincon, GA 31326

Dear Reverend Dees,

Please accept this letter as my humble appreciation to you and the members of the Aging Services Advisory Council for the honor you bestowed upon me in recognition of my service. You have and will continue to do an outstanding job as our Chairman. As you know, the Advisory Council has an awesome responsibility in working toward the improvement of services and programs for our regions senior citizens. It is people like you and the other Advisory Council members that help to vanguard the services and care of our elderly population. It is compassing to know that you and others have devoted extra time in serving on this council to ensure that this happens. I also want to thank you for attending the HR DC board meetings from time-to-time to bring our board of directors updates on the work of the Advisory Council.

Again thank you from the Advisory Council for your recognition of my service. It truly is an honor for me to have had the opportunity to work with leaders such as you during my almost 40 years of service to Coastal Georgia. It has truly been a rewarding and humbling experience.

Sincerely,

Vernon D. Martin, AICP
Executive Director

VDM/ch

OCTOBER 15, 2007
Reverend Lloyd E. Dees
P.O. Box 668
Rincon, GA 31326

Mr. R. Gerald Turner, President
Southern Methodist University
P.O. Box 750100
Dallas TX 75278

Dear President Turner,

I am a retired clergy member of the New York Annual Conference of the United Methodist Church. I am writing to express my deep concern about the idea of having the Bush Presidential Library located on the campus of Southern Methodist University. In my opinion, it would begin a practice of political partisanship.

It has been reported that at least one member of the Board of Trustees of Southern University is a powerful financial supporter of President Bush. Furthermore, I understand that this same trustee is the C.E.O. of a major oil company, and is seeking to secure a deal that will give his company a distinct advantage in the supply of Iraqi oil.

I do not believe that a university bearing the name "Methodists" should put itself in the position to be accused of practicing partisan politics and embracing a trustee whose company is seeking to profit from the spoils of a very unpopular war.

I write to you in the cause of justice and peace.

Yours truly,
Rev. Lloyd E. Dees

cc. General Secretary, Board of Global Ministries
General Secretary, Board of Higher Education and Ministry
General Secretary, Board of Church of Society
General Secretary, General Commission on Racc
Bishop Alfred Norris

SMU
Office of the President

October 23, 2007

Reverend Lloyd E. Dees
P.O. Box 668
Rincon, GA 31326

Dear Reverend Dees,

We have received your letter with your thoughts on the Bush Presidential Library at SMU. Obviously, your view of the value of having the Presidential Library as a resource for future research is different from ours.

I was a graduate student at the University of Texas when it was announced that the LBJ Library would be placed on that campus. I remember well the demonstrations and heated outcry against it. Now, much of the same would occur if serious efforts were undertaken to remove it from campus. I think that memory is what encouraged the UT Trustees to compete with SMU for the current President's Library. We are, hopefully, close to completing negotiations with the Bush Presidential Library Foundation; therefore, I hope the LBJ-UT Austin experiences are predictive of what will be ours.

Thank you for your letter.

Best wishes,

R. Gerald Turner
President

Southern Methodist University • P.O. Box 750100 • Dallas, TX 75275-0100

United States Senate
WASHINGTON D.C.

January 17, 2008

Rev. Lloyd E. Dees
P.O. Box 668
Rincon, GA 31326

Dear Rev. Dees,

I wish you well as you prepare for this year's "Senior Week" at our state Capitol. During the last week of February, your group will have the perfect opportunity to watch the legislative process in action.
I remember how much I enjoyed my time serving in the Georgia General Assembly. I hope that the participants of this event will have an equally unforgettable experience as they learn more about our state government.

I greatly appreciate your dedication in leading this trip and I know it will be even more successful than it was last year.

With warmest personal regards,

Sincerely,

Johnny Isakson
JI/kem

SEPTEMBER 6, 2010
Card received

Dear Lloyd,

Your thoughtfulness was just the magic needed most at a time greatly needed. Thank you my friend for thinking of me.

We have gone through a very difficult spell of great heat and then a lot of rain causing property damage. But, thank God we have survived.

This year I had to put on a new roof, a new deck, and new siding for the house and it has all been paid for, thanks to sufficient insurance.

I think of your folks regularly and hope all is going well. Our present pastor, who succeeded Rev. Grady, Rev. David Jefferson is doing a fine job. Incidentally Rev. Grady recently lost his mother. There has been a great number of deaths among my close friends, and sometimes I wonder why God has been so good allowing me to live, and continue doing church and social work so long. But it does keep me out of trouble (smile).

My love to you, Dolores and Janet. I'm so proud of my godchild, and I'll be getting in touch with her.

God's blessings to you all,

Nancy
[Nancy Fowlkes, Janet's Godmother]

NOVEMBER 4, 2010

The State Senate
Atlanta

Jack Hill
Senator
POST OFFICE BOX 486
FOURTH DISTRICT
REIDSVILLE, GEORGIA 30453

Rev. Lloyd E. Dees
P.O. Box 668
Rincon, Georgia 31326

Dear Rev. Dees,

Thank you so much for the enlarged, framed photo of us. I have placed it in my office in Reedsville for all to see!

You are so thoughtful! I certainly hope to see you over the next few months—if not in Effingham County then maybe at the Martin Luther King Jr. Breakfast or possibly at the General Assembly if you all can come up.

Best wishes for a blessed holiday season!

Sincerely,

Jack Hill

DUSTY ZEIGLER
Chairman at Large
DAVID R. CRAWLEY JR
County Administrator
PATRICIA R. CRAWLEY
County Clerk
ERIC R. GOTWALT
County Attorney
Effingham County Board of Commissioners
ROBERT BRANTLEY
VERA JONES
STEVE MASON
REGINALD LOPER SR.
PHIL KIEFER
District 1 District 2 District 3 District 4 District 5

June 24, 2011

Rev. Lloyd E. Dees
P. O. Box 668
Rincon, GA 31326

Re: Area Agency on Aging

Dear Rev. Dees:

At their June 21, 2011, Commissioners Meeting, the Board reappointed you to continue serving on the Area Agency on Aging.

If you have any questions, please do not hesitate to contact me at 912-754-2123.

Sincerely,

Patricia Crowley
County Clerk

601 N Laurel Street • Springfield, Georgia 31329
(912)754-2123 • Fax (912)754-4157

CONGRESS OF THE UNITED STATES
HOUSE OF REPRESENTATIVES
COMMITTEE ON ENERGY & COMMERCE
COMMITTEE ON VETERANS' AFFAIRS
OVERSIGHT AND INVESTIGATION

JOHN BARROW
12TH DISTRICT OF GEORGIA

July 5, 2011

Rev. Lloyd E. Dees
P.O. Box 668
Rincon, GA 31326-0668

Dear Rev. Dees,

Thank you for contacting me in support of preserving Medicare and Social Security. You have my steadfast support.

When Medicare was created back in 1965, only about half of folks over the age of 65 had any health insurance, and many of those only had very limited coverage for inpatient services. Today, millions of Americans benefit from the insurance Medicare provides, and thousands of folks right here in Georgia's 12th district count on Medicare as their only source of medical care.

Like Medicare, Social Security is another critical program that our seniors have paid into for decades, and I'm opposed to cutting benefits or privatizing the program. Despite recent claims, Social Security isn't in imminent danger of going bankrupt. Today, the total revenues of the program are higher than total payouts, and the nonpartisan Congressional Budget Office tells us that Social Security will continue to be fully solvent for decades.

We have to restore fiscal discipline to the nation's finances, but I refuse to place the burden of fiscal reform on our seniors and vulnerable populations. I believe we can reach agreement on a budget for next year, and I'm committed to doing so while preserving Medicare and Social Security.

Thanks again for caring enough to get involved, and please don't hesitate to contact me again in the future.

Sincerely,
John Barrow

AUGUST 15, 2011

Rev. Lloyd E. Dees
P.O. Box 668
Rincon, GA 31328

Dear Reverend Dees,

This letter is written to you to invite you to lunch to introduce the new President-Dean of Gammon Theological Seminary, Rev. A.D. Mosley. This event will be held at Skidaway Island United Methodist Church, Savannah, GA at noon on Thursday, September 22nd, 2011. The church is located at 51 Diamond Causeway, Savannah, GA 31411. Gammon Theological Seminary is a United Methodist Seminary at the Interdenominational Theological Center in Atlanta, GA. Gammon, known as "the school of the prophets," trained students, who are primarily United Methodists, for ministry in the United Methodist Church.

As a member of the Board of Directors of Gammon, I am sponsoring this event to give you an opportunity, not only to have a catered lunch, but to become familiar with the story of Gammon Theological Seminary. Reverend Mosley will give a short briefing on Gammon Theological Seminary and outline his vision and plans for the future growth of the institution. He will be placing emphasis on increasing the enrollment of Gammon Theological Seminary as well as establishing a Merit Scholars Program. We envision that scholarships will be offered to highly qualified students who are certified candidates for the ministry and come highly recommended by their local church pastor, campus minister, or other affiliate ministry.

I have invited all the United Methodists pastors in Chatham County and a number of fellow laypersons of the United Methodist Church. Reverend William (Mike) Huling, District Superintendent of the Savannah District and several alumni of Gammon will be in attendance. It is my hope that you will calendar this event and meet us on Thursday, September 22nd at noon at Skidaway Island United Methodist Church. We will terminate the lunch by 1:30 PM or before.

Please RSVP (912-414-1024) by Friday, September 9th so that the number of people attending will be provided to the caterer.

Thank you in advance for attending this affair. We anticipate that you will learn more about Gammon Theological Seminary and ways that you and/or your church may support this institution in the future. If you have any questions, please contact me at the number listed below.

Yours in Christ,
Bill Lyght
105 North Sheftall Circle
Savannah, Georgia 31410
912-414-1024
Member of Asbury
United Methodist Church

COASTAL
REGIONAL
COMMISSION
OF GEORGIA

AREA AGENCY ON AGING
Serving the Cities and Counties of Coastal Georgia since 1964

April 1, 2013

Dear Coastal Area Agency Advocates:

I want to thank you for giving your time and talents to this year's Advocacy Committee. The Georgia State Alzheimer's Association said we were a big "hit." The following information is an update on the Georgia Alzheimer's and Related Dementia State Plan Task Force that was fervently advocated at the Capital.

Legislative update:

SB14: Georgia Alzheimer's and Related Dementia State Plan Task Force sponsored by Senator Unterman (45th), Senator Wilkinson (50th), Senator Crosby (13th), Senator Hill (4th), and Senator Orrock (36th). It passed out of both Houses and is awaiting the Governor's signature.

We are not finished. By 2050, up to 16 million Americans will have Alzheimer's disease, creating an enormous strain on the health care system, families, and the federal budget. Talk with your legislators this week. Remind them that a state Alzheimer's Disease Plan creates the infrastructure and accountability necessary to confront the sweeping economic and social impact of this disease. I have enclosed some resources and talking points. Also enclosed is the picture of our 2013 Advocacy group with the Governor.

The next step for the Advocacy Academy will be addressing the Coastal Regional Delegation in the November/December timeframe in preparation for the 2014 Legislative Session. If you are interested in being part of the Legislative Committee, please contact Deborah Scariano at 912-437-0845.

Thank you again for your "voice." We couldn't do it without you!

Sincerely,

Deborah Scariano

April 1, 2013

Two Peachtree St. N.W. Suite 32-270, Atlanta, Georgia 30303-3142

(404) 657-5343 Fax (404) 657-1722
Visit www.gcoa.org
GEORGIA COUNCIL ON AGING

Rev. Lloyd E. Dees
P.O. Box 668
Ricon, GA 31326

Dear Rev. Dees,

The Georgia Council on Aging is pleased to announce that you have been nominated by the Coastal Area Agency on Aging as one of our "Martha Eaves Advocating for Positive Change" Award recipients. This award recognizes adults, (60 and above) from across the State who have devoted time and energy advocating for positive change at the local, state or federal level. By creating this award and recognizing role models for local involvement, it is hoped that others will be encouraged to become advocates for issues concerning older adults in their own communities.

We would like to invite you, free of charge, to our April 25th Coalition of Advocates for Georgia's Elderly (CO-AGE) meeting where you will be recognized. The meeting details are included in this packet. As a courtesy, a copy of this award letter has also been sent to the Coastal Area Agency on Aging. Congratulations and we look forward to meeting you on April 25th!

Sincerely,

Patty Lyons, CO-AGE Chair

Georgia's Generations Sharing Their Gifts

BERMUDA PROGRESSIVE LABOUR PARTY

ALASKA HALL, COURT STREET, HAMILTON 5-27, BERMUDA

MAILING ADDRESS:
P.O. BOX 1367
HAMILTON 5,
BERMUDA

Telephone: 2-2264
Cables: P.L.P. BERMUDA

May 2, 1983.

Rev. Lloyd E. Dees,
St. Marks United Methodist Church,
Ocean Ave and Beverley Road,
Brooklyn, N.Y. 11226,
U.S.A.

Dear Rev. Dees,

The officers of our Party are delighted to have you accept our invitation to be our Father's Day speaker this year. This gives us the opportunity of reaquaintance and you the chance to reunite with old friends again.

We would prefer if you could arrive in Bermuda not later than Friday, June 17 and we would provide accomodation for you while here as well as air fare between here and New York. We hope you will accept a small remuneration from us for your services as it is our custom so to do.

We thank you for your promptness in despatching your resume for use in advertising for we have already received it. Inform us of your definite dates of travel so we can make reservations and we will wire the ticket through to you in time for your departure.

Thanks again as we look forward to your visit.

Yours truly,

E. M. Lovette Brangman, (Mrs.)
Secretary General

EMLB:lc

Lawrence Public Schools

Alvin J. Baron

Maria R. Petraglia

Peter J. Weber

April 28, 1987

Rev. Lloyd Dees, Pastor
St. Paul's Methodist Church
200 Redwood Avenue
Inwood, NY 11696

Dear Reverend Dees:

Last night's third community meeting of the Superintendent's Advisory Committee on Minority Concerns was very exciting for me because it was our first formal attempt at parent education. I was very pleased with the turnout which, although somewhat smaller than the previous ones, made for very effective workshop sizes.

As I look back over the almost two years of meetings and programs, I am pleased that the Superintendent's Advisory Committee is no longer an ad hoc organization. I think that the group has achieved a somewhat more formal and permanent status and one which I believe is extremely important to the well being of the District. We have begun a very long journey, and I look forward with great optimism and anticipation to our continued association.

I think last night's meeting did a great deal to carry out the original goals of the Committee; namely, to open communication with parents and to provide information to them about ways to interact positively with the schools. Your participation on the Testing Panel helped to make the meeting a success. Your insightful comments and frank discussion made for a very effective presentation.

In behalf of the Board of Education, I wish to thank you for the many hours of planning which preceded last night's meeting as well as for your participation as a panelist.

Sincerely yours,

Alvin J. Baron
Superintendent

AJB:JB

c.c. Members of the Board of Education

Lawrence Public Schools

BOARD OF EDUCATION
Pasquale Ferraro, Jr.
Alvin S. Katz
Barbara Berkowitz
Anita Cuchel
Diane Nelson
Janet M. Rose
Arthur H. Sobel
Elliott Norwalk
Mildred E. Magnusson

Post Office Box 477
Lawrence, New York 11559

February 1, 1988

Rev. Lloyd Dees
Freeport United Methodist Church
46 Pine Street
Freeport, N.Y. 11520

Dear Rev. Dees:

In behalf of the Board of Education, I would like to thank you for your many contributions to the Lawrence Public Schools. You served as a member of the Continuing Education Advisory Committee making suggestions for enriching our offerings to the community. As an initiator and founding member of the Superintendent's Advisory Committee for Minority Concerns, you were instrumental in establishing communication between the administration, Board and the minority community at large. We always appreciated your participation at High School graduation ceremonies.

The Board wishes to acknowledge the significant manner in which you enriched community life in the District and extends good wishes for happiness and success to you, Mrs. Dees and the children.

Sincerely,

PASQUALE FERRARO, JR., PRESIDENT
Lawrence Board of Education

ALVIN J. BARON
Superintendent

PF:mem
c.c. Members of the Board of Education

LAWRENCE UNION FREE SCHOOL DISTRICT

PO Box 668
Rincon, GA 31326
November 1, 1999

Bishop Robert C. Morgan, President
Council of Bishops
The United Methodist Church
2000 Warrington Way
Louisville, Kentucky 40222

Dear Bishop Morgan,

"Grace be to you and peace from God our Father and from the Lord Jesus Christ."

I am a recently retired member of the New York Annual Conference- having served fifteen years in the African Methodist Episcopal Church and twenty-seven years in the United Methodist Church.

My wife and I are now living in Rincon, Georgia- not far from Savannah. My new status and the summer season provided us with the opportunity to visit and worship in several United Methodist Churches in and around Savannah. While worshipping one Sunday morning in one of our "historic" churches in downtown Savannah, I was forcefully awakened to what I knew deep inside and I am sure that all the Bishops of our Church know as well. Many of our local churches are practicing segregation on Sunday mornings. So, we worshipped in churches where we were the only Blacks in attendance and churches where there were no Whites in attendance.

It has been 31 years since the dissolution of the Central Jurisdiction, but, our goal of "One United Church" is far from being reached. I believe it is a noble goal still, and that it should be pursued with vigor and commitment.

It seems to me that the upcoming meetings of the Council of Bishops and the General Conference of early next year will provide excellent opportunities for our Bishops to re-articulate our goals and aims, and to encourage the Church to re-vitalize its efforts to walk the road that leads towards "one-ness." This- I believe- would be a powerful witness of our Church for the 21st century.

Your faithful servant,

Lloyd E. Dees

cc: The United Methodist Bishops in the United States

THE UNITED METHODIST CHURCH

INDIANA AREA

WOODIE W. WHITE, *Resident Bishop*

DR. JAMES J. JONES, *Executive Assistant*

September 12, 2003

Reverend Lloyd E. Dees
P.O. Box 668
Rincon, Georgia 31326

Dear Lloyd,

Thanks for your continuing commitment to the eradication of Racism.

You will be pleased to know that the Council of Bishops has identified the issue of Racism as one of our priorities for the quadrennium. A rather comprehensive effort is in the works and will be implemented across the Church.

Here in Indiana, I prepared an Episcopal Pastoral Letter on Race, which was to have been read in every congregation. Additionally the 18 Districts in the Indiana Area will have or already have had a day long District Event on Racism. I prepared a video that was used, and follow-up efforts are anticipated after each District Event.

We are definitely still addressing the issue forthrightly, even if you don't see anything in the Church press.

Thanks for your reminder!

Sincerely,

Woodie W. White

WWW/kj

LONG ISLAND EAST DISTRICT

Rev. Dr. Allen N. Pinckney Jr.
District Superintendent

357 MacArthur Boulevard Hauppauge, N.Y. 11788-3002 Telephone 631-366-2396 Fax 631-366-4842

March 26, 2002

Rev. Lloyd Dees
P.O. Box 668
Rincon, Georgia 31326

Dear Rev. Dees

Thank you for your letter and your concern regarding the issue of cross cultural/racial appointments. You have clearly given critical thought to the matter and have articulated some very important concerns. As one who has served in cross cultural/cross racial appointments, I am deeply aware of the need for the cabinet and our conference to provide strategic leadership in addressing this critical area in the life of our church.

It is not easy as you have pointed out, and does require tremendous courage to withstand the forces of opposition that prefer to maintan the status quo. I would ask that you keep the appoint cabinet and Bishop in prayer. Please understand that in addition to this very significant issue, the appointment making process presents very complicated factors and dynamics that the cabinet constantly struggles with.

I ask that you pray that the Holy Spirit will grant us the discerning power to appropriately and creatively match ordained clergy with the very diverse churches that comprise our conference.

Yours in Christ

Rev. Dr. Allen N. Pinckney Jr.
District Superintendent Long Island East

ANP/bma

GENERAL COMMISSION ON RELIGION AND RACE
THE UNITED METHODIST CHURCH
100 Maryland Avenue, N.E., Suite 400 (United Methodist Building) Washington, D.C. 20002-5620
202-547-2271 ♦ 202-547-4828 (Self Determination Fund) ♦ 202-547-0353 (Fax)
E-mail: gcorr@crols.com / Website: www.umc.org/gcrr

Chester R. Jones
General Secretary

Mable Pone
Office Manager

Associate General Secretaries
Kenneth Deere
Erin Hawkins
Yolanda Pupo-Ortiz
James E. Taylor
Kathleen A. Thomas-Sano

July 12, 2002

Rev. Lloyd E. Dees
P.O. Box 668
Rincon, GA 31326

Dear Rev. Dees:

Thanks for sending me a copy of your letter to Bishop Watson. As you know racism is still the unfinished agenda of the Church. I really appreciate your letter showing a deep interest in the subject of race relations. I will be with Bishop Lyght next week and will share this information with him.

Again, thanks for your letter of support.

In Christ,

C.R.J.
Chester R. Jones
General Secretary

CRJ:msp

Dictated by Chester R. Jones, signed in his absence to avoid delay

President, Bishop Elias G. Galván ♦ 2112 3rd Avenue, Suite 301 ♦ Seattle, WA 98121
Vice President and Chairperson, Funding Committee, ♦ Bishop Charlene P. Kammerer ♦ P.O. Box 18750 ♦ Charlotte, NC 28218
Secretary, Rev. Vicki Woods ♦ 211 W Broadway ♦ Bangor, ME 04401

KENTUCKY ANNUAL CONFERENCE
THE UNITED METHODIST CHURCH
LOUISVILLE AREA

7400 FLOYDSBURG ROAD
CRESTWOOD, KENTUCKY 40014
502-425-4240

JAMES R. KING, JR.
RESIDENT BISHOP

RHODA A. PETERS
PROVOST

July 26, 2002

Rev. Lloyd E. Dees
P. O. Box 668
Rincon, Georgia 31326

Dear Rev. Dees:

Thank you for your letter of July 10. I appreciate your concern for our moving ahead in the United Methodist Church toward our goal of "one united church."

We are working toward cross-racial appointments in Kentucky and, in fact, have made some over the past few years. I appreciate knowing that you are available for "interim" and short-term work and will keep your letter on file, should such a need arrive.

Blessings on you in your ministry on behalf of the whole church.

Sincerely,

James R. King, Jr.

JRK/rp

Office of the President

October 23, 2007

Reverend Lloyd E. Dees
P.O. Box 668
Rincon, GA 313326-0668

Dear Reverend Dees:

We have received your letter with your thoughts on the Bush Presidential Library at SMU. Obviously, your view of the value of having the Presidential Library as a resource for future research is different from ours.

I was a graduate student at the University of Texas when it was announced that the LBJ Library would be placed on that campus. I remember well the demonstrations and heated outcry against it. Now, much of the same would occur if serious efforts were undertaken to remove it from campus. I think that memory is what encouraged the UT Trustees to compete with SMU for the current President's Library.

We are, hopefully, close to completing negotiations with the Bush Presidential Library Foundation; therefore, I hope the LBJ-UT Austin experiences are predictive of what will be ours.

Thank you for your letter.

Best wishes,

R. Gerald Turner
President

Southern Methodist University PO Box 750100 Dallas TX 75275-0100
[illegible]

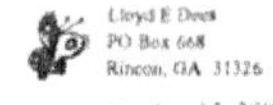

Lloyd E Dees
PO Box 668
Rincon, GA 31326

October 15, 2007

Mr R Gerald Turner, President
Southern Methodist University
PO Box 750100
Dallas, TX 75275

Dear President Turner:

I am a retired clergy member of the New York Annual Conference of the United Methodist Church.

I am writing to express my deep concern about the idea of having the Bush Presidential Library located on the campus of Southern Methodist University. In my opinion, it would begin a practice of political partisanship.

It has been reported that at least one member of the Board of Trustees of Southern University is a powerful financial supporter of President Bush. Furthermore, I understand that this same trustee is the C.E.O. of a major oil company, and is seeking to secure a deal that would give his company a distinct advantage in the supply of Iraqi oil.

I do not believe that a university bearing the name "Methodist" should put itself in the position to be accused of practicing partisan politics and embracing a trustee whose company is seeking to profit from the spoils of a very unpopular war.

I write to you in the cause of justice and peace.

Yours truly,

Rev. Lloyd E. Dees

Cc: General Secretary, Board of Global Ministries
General Secretary, Board of Higher Education and Ministry
General Secretary, Board of Church of Society
General Secretary, General Commission on Race
Bishop Alfred Norris

GEORGIA COUNCIL ON AGING

Two Peachtree St. N.W., Suite 30-270, Atlanta, GA 30303-3142
(404) 657 5240 Fax (404) 657 1722
Visit www.gcoa.org

April 1, 2013

Rev. Lloyd E. Dees
P.O. Box 668
Rincon, GA 31326

Dear Rev. Dees,

The Georgia Council on Aging is pleased to announce that you have been nominated by the Coastal Area Agency on Aging as one of our "Martha Eaves Advocating for Positive Change" Award recipients. This award recognizes adults, (60 and above) from across the State who have devoted time and energy advocating for positive change at the local, state or federal level. By creating this award and recognizing role models for local involvement, it is hoped that others will be encouraged to become advocates for issues concerning older adults in their own communities.

We would like to invite you, free of charge, to our April 25th Coalition of Advocates for Georgia's Elderly (CO-AGE) meeting where you will be recognized. The meeting details are included in this packet. As a courtesy, a copy of this award letter has also been sent to the Coastal Area Agency on Aging.

Congratulations and we look forward to meeting you on April 25th

Sincerely,

Patti Lyons

Patti Lyons, CO-AGE Chair

Georgia's Generations Sharing Their Gifts

CONGRESS OF THE UNITED STATES
HOUSE OF REPRESENTATIVES

COMMITTEE ON ENERGY & COMMERCE

COMMITTEE ON VETERANS' AFFAIRS

JOHN BARROW
12TH DISTRICT OF GEORGIA

July 5, 2011

The Rev. Lloyd E. Dees
PO Box 668
Rincon, GA 31326-0668

Dear Rev. Dees,

Thank you for contacting me in support of preserving Medicare and Social Security. You have my steadfast support.

When Medicare was created back in 1965, only about half of folks over the age of 65 had any health insurance, and many of those only had very limited coverage for inpatient services. Today, millions of Americans benefit from the insurance Medicare provides, and thousands of folks right here in Georgia's 12th District count on Medicare as their only source of medical care.

Like Medicare, Social Security is another critical program that our seniors have paid into for decades, and I'm opposed to cutting benefits or privatizing the program. Despite recent claims, Social Security isn't in imminent danger of going bankrupt. Today, the total revenues of the program are higher than total payouts, and the non-partisan Congressional Budget Office tells us that Social Security will continue to be fully solvent for decades.

We have to restore fiscal discipline to the nation's finances, but I refuse to place the burden of fiscal reform on our seniors and vulnerable populations. I believe we can reach agreement on a budget for next year, and I'm committed to doing so while preserving Medicare and Social Security.

Thanks again for caring enough to get involved, and please don't hesitate to contact me again in the future.

Sincerely,

John

John Barrow

AREA AGENCY ON AGING

Serving the Cities and Counties of Coastal Georgia since 1964

April 1, 2013

Dear Coastal Area Agency Advocates:

I want to thank you for giving your time and talents to this years Advocacy Committee. The Georgia State Alzheimer's Association said we were a big "hit." The following information is an update on the Georgia Alzheimer's and Related Dementia State Plan Task Force that was fervently advocated at the Capitol.

Legislative Update:

SB 14: Georgia Alzheimer's and Related Dementia State Plan Task Force Sponsored by Senator Unterman (45th), Senator Wilkinson (50th), Senator Crosby (13th), Senator Hill (4th), and Senator Orrock (36th). It passed out of both Houses and is awiting the Governers signature.

We are not finished. By 2050, up to 16 million Americans will have Alzheimer's disease, creating an enormous strain on the health care system, families, and the federal budget. Talk with your legislators this next week. Remind them that a state Alzheimer's Disease Plan creates the infrastructure and accountability necessary to confront the sweeping economic and social impact of this disease. I have enclosed some resources and talking points. Also enclosed is the picture of our 2013 Advocacy group with the Governer.

The next step for the Advocacy Academy will be addressing the Coastal Regional Delegation in the November/December timeframe in preparation for the 2014 Legislative Session. If you are interested in being part of the Legislative Committee, please contact Deborah Scariano at 912-4737-0845.

Thank you again for your "voice." We couldn't do it without you!

Sincerely,

Deborah Scariano

Chapter 11

Pictures/News Articles

Rev. and Mrs. Dees Wedding, September 14, 1957

Page 4 The Royal Gazette, Wednesday, March 25, 1970

Prices too high — pastors to stage fast over Easter

Two Bermuda A.M.E. pastors are to undergo a four-day fast over Easter as a protest against increasing high prices for food and housing.

They are the Rev. Lloyd E. Dees, of Bethel A.M.E. Church, Shelly Bay, and the Rev. John E. Brandon, of Allen Temple A.M.E. Church, Somerset.

Their fast will start at midnight tonight, and continue through to midnight Sunday.

During that time they will eat sparingly of bread, and drink a little water. No other food or sustenance will pass their lips.

News of the fast came yesterday in a "joint statement."

In it, they said "We are taking this action mainly for two reasons: (1) We hope that the general public will become more aware of the increasing high prices being paid for such basic commodities as food and housing; (2) We hope that the Government will be moved to take some action in regulating prices, and instituting a degree of price control."

Mr. Dees told The Royal Gazette that during the fast, both he and his colleague would be "confined" to their parsonages as much as possible.

"We feel that such action as this is very much part of our job. We are not trying to start a petition of protest. We will let people be led by their own consciences. There is no question of a mass demonstration."

The Royal Gazette, March 25, 1970

Monday March 30, 1970 / Page 3 The Royal Gazette

Pastors' appeal for costs cut

The two ministers who last night ended a four-day fast in protest at rising prices appealed to Bermuda merchants to voluntarily reduce costs.

The Rev. John Brandon and the Rev. Lloyd Dees, both pastors of the A.M.E. Church, declined an open invitation to have talks with the Member for Finance, the Hon. Jack Sharpe, and said in a joint statement:

"We do not intend to confuse our position as ministers of the Gospel, for we are not politicians.

"We as pastors speaking on behalf of those who suffer under the present price crisis would first of all call upon the merchants of the community to take some voluntary steps to reduce the crisis."

"Secondly, we urgently implore the Government to begin immediately to set up guidelines for some regulatory procedure to halt spiralling prices in Bermuda."

The important question, they said, is not whether or not some kind of price control will work, but rather how are people being affected under the present situation.

"What happens to the average citizen when he has to suffer outrageous discrepancies in prices from week to week and place to place when his wages remain unchanged?"

Although the fast ended at midnight Mr. Brandon said he would be eating only soup and crackers for the next few days before going back to regular eating.

"I have not suffered any adverse affects, just a feeling of being tired," he said.

"It has made me more determined than anything else to see this thing through."

Mr. Brandon said he would continue to limit his eating habits in protest at the situation.

The Royal Gazette, March 30, 1970

The Bermuda Recorder
Hamilton, Bermuda
Saturday, April 18, 1970

Page 1 & 2

VOLUME 46

Page 1

Pastors Issue Open Letter To Governor

The Rev. John E. Brandon, Pastor of Allen Temple A.M.E. Church and Rev. Lloyd E. Dees, Pastor of Bethel A.M.E. Church have co-authored the following open letter to His Excellency the Governor. Both of these Pastors have been in the news recently as a result of their silent price protest vigil which they staged on the grounds of the House of Assembly last Friday and this past Wednesday. They both feel that it is their responsibility to their respective congregations, many of whom they stated are feeling the pinch of the spiraling cost of living. To them pastoring is to concern oneself with the whole man. Consequently, they have been quietly attempting to focus attention on a problem which they feel is vitally important to their individual members and the general public.

"We take time to write this letter to you at a most critical moment in the history of Bermuda. It is with a great deal of urgency that we address you. We know that you are aware of recent events with respect to high and rising prices. You also know that on two occasions we took our cause to the House of Asembly in a most peaceful manner and that little has been said—and nothing has been done to bring about a positive change in the present price-crisis as it exists in Bermuda. We are writing you to impress upon you our deep concern about this situation.

"One of the expressions which we have had from members of government is that they are unable to do anything about high and rising prices. However, we take the position that government can do something about this issue. The crucial question is whether or not government is **willing** to do something about this most important matter. It appears to us that government has been doing whatever it desired to do at any given time. We wonder why government feels incapable of acting at the present time on the price issue. We also wonder if government is really concerned about the welfare of all the people. The impression one gets is that members of government are oblivious to the needs of the people. We hope that ~~this is~~ not true. We must admit, however, that there are a few members of government who agree that high and rising prices should be dealt with. But these same members state that they can do nothing about regulating or controlling prices. We happen to know that there is a degree of price-control on certain commodities at the present time. If government can control prices in these areas, why can it not do same in the area of food and rent?

"We noted with much interest the government's budget for the fiscal year 1970-71, and were quite amazed that $3,500.00 a year were approved for the feeding of your horses. Could it be that government 's more concerned about feeding horses than it is about feeding babies?

"With respect to government's alledged inability to do certain things, can you tell the public, Sir, how government was able to approve $9.600.00 a year for your entertainment allowance and $800.00 for the acting Governor?

"The Member for Finance has stated (as reported in the Bermuda Sun, Saturday, April 11, 1970) that, 'There is no duty levied on basic commodities.' But he has failed to let the public know what these basic commodities are and whether merchants are selling these "basic commodities" as if duty is being levied. Do you think that in light of the price-crisis that such a disclosure

(Continued on Page 4)

The Bermuda Recorder, April 18, 1970

Page 28

The Bermuda Recorder
Hamilton, Bermuda
Saturday, April 18, 1970

Pastors Issue

(Continued from Page 1)

would be in the interest of the public ?

"We are writing you, Sir, because we trust that you will use the influence of your office to affect some positive change in this critical situation. As we have stated earlier, we will be relentless in our effort to bring about a positive change in the present crisis of prices.

"We hope that the government is not misled by the apparent silence of many individuals on this matter of prices. Many are simply afraid of reprisals if they speak the truth openly. This to us is an indication of the kind of fear that pervades the whole community—a most unhealthy atmosphere.

"Our concern is that you will grasp the significance of this matter and be moved to address yourself to it in a meaningful way.

"We hope that you will take under consideration the peaceful means we are using to dramatize the sad state of things when it comes to outrageous prices in Bermuda. This is the way we would like to affect change.

Yours for a peaceful solution
to high and rising prices,

John E. Brandon,
Allen Temple A.M.E. Church.
Lloyd E. Dees,
Bethel A. M. E. Church."

The Bermuda Recorder (page 2), April 18, 1970

CERTIFICATE OF RECOGNITION

THIS RECOGNIZES THE ATTENDANCE AND PARTICIPATION OF

LLOYD DEES

IN THE **NATIONAL CHRISTIAN EDUCATION TRAINING FOR ETHNIC MINORITY CHURCHES** ON

FEBRUARY 10-13, 1978

ASSISTANT GENERAL SECRETARY
SECTION ON ETHNIC MINORITY LOCAL CHURCH

OCIATE GENERAL SECRETARY
DIVISION F EDUCATION

BOARD OF DISCIPLESHIP
THE UNITED METHODIST CHURCH

February 21, 1978
DATE

Certificate of Recognition for Attendance and Participation in the National Christian Education Training for Ethnic Minority Churches, February 21, 1978

Bishop Roy Sano with Rev. Dees, 1992

Texas Southern University

Weekend College and Continuing Education

Certificate

to

LLOYD E. DEES

IN RECOGNITION

OF PARTICIPATION IN

"TRUTH AND RELEVANCE: THE CASE FOR A MULTICULTURAL CURRICULUM"

.1 CONTINUING EDUCATION UNITS (C.E.U.'S)

1 CLOCK HOUR

CONDUCTED AT

Texas Southern University

Course Director

JULY 22, 1991

Date

Director of Continuing Education Program

Certificate of Participation in Continuing Education Units conducted at Texas Southern University, July 22, 1991

March 6, 1992

BERMUDA TIMES 12

AROUND THE COMMUNITY

VISITING MINISTERS: Rev. Dr. John Brandon and Rev. Lloyd Dees, founders of Bermudians for Reconciliation recentlyh returned to the island for rest and relaxation.

Around the Community–Rev. Brandon (left) and Rev. Dees (right), March 6, 1992

Shangri-La and Rev. Dees, circa 1997

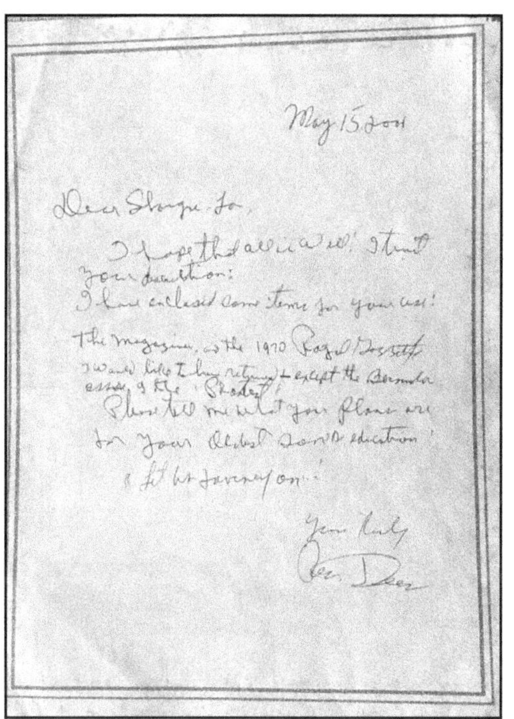

May 15 2001

Dear Shangri-La,

I hope that all is well! I trust your [illegible]:

I have enclosed some items for your use!

The magazine, and the 1970 Royal Gazette

I would like to have returned — except the Bermuda essay, & the 'Shades'!

Please tell me what your plans are for your oldest son's education!

[illegible] journey on!

Yours Truly

Rev. Dees

Note to Shangri-La, May 15, 2001

Rev. Dees and my brother, Coolidge "Danny" Durham, when Rev. Dees visited Bethel. My brother later became an A.M.E. minister, Rev. Coolidge (now deceased), June 15, 2003

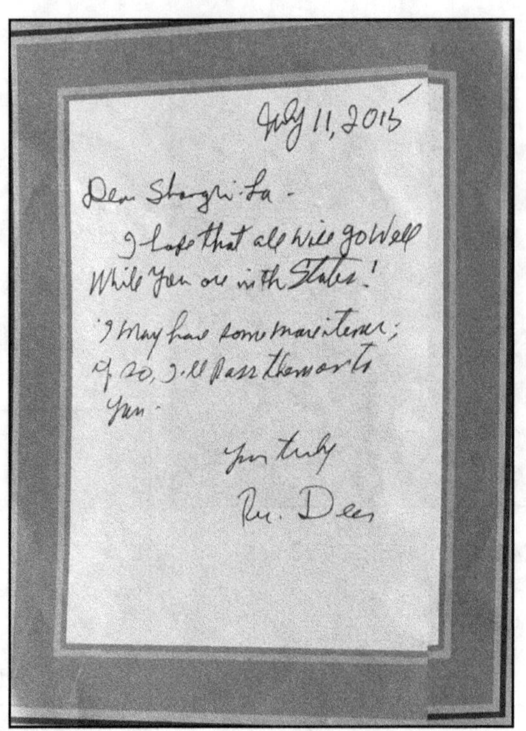

July 11, 2015

Dear Shangri-La -

I hope that all will go well
While you are in the States!

I may have some more items;
if so, I'll pass them on to
you.

Yours truly

Rev. Dees

Note to Shangri-La, July 11, 2015

Rev. and Mrs. Dees, 2013

The Chimes of Hope Concert, June 17, 2003

The
Solid Rock Foundation

Presents

The Chimes of Hope Concert

An Evening of Classical and Sacred Music

Featuring

Reverend Lloyd E. Dees, Vocalist

Dr. Anne Yarrow, Violinist

Tuesday, June 17, 2003
8:00 PM

St. Paul Centennial Hall - No 15
Court Street
Hamilton, Bermuda

The Solid Rock Foundation

Executive Director: Mrs. Shangri-La Durham-Thompson

Treasurer: Mrs. Tonia Minors

Secretary: Ms. Kellianne Gibbons

Technical Director: Ms. Quemande Brangman:

Publicity: Mrs. Edna Dill

Member at Large: Mrs. Julia Durham, JP

Ushers

Mrs. Marjorie Whitter- Head Usher

Ms. Renee Wilson

Mrs. Annette Whitter

Mr. David Lovell

Mr. Eric Whitter

I am honoured to hold this concert under my drama group, The Solid Rock Foundation. Although it is true that Rev. Dees did much for me, it is also true that he did so much for Bermuda. He went on a hunger strike to protest the rising cost of living in Bermuda in 1971 and organized a march on parliament. Because of his belief in working for justice, the Bermuda Reconciliation Organization was born. Today we have a consumer Affairs Bureau. Therefore, since he did so much for all of us, I would like for us to do something for him and filling the concert hall would be a nice way of showing our appreciation. Additionally, the concert promises to be an inspirational one.

Shangri-La

Dr. Anne Yarrow - Violinist

Anne Yarrow, violinist, conductor and college professor holds Bachelor and Master Degrees in music from Yale University, School of Music where she was a scholarship student of Joseph Fuchs. She has done further studies with Helen Airoff Dowling in New York and Switzerland; Nadia Boulanger in France and Maxim Jacabsen in Portugal. She also received a Ph D. in Musicology and Violin Performance from New York University.
Dr. Yarrow was a member of several violin-piano duos specializing in the 19th Century Romantic Repertoire and of The Musinger Players, a vocal-insrtumental chamber ensemble consisting of soprano, tenor, clarinet, oboe, violin, and piano. As an Edvard Grieg scholar, she gave a presentation at Grieg's Sesgnicentennial Celebration in Bergen, Norway in 1993 - one of three scholars invited from trhe United States. In the 1990s to the present, she has been active in performing and promoting the works of living composers. In addition to a concert career, Dr. Yarrow is currently on the music faculty of Molloy College in New York, where she founded and conducts the Molloy College Community orchestra.
For the past three years, Anne Yarrow has been recording and producing C.D's in Switzerland and New York with Swiss pianist Caspar Dechmann and American composer/pianist Herbert Rothgarber. Just released is a solo album entitled Adoration - 18 short works for violin and piano with Dechmann and Rothgarber at the piano. Her latest musical endeavor, Chimes of Hope, with Reverend Lloyd Dees and Laurel Tompkins, represents a fusion of music and ministry, designed to bring healing and reconciliation to all peoples

Laurel Tompkins
(Pianist)

Laurel Tompkins, pianist, organist, and teacher, graduated from Westminster Choir College in Princeton, New Jersey where she received a Bachelor of Music Education, majoring in organ. For many years, she taught music in the public schools on Long Island and has served as organist and choir director at numerous churches in the New York area. While at Westminster, she performed under the direction of several outstanding conductors, including Eugene Ormandy and Leonard Bernstein.

Laurel has accompanied numerous vocalist and instrumentalists, and presently plays with the Suffolk Y chamber group on Long Island. Throughout her live, she has shown a versatile interest in all the arts and has exhibited and sold professionally her crafts and floral arrangements. Among her other interests, Laurel Tompkins is a yoga practitioner, canine companion trainer, and spiritual healer. She brings to Chimes of Hope a long time association as concert partner with violinist Anne Yarrow, and a music ministry as a church organist with Reverend Lloyd Dees, dating back to the years when he served as Pasteur of the Freeport United Methodist Church on Long Island.

The Chimes of Hope Concert, June 17, 2003

Reverend Lloyd E. Dees

Reverend Lloyd E. Dees, a native of Alabama, is married to Delores Mills Dees; they have a daughter, Janet and a son, Jason - who was born in Bermuda.

Rev. Dees has an undergraduate degree in philosophy and a master of Divinity in Biblical Studies from the International Theological Center, Atlanta, Georgia; and he has done further studies at Princeton Theological Seminary, New Jersey, and the Union Theological Seminary, New York.

Reverend Dees has held several positions during his ministry: Social Investigator, New York City Department of social services; Executive Director, Commission on Human Rights, Wheeling, West Virginia,; Campus Minister, North Carolina A&T State University at Greensboro. But his great love is that of being pastor to the local church and the community in which the local church is located.

In 1960, Reverend Dees came to Bermuda to be pastor to Bethel AME Church in Shelly Bay. And in soul and spirit he has never left. He became known throughout the Island for his ministry at Bethel and for other community activities. During Holy Week, 1970, he and Reverend John E. Bandon, the pastor of Allen Temple AME Church in Somerset, went on a fast- eating only bread, and drinking water, to protest the high cost of living in Bermuda. The same two ministers were co-founders of Bermudians for Reconciliation - which Randolph Hayward became president - to focus on this and other issues. Through the efforts of this organization, and other supporters and friends, the Bermuda Government was persuaded to establish a Bureau of Consumer Affairs.

Since 1979, Reverend Dees has been an ardent supporter of the Progressive Labour Party, and has participated in many of its activities, He came in January, 1998 for the great victory celebration, and presented a poem to Premier Jennifer Smith - which he had written especially for the occasion, titled: "An ode for the Premier of Bermuda". Now, Reverend Dees is returning to Bermuda to sing - which is a surprise to many people. This time, he has composed a song titled: BERMUDA SONG. He will sing and dedicate the song to the Premier, who will be present at the concert on June 17th.

When asked about his singing, he said, "It is just something that I like to do'. I sang in the Sunday School Choir; my high school choir, and my seminary Glee Club". He gives thanks to the many organist who have nurtured his soul in the many churches in which he has been a pastor.

M.C. Shangri-La Durham-Thompson

Programme
The Chimes of Hope

Lloyd E. Dees
Voice
Anne Yarrow
Violin
Laurel Tompkins
Piano

I. Invocation: .... Reverend Conway Simmons,
Pastor: St. Paul A.M.E. Church, Hamilton, Bermuda

II. Greetings: .... The Honourable Lois Browne-Evans

III. Largo .... Veracini
IV. Melodie .... Gluck
V. Allegro .... Vivaldi

VI. Balm in Gilead .... African American Spiritual
VII. Because He Lives .... Gaither
VIII. Pilgrim's Journey .... Anonymous

IX, Adoration .... Borowski
X. Sicilienne .... Paradis
XI. Intrada .... Moffat

XII. Home in 'Dat' Rock .... Traditional
XIII. This Is My Song .... Sibelius/Stone
XIV. Bermuda Song .... Dees
(Dedicated to the Honourable Jennifer Smith, JP,MP, Premier of Bermuda)
XV. *The Premier's Expressions*

**** Intermission ****

XVI. Go Down Moses .... Traditional
XVII Swing Low Sweet Chariot .... Traditional
XVIII. City Called Heaven .... African American Spiritual
XIX. Fix Me Jesus .... Traditional

XX. Deserted Garden .... Price
XXI. Romance .... Wieniawski
XXII Intermezzo .... Schumann
XXIII. Sanatensatz .... Brahams

Presentation – To All Three – Kelly Anne Gibbons

PATRON LIST - REV. DEES

Mrs. Gereen Albouy
Mrs. T. E. Animashaun
Mr. & Mrs. Alfred Augustus
Mrs. Gloria Bascome
Mrs. Phillipa Bassett
Mrs. Laquita Bean
Rev. & Mrs. Lorne Bean
Mrs. Verna Bean
Ms. Violet Brangman
Ms. Waynette Brangman
Mrs. Dawnette Brown
Mrs. Sandra Brown
Mrs. Elsie Browne
The Hon. Dame Lois M. Browne-Evans
Mrs. Aurelia Burch
Mrs. Paulette Burgess
Mrs. Robin Burgess
Rev. Dr. Milton Burgess JP & Mrs. Gloria Burgess
Mr. & Mrs. Randall Butler
Mr. Derek Caines
Rev. & Mrs. Micah Chandler
Mr. & Mrs. Calvin Christopher
Dr. Joseph & Mrs. Marlene Christopher
Ms. Donna Clarke
Dr. Faith Clarke
Mrs. Jean Clarke
Mr. Geddes & Rev. Maureen Clemendor
Mrs. Pamela Coleman
Mr. & Mrs. Clarence Corbin
Mrs. Terry Cox
Mr. & Mrs. Arthur Daniels
Mr. & Mrs. William DeShields
Mr. & Mrs. Randolph Dickinson
Mrs. Edna Dill
Rev. Howard & Rev. Emily-Gail Dill
Mrs. Margaret Donawa
Mr. Coolidge & Mrs. Julia Durham Sr., JP
Mr. Coolidge & Mrs. Paula Durham Jr.
Mrs. Shelby Durham-Jackson
Dr. Donna-Gay Durham-Pierre
Presiding Elder, Rev. Malcolm L. Eve, JP
&
Mrs. Elvia Eve
Mr. & Mrs. Elroy Eve
Mr. & Mrs. Roland Francis
Mrs. Una Francis
Mrs. Thelma Francis
Ms. Joan Furbert Forde
Mr. Glen & Mrs. Deonn Fubler
Mrs. Eloise Furbert JP
Ms. Lynell M. Furbert JP
Mr. & Mrs. Sheldon Fox
Mr. & Mrs. Sheldon Fox
Mrs. Greta Gibbons
Mrs. Henrietta Gibbons

Ms. Karla Gibbons
Ms. Kellianne Gibbons
Mrs. Shawnette Griffin
Rev. & Mrs. Rodney Grimes
Mr. & Mrs. Gerald Harvey
Mr. Randolph Hayward
Mr. & Mrs. Conrad Henry
Mr. Randolph Horton JP, MP
Mrs. Karen Hurdle
Ms. Robin Ingham
Dr. Hermoine Jackson
Mr. & Mrs. Claude James
Mr. & Mrs. Austin John
Dr. Vincent & Mrs. John
Mr. Sherwin Jones
Rev. & Mrs. Philip Knights
Mrs. Nathley Landy
Mr. & Mrs. Leroy Lewis
Rev. Dr. Larry Lowe MP & Mrs. Lowe
Mr. Stephen & Mrs. Carolla Lowe
Mr. & Mrs. Willard Lightbourne
Ms. Jennifer Manders
Mr. & Mrs. Quinton Manders
Mrs. Ross Manders
Mr. Lloyd Matthew
Ms. Linda Merritt
Mr. Patrick McDonald Mills
Mr. Malcolm Ming
Mrs. Tonia Minors
Imani Myers
Ms. Virginia Outerbridge
Mrs. Alice Pearman
Ms. Chris Pearman
Mr. & Mrs. Lionel Phillips
Mrs. Margaret Postlewaite
Ms. Terry Pringle
Mrs. Brenda Raynor
Mr. Llewelyn Richards
Mr. & Mrs. Beresford Richardson
Mr. & Mrs. Darius Richardson
Mr. & Mrs. Denny Richardson
Mr. Eugene Richardson
Mrs. Leslie Robinson
Mr. R. Reid Robinson
Mrs. Windfield Robinson
Mrs. Hilda Romaine
Rev. Dr. Leonard Santucci JP
Mrs. Muriel Santucci
The Hon. Alex Scott MP & Mrs. Scott
Ms. Anette Simmons
Rev. Conway & Mrs. Simmons
Mr. Cyril S. Simmons
Ms. Malinda Simmons
Mr. & Mrs. Norbert Simmons
Mr. Ottiwell Simmons MP & Mrs. Simmons
Mr. & Mrs. Stuart Simmons
Mrs. Pearl Simmons, JP
Ms. Carol Smith

The Chimes of Hope Concert, June 17, 2003

Rev. Charles A. Smith
Mr. & Mrs. Cecil Smith
Mrs. Edna Smith
Mr. Leon Smith
Mr. & Mrs. Osrola Smith
Rev. Ruth VanLowe Smith
Mr. & Mrs. Neville Somner
Mr. Burgon Spencer
Mrs. Cynthia Stovell
Mr. Leon McPhee Stovell
Mrs. Sheila Swan
Mrs. Valerie Symonds
Mr. Stanton Thompson
&
Mrs. Shangri-La Durham-Thompson
Mrs. Elizabeth Trott
Mr. Gilbert Trott
Mr. Marvin Trott
Mr. Perry Trott
Mrs. Thelma Trott
Mrs. Bernadette Tucker
Mrs. Dorothy Tucker
Ms. Gina Tucker
Mrs. Gloria Tucker
Mr. & Mrs. Morris Tucker
Mr. & Mrs. Sean Tucker, JP
Mrs. Lynn Tucker
Mrs. Shirlene Tucker
Mr. Derek Tully
Mr. & Mrs. Dennis Wainwright
Mr. Eugene & Mrs. Rosa Wainwright
Rev. & Mrs. D.wain Wales
Mr. McNeil Warner
Mrs. Cheri Whitter
Mr. Larry & Mrs. Lesiline Williams
Mrs. Renee Wilson
Mr. & Mrs. Roy Wright
*
Mr. & Mrs. Jerry Coulter
Mr. & Mrs. Donald Evans
Rev. Constance Jackson
Ms. Clara Kearse
Ms. Addie Robinson
Mr. & Mrs. Richard Shinhoster
Bishop and Mrs. Forrest Stith
Mrs. Debra Trott
Ms. Terrylynn Weeks
Mr. & Mrs. Ross Tuzo

Acknowledgments

We are grateful to the following persons who by their direct efforts have made the presenting of the Chimes of Hope concert possible:

Mrs. Shangri-La Durham Thompson — **Mr. Randolph Hayward**
Mrs. Delores D. Willis — **Mrs. Julia Durham, JP**
Mr. Jason Dees — **Mr. Martin Dees, Jr.**

We wish, also, to thank the hundreds of others who have lent financial support as patrons and purchasers of ads, and support in others ways. Finally, we are most grateful to those who attended the concert; and we hope that the music was inspiring to all.

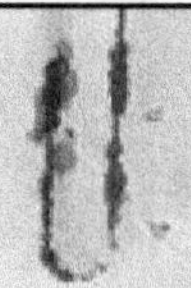

CURRICULUM VITAE

Lloyd E. Dees - Ordained Elder - Methodist Church 1968

163 So. Long Beach Avenue
Freeport, NY 11520
Telephone: 516-378-0911

Married to: Dolores Dees
Children: Jason
Janet

FORMAL EDUCATION:

Bachelor of Arts	Shelton College, Ringwood, New Jersey Major in Philosophy
Master of Divinity	Interdenominational Theological Center Atlanta, GA Emphasis on Old Testament Studies
Master of Sacred Theology	Princeton Theological Seminary Christian Social Ethics (1/2 requirement)

CONTINUING EDUCATION

Congress of Evangelism - United Methodist
1990 - Chicago
1991 - Atlanta
1993 - Houston

Workshop on Preaching - Auburn Theological Seminary - New York City - Spring 1986

Institute on Religion and Social Studies - Jewish Theological Seminary - New York City - 1987, 1989, 1993

United Methodist Bishops Convocation on "Critical Issues - 1986-1994

EMPLOYMENT EXPERIENCE

Pastor	Freeport United Methodist Church - June 1987-to present Freeport, New York
Pastor	St. Paul's United Methodist Church - June 1983-June 1987 Inwood, New York
Pastor	St. Marks United Methodist Church - June 1980-June 1983 Brooklyn, New York (A congregation made up of many nationalities - the majority of which was from the Caribbean area.)
Pastor	Trinity United Methodist Church - June 1977-June 1980 White Plains, New York
Pastor Director	Taft United Methodist Church - June 1975-June 1977 Taft Community Center, New York, New York

Rev. Dees Vitae, 1968

	First Vice-President Five Towns Community Center Inwood, New York	May 1986-May 1987
	Superintendent of Schools Advisory Committee - District #15 Lawrence, New York	June 1986-1987
	Joint Review Committee The United Methodist Church New York Annual Conference	1985
President	Black Clergy Caucus The United Methodist Church New York Annual Conference	December 1984-1988
Member	Equitable Salary Commission The United Methodist Church New York Annual Conference	1986-1993
Chairperson	Equitable Salary Commission The United Methodist Church New York Annual Conference	1993-1994
Chairperson	Committee on Fundraising and Public Relations Habitat For Humanity Nassau County, New York	1991-1994
Member	Freeport Family Service Center Board of Directors Freeport, New York	1993-1994
President	Freeport Interfaith Clergy Council Freeport, New York	1994

PROFESSIONAL ASSOCIATION

International Society of Theta Phi - an organization of theological and religious scholars.

AWARDS

Henry McNeil Turner Preaching Award for outstanding achievement in homiletics.

Sammye F. Coat Merit Award for outstanding achievement during seminary career.

Rev. Dees Vitae, 1968

Pastor	Woodycrest United Methodist Church - June 1974-June 1975 Bronx, New York
Pastor Executive Director	Simpson United Methodist Church - March 1973-June 1974 Wheeling Human Rights Commission Wheeling, West Virginia (I was chosen to assist in organizing the first Human Rights Commission for the City of Wheeling, and to serve as its Interim Executive Director.)
Pastor	Epworth United Methodist Church - June 1972-March 1973 Gastonia, North Carolina and Kelly Chapel United Methodist Church Bessemer City, North Carolina
Director	United Campus Christian Ministry - February 1971-March 1973 North Carolina A&T State University Greensboro, North Carolina (The United Campus Christian Ministry was an ecumenical venture, designed to serve the spiritual, and religious needs of faculty and students at a state university.)
Pastor	Bethel African Methodist Episcopal Church - June 1969-June 1971 Shelley Bay, Bermuda
Pastor	Fisk Chapel African Methodist Church - June 1968-June 1969 Fair Haven, New Jersey
Youth Counselor	City-Wide Coordinating Committee - Summer 1966 New York City
Social Investigator	New York City Dept. of Social Services - 1963-1965 (I had responsibility for determining the eligibility of persons to receive public assistance, and of maintaining an active caseload of eight-five clients.)
U.S. Army P.F.C.	(Ten months in Berlin, Germany) - May 1951-1953

ACTIVITIES

Member	Superintendent of Schools Advisory Committee White Plains, New York	1978-1980
	Board of Trustees White Plains Public Library	1978-1980
	Citizens Advisory Committee Community Development Fund City of White Plains	1977-1980
	Board of Directors Westchester Day Care Council White Plains, New York	1978-1980
	Board of Ordained Ministry The United Methodist Church New York Annual Conference (Executive Committee)	June 1978-1986

Rev. Dees Vitae, 1968

Acknowledgments

Completing this work has been a decade-long labor of love, fulfilling a promise to my mentor and friend, Rev. Lloyd E. Dees. My commitment was always to please and honor God. He wanted you, the reader, to be blessed by it. May we find inspiration in his story to stay strong in our Faith and our efforts to make a difference.

This journey, though challenging and at times seemingly insurmountable, deepened my communication with God, as I constantly sought His wisdom and guidance. Ralph Waldo Emerson once said, "It's not the destination, it's the journey." Truly, this has been a journey and a walk of faith. I am profoundly grateful to God for allowing me to serve as the conduit for this work and for placing supportive individuals along my path.

My heartfelt thanks go to Rev. Dees' wife, Dolores, for her gracious patience regarding the timeline of this project. I also appreciate his daughter, Janet, who reviewed excerpts and offered valuable insights, such as highlighting the significance of the Black Doll Study by psychologists Mamie and Kenneth Clark in the 1940s and 50s, which influenced her father's protests. Acknowledgment is also due to Rev. Dees' son Jason for his readiness to assist, and to Rev. Brandon's son, Marcus, for promptly providing helpful information.

My mother, Mrs. Julia Durham, has been a constant source of love and support, always believing in me as she did in Rev. Dees and his humanitarian efforts. I am equally thankful for my wonderfully supportive husband, Mr. Stanton Thompson Sr., who has unwaveringly believed in me and supported all my endeavors, never complaining about the books and papers scattered around my workspace. He is also an exemplary father and grandfather.

To my sons, Stanton Jr., who often remarked, "You're on that computer again," and Shan-on, whom I hold dear, thank you for your encouragement. To my daughter-in-law, Dr. Nyshawana Francis-Thompson, and my beautiful granddaughter, Nina Solei Thompson, thank you for your love and support. I hope you all read this work and are inspired to make a difference as you journey through life.

I am blessed with the best sisters: Mrs. Shelby Durham-Jackson and Dr. Donna Durham-Pierre. You make me proud. I only wish our brother, Rev. Danny, were here. To his beloved wife, my sister-in-law Paula, my nephew Coolie, and my niece Kenya, Donna's daughter, your love and support have enriched my life.

Family means the world to me, and having acknowledged them, I must also thank others who contributed to the completion of this work. Mr. Rolfe Commissiong and Mr. Philip Perinchief were invaluable resources, offering expertise that greatly enriched this project. Thank you.

Thank you also to contributors Rev. Dr. John Brandon, Mr. Marcus Brandon, Mr. Martin Dees, Dr. Anne Yarrow for their input, and to Rev. Howard Dill for the Foreword. I thank Rev. Dr. Lois Poag Ray for her review. I appreciate contributions from Mr. Chris Furbert (President of the Bermuda Industrial Union), my mother, Mrs. Julia Durham, Rev. Dr. Wendell Christopher, Rev. Trevor Woolridge, Rev. Dr. Larry Dixon, Ms. Betty Monroe, Julien Leotaud, Ms. Linda Hendrickson, and Mrs. Eloise Furbert. I cherish the wonderful afternoons spent with Mr. Lionel Simmons and his lovely wife, Cecille Snaith-Simmons. Lionel took the time to photograph images for this publication, and Cecille kindly verified some references on my behalf. To my web designer, Stephan Johnstone, thank you. To Isak Foy, thank you for trying to verify information for me.

Writing this book was challenging, but I was blessed by many people who God placed in my path, including my inspirational friend and fellow author, Mrs. Margaret Giloth, and her niece, Britney Bannister. As the radio host for *The Need to Lead* on Magic 102.7, I have called on Margaret on many occasions. She shared her book with the radio audience and introduced me to her, now my, wonderful editor, Mrs. Barbara Dee of Suncoast Digital Press, who lightened my burden and ensured that this work finally came to publication. Margaret, thank you for your encouragement and support on the last legs of this journey. You assured me that Barbara Dee and her phenomenal team would make a difference, and they certainly have. A special thanks to Ketti Harris for her tireless work managing and formatting all the many pieces of history we endeavored to include. I profusely thank Elijah Toten for his work in formatting this book to ensure it was ready for publication. God is so good! Thank you, Barbara, for guiding me and being such an awesome support. Your encouragement when I was down will never be forgotten.

There are so many people who have supported me in this venture, and I want to recognize all of them. If you helped in any way, I thank you. To all of you—family, friends, church family, new friends, and readers—as you digest this work, I pray that your souls will be enriched and that you will be tremendously blessed as you journey through this life and make a difference.

About the Author

Dr. Shangri-La Durham-Thompson is a renowned educator, leader, author, artist, and radio host, whose career embodies excellence in communication, creativity, and leadership. With an unwavering commitment to authentic expression, she uses her gifts and talents for the glory of God.

Dr. Durham-Thompson's distinguished academic achievements include: a Bachelor of Arts in Speech and Theatre Education—North Carolina Agricultural and Technical State University (N.C. A&T); a Master's in Public Speaking—University of North Carolina at Greensboro (UNC-G); a Master's in Curriculum and Administration—Miami University, Oxford, Ohio; and a Doctorate in Educational Leadership—St. John's University, Jamaica, New York.

Her extensive career in education spans roles as a teacher, principal, and Education Officer for the Arts and Leadership within Bermuda's Department of Education. She has also served as the Bermuda Conference Superintendent for eleven A.M.E. church schools. She is the host of *The Need to Lead*, a weekly radio show that explores the principles of leadership and their real-world applications.

Dr. Durham-Thompson's impact on education includes her tenure as an elementary teacher, high school English and drama teacher, acting middle school assistant principal, and elementary principal. As the Officer of the Arts and Leadership at the Bermuda Department of Education, she founded "Spring into the Arts," a five-day festival that continues to celebrate student creativity. She has been an adjunct professor of public speaking and business communication at Bermuda College and Mount St. Vincent University, Bermuda campus.

Dr. Durham-Thompson's contributions have earned her numerous awards including: Outstanding Contribution to the Quality of Life in Bermuda—Seventh-Day Adventist Church; Community Award—New Testament Church of God; J. Daniel Smith Achievement Award—

Allen Temple A.M.E. Church; Service Awards from A.M.E. Churches in 1990, 1997, 2001, and 2012; Cultural Award—Progressive Labour Party; Paul Harris Award and Leadership Award—Pembroke Rotary Club, where she is a past president and active member; Commendations from the Bermuda Senate (1992, 1994, 1996, 1999, 2000, 2003); and the Queen's Badge and Certificate of Honour—Queen Elizabeth II, in recognition of her lifelong dedication to education and leadership.

As a playwright and poet Dr. Durham-Thompson has worked to preserve Bermuda's cultural identity and her works celebrate themes of faith, leadership, and connection.

She is the daughter of Julia (Furbert) Durham and Coolidge George Durham (deceased) and sibling to Dr. Donna Durham-Pierre, Mrs. Shelby Durham-Jackson and Rev. Coolidge "Danny" Durham (deceased). She is the devoted wife of Mr. Stanton Thompson, Sr. They have two sons, Stanton Jr. and Shan-on, and she is the mother-in-law of Dr. Nyshawana Francis-Thompson and grandmother to Nina Solei.

Dr. Durham-Thompson lives by biblical principles, particularly Matthew 6:33: "Seek ye first the kingdom of God, and his righteousness, and all these things shall be added unto you."

With decades of leadership experience, Dr. Shangri-La Durham-Thompson's lifelong mission remains clear—to educate, inspire, and uplift others through words, art, and leadership, leaving an indelible mark on Bermuda and beyond.

Other works by the author:

- *Battle for Freedom – Anthology of Poetry and Drama*

Some of the plays in this anthology include:

- The Theatre Boycott
- Battle for Freedom (Historical Fiction on the history of the A.M.E. Church in Bermuda)
- Man Our Brother
- F.S. Returns (A history of the Berkeley Institute)
- Home for Christmas
- Rufus (Retelling the Life of an A.M.E. Pastor)
- In Unity is Strength (A history of the Bermuda Union of Teachers)
- The Songbirds (Performed in Philadelphia at the request of the Bishop)
- Daniell's Choice (Concerning the Aids Epidemic)

Children's Books:

- The Princess Solei Series:
  - Presenting Princess Solei on her First Birthday
  - Princess Solei Learns of that First Christmas Day
  - Princess Solei Adopts a Grandmother

Poetry From the Heart:

Additionally, her poems have been included in the following:

- L. Frederick Wade, in *Words and Pictures*, by Dale Butler, JP, 1997
- *Bermuda's First Anthology of Poetry*, Bermuda Department of Cultural Affairs

Plays:

- *Presenting Mazumbo* (A play concerning the life of Dr. E.F. Gordon)

Website: drshangrila.com

Youtube: https://www.youtube.com/@shangri-ladurham-thompson2512

References

"A Lasting Voice." *Effingham Living*, 2013: 52-57.

"Action Call." *Bermuda Sun* 13 November 1971.

Anderson, V.R. *My Soul Shouts*. Judson Press, 2002.

"Assemblymen debate role of the church in political affairs." *The Royal Gazette* 25 April 1972.

"PLP Adopts Brown and Butterfield as Election Candidates." *Bermuda Industrial Union The Workers Voice* 5 June 1992: 17(19).

"Bermudians for Reconciliation reply to Member's Reply." *The Royal Gazette* 24 February 1972: 7.

"Big debate on the cost of living." *The Royal Gazette* 24 February 1972: 7.

"Bishop Ernest Lyght, city officials, and area clergy participate in renaming of city street to Dr. Martin Luther King, Jr. Blvd." *The United Methodist Review, The Vision* 15 (6 February 1998): 4.

Dees, L., and Brandon, J. *The Protest* (1971): 8.

Dees, Rev. L. "Drugs." *The Bermuda Recorder* (n.d.).

Dees, Rev. L. "Commentary from an old friend, A Glance Backward and a Look Forward." *The Workers Voice* 14 October 2005.

Dees, Rev. L., and Brandon, Rev. J. "Special Issue on Bermuda." *The Protest* (1971): 1-15.

Dees, Rev. L., and Brandon, Rev. J. *The Protest* (1969).

Dees, Rev. L., and Brandon, Rev. J. *The Protest* (1970a): 1-14.

Dees, Rev. L., and Brandon, Rev. J. *The Protest* (1970b): 1-15.

Durham-Thompson, Dr. S.-L. *Battle for Freedom*. University of Toronto Press for the Writer's Machine, 1994.

Falk, B. "Fireman Tells of Biased Treatment." *The Weekly* (1977).

Harris, S. "The Rev. Lloyd Dees of Trinity United Methodist Church, White Plains." *New York Times* (1996, 12 July 1996).

"Highlights in the History of Trinity United Methodist Church, Assumes Duties." *The Reporter Dispatch White Plains, Religious News* June 1977.
Hodgson, Dr. E. *Second Class Citizens; First Class Men* 3rd ed. The Writers' Machine, 1997.
"Human Rights Director Resigns." *The Intelligencer* 17 May 1974.
Ira Philip. "A Holiday to Remember." *The Royal Gazette* 8 January 1999: 2.
Leheny, A. "Rights Unit Awaiting Hiring Practice Reply." *The Intelligencer* 17 May 1974.
"Living Costs Prohibitive?" *The Bermuda Recorder* 22 December 1970.
Lovett, D. "A Lifetime of Advocacy." Coastal Regional Commission of Georgia. The Pelican Brief. March 2013.
"Lower food and housing prices." *The Royal Gazette* 11 April 1970.
Maxwell, J.C. (2007). *The 21 irrefutable laws of leadership: follow them and people will follow you* 10th Anniversary Edition. 1998. 155-168. Thomas Nelson. (Original work published 1998)
"Ministers Plan Assembly Vigil Tomorrow." (1971, April 14). The Royal Gazette, 1.
On Parliament Hill, "Vigil Pastors make appeal to supporters." (1970, April 20). The Royal Gazette, 1.
Pastors' appeal for costs cut. *The Royal Gazette* 30 March 1970: 3.
"Petition Against High Prices." *The Bermuda Recorder* 18 September 1971.
"Postponed debate on petition." *Bermuda Sun* 13 November 1971.
"Prices too high - Pastors to stage fast over Easter." *The Royal Gazette* 25 March 1970: 4.
"Protection for the Consumer." *The Bermuda Sun* 13 November 1971: 4.
"Record Budget." *Bermuda Mid-Ocean News* 26 February 1972: 1-3.
"Reverends Brandon and Dees make presentation to Premier Jennifer Smith." *The Workers Voice* 15 January 1999: 23(11).
"Second balloting against high prices yesterday." *The Royal Gazette* (n.d.): 15.
"Simpson U. M. Pastor is Wheeling Human Rights Director." *The Intelligencer* (n.d.).
Stout, D. "Minister is Released in Child Abuse Case." *New York Times* 12 July 1996.
The Bermuda A.M.E. Church School Memoirs Jostens': 2015: 35.
"We are willing to die: Cadre." *The Royal Gazette* 14 October 1974.
"We don't want a Gestapo- Prices Group." *Bermuda Sun* 6 November 1971.
Zastudil, M. "Blacks' Struggle Not Over, Rev. Dees Speaks to the NAACP." *The Intelligencer* (n.d.).

Index

A

Allen, Richard, pg. 89, 241

Anderson, Vinton Randolph, pg. 73

Anderson, Vivienne L., pg., 73, 92

Annex Store, pg. 3

Astwood, Lt. Col. J.C, Speaker, pg. 37

B

Ball, Barbara, Dr., pg. 42, 44

Barber, George Wilbur, Bishop (1898-1970) pg. 85, 218

Barcilon, Hector, pg. 33

Baron, Alvin, pg. 283, 284

Barrow, John, Congressman, pg.108, 157, 158

Battle for Freedom, pg. 19, 87

Bayard, Rustin, pg. 215

Berkeley Educational Society, The, pg. 226, 227

Berkeley Institute, The, pg. 18, 88

Bermuda A.M.E. Church School Memoirs, 2015, pg. 12

Bermuda Industrial Union, (BIU), pg.8, 40, 134

Bermuda Ministerial Association, pg. 68

Bermuda Musical and Dramatic Society (BMDS), pg. 74

Bermuda Population Trend Report, pg. 3

Bermuda Recorder, The, pg. 29, 87

Bermuda Song, pg. 138

Bermuda Sun, The, pg. 31

Bermuda Workers' Association, pg. 222

Bermudians for Reconciliation, The, pg. 3, 29, 32, 36, 54, 56, 107, 129, 130, 140, 163

Bethel A.M.E. Church, Lansdowne, PA, pg. 67

Bethel A.M.E. Church, Shelly Bay, Bermuda, pg. 2, 225

Bethel A.M.E. Church, Greensboro, North Carolina, pg. 97

Birch, David, Rev. pg. 101, 102

Black Beret Cadre, pg. 25, 26, 86, 222

Blake, Eugene Carson, Dr, pg. 90

Blakeney, Glenn, pg. 6

Blyden, Francella, pg. 132

Bradford, Henry Jr., pg. 157 , 265, 267

Brandon, John, Rev., pg. 18, 24, 27, 51, 53, 77, 129, 163, 203

Brandon, Marcus, pg. 20, 170

Brandon, Micah pg. 21

Brandon, Minnie, pg. 170

Brangman, Lenamae, pg. 132

Brangman, Lovette, pg. 121, 283
Bronson, Oswald, P. Sr, pg. 152, 156, 258
Brown-Evans, pg. 53, 55, 97, 122, 136, 141
Brown, Lee, Mayor, pg. 156, 257
Bruno, Harry, pg. 100
Buchanan, George, Rev. pg. 55
Burgess, Norris, pg. 16
Burrow, John, pg. 270, 279, 289
Burrows, Marsha, pg. 136
Burrows, Reginald (PLP) pg. 46
Burns, Jon, pg. 114
Burt, David, Hon, Premier, pg. 173
Butler, Dale, pg. 19, 87

C

Carolina Peacemaker, pg. 74
Cann, Eustace, Dr., pg. 123
Cann, John, William, pg. 221
Carmichael, Stockley, pg. 215
Chaffy, Robert B. pg. 18
Christopher, Wendell, Rev., Dr., pg. 172
Chimes of Hope, pg. 110, 134
Chin, Noel N. Rev., pg.154. 251
Clark, Maimie & Kenneth, Drs., Black Doll Study, pg. 4
Commissioner of Consumer Affairs, pg. 31, 32
Commissiong, Rolfe, JP, pg. 7, 19
Commissiong, Rudolph, pg. 9
Commissiong, Vera, pg. 9
Cone, James, H. pg. 79, 89, 192, 232
Consultation on Church Union (COCU), pg. 75, 76, 89, 90, 186, 187
Consumer Affairs Bureau pg. 21, 132, 141
Consumer Protection Legislation, pg. 27
Conway, Samuel, pg. 241
Corbin, Doris, pg. 74
Coston, Pat, pg.96
Cox, William (UBP), pg. 46
Crowley, Patricia, pg. 158, 278

D

Dey, Connie, pg. 74
Dees Benevolent Society, pg. 132
Dees (Mills), Dolores, pg.6, 12, 20, 106, 128, 133, 139, 164, 167, 168
Dees, Janet, pg. 6, 109, 152, 163, 164, 167, 168
Dees, Jason, pg. 6, 15, 109, 163, 164, 165, 167, 168
Dees, Martin, pg.169
Dill, Edna, pg. 132
Dill, Emily-Gail, Rev. Dr., JP, MP, pg. 53
Dill, Howard, Rev. & Presiding Elder, pg. 53
Districts in the A.M.E. Church, pg. 85
Dixon, Larry, Rev., Dr., pg. 171
Dodson, Owen, pg. 16
Douglas, Rosalie, (Somerset) pg. 21, 141
Dowdy, Lewis, C, Dr., A&T Chancellor, pg. 97
Dowling, Henry, Dr. pg. 67
Dowling, W. Berkeley, pg. 88, 229
Duckett, George, pg. 24, 24
Durham, Coolidge 'Danny' pg. 94, 129
Durham, Coolidge George, pg. 16, 128
Durham-Jackson, Shelby, pg. 11,17, 73, 95, 127, 128, 129, 162
Durham, Julia, pg. 16, 135, 140, 162, 163, 170
Durham-Pierre, Donna, Dr., pg.17, 94, 129
Durham-Thompson, Shangri-La, Ed.D, pg. 124, 127, 130, 141, 163, 166, 171, 307

E

Eckford, Elizabeth, pg. 211
Edness, Quinton, (UBP) pg. 45
Effingham County, pg. 108, 113

Enoch, Hendry, pg. 165
Essien-Udom, E.U., pg. 235
Evans, Lloyd, Rev., pg. 105
Eve, Malcolm, pg.95
Eve, Malcolm, Presiding Elder, Rev., pg. 95

F

Fairfield Baptist Church, pg. 90
Falk, Bill, pg. 102
Farmer, Jones, pg.215
Foster, Rev. Thomas, pg. 59
Ferraro, Jr. pg. 152
Foster, Rev. pg. 57, 58
Fox Chase Laboratories, pg. 94
Francis Patton Elementary School, pg. 16
Frazier, John, K. Rev., pg. 118
Freedom Democratic Movement, pg. 65
Ford (Furbert) Joan, pg. 96
Fowlkes, Nancy, pg. 276
Furbert, Chris, pg. 68, 134, 173
Furbert, Eloise, pg. 171
Furbert, Frederick Shirley pg. 88, 89, 94
Furbert, Laverne, pg. 127

G

General Conference, pg. 91, 92
Ghandi, Mahatma, pg. 111
Gibbons (Smith), Kelly Anne, pg. 137
Gordon, Clark, pg. 118
Gordon, Edgar Fitzgerald, Dr, pg. 86, 11, 222
Greensboro four (McNeil Joseph, McCain, Franklin; Blair, Ezell, Jr.; Richmond, David), pg.96

H

Harris, Susan, pg. 105
Hartsdale Fire Department, pg. 103
Hall, Julian, pg. 19
Hayward, Randolph, pg. 127, 135, 140, 163
Hendrickson, Linda, pg. 173
Higgs, Shearin O., pg. 103
Hill, Carol, pg. 16
Hill, Jack, State Senator, pg. 108, 114, 158, 277
Hodgson, Eva, Dr. pg. 9, 86, 121, 220
Hodgson, Arthur, pg. 74
Holden, Robert, pg. 161
Horton, Randolph, pg. 127, 133, 137, 134
Howard University, pg. 94
Hughes, Langston, pg. 17, 18, 84
Hutchinson, William, W., pg. 156, 262

I

Intelligencer, pg. 115
Interdenominational Theological Center (ITC) pg. 72, 154, 156
Isakson, Johnny, Senator, pg. 108, 275

J

Jackson, J.H.R, M.C.P, pg. 228
Jackson, Jessie, pg. 97
Jackson. Melvin, pg. 73, 95, 129
John W. Dodd Junior High School, pg. 152
Johnson, J.A., Rev., pg. 228
Joint Statement, pg. 21
Jones, Chester, R., pg. 156, 263, 286
Jones, Douglas, pg. 239
Jones, Noel, Bishop, pg. 161

K

Henner, Herman. Pg. 241
Kilimanjaro, John Marshall, Dr. pg. 74
King James, Jr. pg. 156, 264, 286

King, Joseph, W., pg. 153
King, Martin Luther, Dr. pg. 19, 52, 213, 214
Koch, Edward, I., pg. 153, 212, 213

L

Leheny, Andy, pg. 99
Leotaud, Julien, pg. 173
Lewis, John, pg. 213
Lincoln, C. Eric, Dr, pg. 232
Lowe, Wilbur M. (Larry), Jr. pg. 56
Lovette, Dionne, pg. 106
Lyght, Ernest S. Bishop, pg. 154, 156, 157, 259, 268, 280
Lyons, Patty, pg. 159, 282, 288

M

Magic, 102.7 radio, pg. 66
Mandela, Nelson, pg. 60
Margaret Walker, pg. 83
Marshall, Ralph, U.B.P., pg. 38
Martin, Vernon D., pg. 157, 271, 272
Maslow, Abraham pg. 83
Master's Toy Department pg. 4
Maxwell, John, 21 Irrefutable Laws of Leadership, pg. 6, 10, 95
Mazumbo, pg. 87
Mckelvey, Walter H., pg. 154, 255
McNeil, Leila, pg. 5
Mercer, Linda, pg. 112
Meredith, James, pg. 84, 124
Medical Radio, pg. 67
Miami University, Oxford, Ohio, pg. 94
Mid Ocean News pg. 24
Mills, Thomas H. Jr., pg. 156, 261
Minority Hiring Practices, pg. 100
Monroe, Betty, pg. 172
Monk, Rev. Theopolis, pg. 8
Morgan, Harding, pg. 152
Morgan, Robert C, Bishop, pg. 254
Morton, Stanley, pg. 51, 52, 53

N

National Association for the Advancement of Coloured People, (NAACP) pg. 25, 17, 117
Need to Lead, The, pg. 67, 95
North Carolina Agricultural & Technical State University (A&T) pg. 74, 87, 93, 95, 97, 98

O

One Bermuda Alliance (OBA), pg. 65
Orr, Grace, L., pg. 250
Ottley, Marina, pg. 132

P

Parks, Rosa, pg. 211
Parris, Sharon, Dr. pg. 19, 20, 83
Payne Theological Seminary, Ohio, pg. 94, 128
Pearman, James E. Hon, pg. 45
Perinchief, Philip, pg. 24, 56, 58-66,
Perry, Fernance pg. 41, 42
People's Movement, pg. 134
Philip, Ira, pg. 87, 130, 132
Phillips, Lionel & Marva, pg. 74
Phillips, Veronica, pg. 15
Pinckney, Allen, N. Jr, Rev. Dr., pg. 156. 260, 285
Piggly Wiggly, pg. 34
Pitt, Mary R., pg. 253
Ponton, Lynelle, pg. 139
Powell, Adam, pg. 215Powell, Richard (Southampton) pg. 21
Progressive Group, The, pg. 8,

Progressive Labour Party (PLP), pg.8, 23, 65, 121, 136, 141
Prospect Primary School, pg. 137
Purell, Ann, pg. 114
Pyke, Leroy, T. pg. 16

R

Race/Racism, pg. 128, 156, 188, 190, 204
Randolph, Asa Philip, pg. 84
Richardson, Anthony, pg. 66
Richards, Lonnie, pg. 141
Robert B. Chaffy, pg. 18
Robinson, Rosalyn, pg. 16
Robinson, Walter, PLP, pg. 37, 140
Royal Gazette, The, 1, 21, 23, 25, 26, 27, 28

S

Saltus, Mel. (Eliyatsoor) pg. 26, 60
Santucci, Leonard, Rev., Dr., JP, pg. 56
Sapp, Hurbert, C., pg. 157, 269
Scott, Alex, Hon, CBE, JP, pg. 178, 162, 141, 163
Scariamo, Deborah, pg. 159, 281
Shockley, Grant S., pg. 234
Sheehy, John, Chief Inspector, pg. 26
Sherman, Marilyn, pg. 152
Seymour, Walter (Southampton) pg. 21
Sharpe, Jack, Hon., pg. 23, 33, 34, 35, 36, 38, 40, 46, 47, 50, 57
Simmons, Colin, pg. 134
Simmons, Conway, Rev. pg. 136
Simmons, Llewellyn, Dr., pg. 66
Simmons, Ottiwell Jr., pg. 19
Simmons-Wade, Ianthia, JP, MP, pg. 98
Simpson United Methodist Church, Wheeling, West Virginia, pg. 98
Silent Vigil, pg. 23
Smith, Calvin, pg. 93, 128
Smith, Charles, Rev., pg. 16
Smith, Hilda, pg. 132
Smith, Jennifer, Dame, DBE, JP, DHuml, pg. 127, 129, 130, 136, 149
Solid Rock Foundation, pg. 134
Spillers, George, pg. 101
St. John's University, Jamaica, Queens, NY, pg. 94
St. Marks United Methodist Church, Brooklyn, pg. 121
St. Paul A.M.E. Church pg. 19
St. Philip A.M.E. Church pg. 88
Stout, Davis, pg. 105
Straut, Charles H. Rev., Dr. pg.154, 250
Student Nonviolent Coordinating Committee, pg. 84

T

Temple University, pg. 94
Thomas, Austin, MP (PLP) pg. 23, 45
Thomas, Ruth, pg. 139
Tompkins, Laura, pg. 136
Thompson, Stanton, Sr, pg. 162
Trinity Methodist Church, White Plains, pg. 104
Trimm, Cindy, Rev., Dr., pg. 56
Trimingham, Deforest MCP. pg. 25
Trott, Elizabeth, pg. 132
Trott, Rebecca, pg. 132
Trott, Winifred, pg. 132
Tucker, Charles Lloyd, pg. 87, 88, 224, 225, 226
Tucker, Henry, Sir, pg. 26, 32
Tucker, W.L., Hon., pg. 121
Turner, Gerald R., pg. 157, 158, 273, 274, 287
Tweed, Nicholas Genevieve, Rev., pg. 134

U

United Bermuda Party, pg. 17, 34
United Church of Christ Ministries, pg. 89
University of North Carolina – Greensboro (UNC-G), pg. 94

V

Viera, Harry, MCP, pg. 24, 44

W

Wade, Frederick, PLP, 41
Warmbrun, Curlene (Furbert)
Warner, Richard, pg. 91
Webster University, pg. 94
White, Kathy Ann, Dr., pg. 95
White, Woodie W. Bishop, pg. 155, 256
Whitter, Eric, pg. 132
Whitter, Pat, pg. 132
Wilkerson, Lois, Rev. pg. 67
Wilkerson, Michael (Evangelist), pg. 67
Wilkins, Roy, pg.84
Wilkinson, David, Hon. (UBP), pg. 52
Williams, A. Cecil, pg. 90, 234
Williams, Frank B., Deputy Commissioner, pg. 25, 26
Williams, Preston N. Dr., g. 235
Wills, Pamela & Prince, pg. 155, 252
Wilmore, Gayraud S. Jr, pg. 234, 236
Winston Salem State University, North Carolina, pg. 94
Woolridge, Lillian, pg. 16
Woolridge, Trevor, Rev. pg. 54, 131
Worker's Voice, pg.129, 136, 139
Wright, Lee, Rev. pg. 118
Wright, Linda, pg. 122

Y

Yarrow, Ann, Dr., pg. 135, 153, 169
Young, Whitney, pg. 110, 135, 170, 214

The Dawn of A New Day

Dedicated with love to

The Premier, The Hon. Jennifer Smith, JP, MP

The Government

And the People of Bermuda

In the midnight of our lives
When darkness
Like a pervasive covering
Blanketed our minds
Bermuda really was another world
Paradise for those selected
Hell perhaps, for those neglected
And those who toiled
Became dejected by life's view
And the darkness whispered
Ensuring division
And the people without vision
Closed their eyes
They closed their hearts
They closed their minds

In the midnight of our lives
When darkness
Like a thief
Stole history
And dismissed those lacking knowledge of their great past
Who gratefully accepted snapshots
From the albums of their lives
Pictures the darkness selected for them to see
Juan De Bermudez
Sir George Somers
Benign slavery

Bedeviled isles
And because all history had no validity
Many stumbled in the darkness
For they could not see their way
And others waited patiently for deliverance

Then the Twilight came
And without choice the darkness lifted
Revealing problems stemming from a neglected past
Divided people with no solutions
An island sinking in pollution
Hearts needing restitution
But hope
Not in vain
Twilight offers a new beginning
The only concrete chance of winning the battle
That could destroy our island home

Twilight, with tears upon the dawning
Oft mistaken as morning dew
Releases the fragrance of the flowers in the air
Produces gentle ocean breezes
Filters the now clear crystal waters
Acknowledges our past
Dispels the myths
Inspires dreams

Twilight admits the road's not easy
So, with God rise to greet the dawn
Then solicits from the rays of breaking day
From your horizon stretch and guide them
For there is much that they must do
Acknowledge God

Respect themselves
And others too

Be encouraged says the Twilight
Free yourselves from darkness past
Diverse people come together in light of day
Transformed by Twilight's cleansing teardrops
Meet the obstacles ahead
With open eyes
With open minds
With open hearts

Today beside the waters
Twilight bids us greet the dawn
And we offer thanks to God for this new day
A chance for a new beginning
A chance to work as one
A chance to enjoy the banquet feast prepared
And we're reminded by the twilight
That when darkness comes it will not last
If we erect our monuments
To Ensure
We never
Forget
Our past

Rejoice Bermuda
In a new beginning
Rejoice
In the dawn of a new day

By Shangri-La Durham-Thompson
January 4, 1999

www.ingramcontent.com/pod-product-compliance
Lightning Source LLC
LaVergne TN
LVHW080309110826
845155LV00023B/96